Additional praise for *Too Big to Ignore: The Business Case for Big Data*

"Today Big data affects everybody and will continue to do so for the foreseeable future. In *Too Big to Ignore*, Phil Simon makes the topic accessible and relatable. This important book shows people how to put Big Data to work for their organizations."
–William McKnight, President, McKnight Consulting Group

"Simon has an uncanny ability to connect business cases with complex technical principles, and most importantly, clearly explain how everything comes together. In this book, Simon demystifies Big Data. Simon's vision helps the rest of us understand how this evolving and pervasive subject affects businesses today."
—Dalton Cervo, co-author of *Master Data Management in Practice—Achieving True Customer MDM* and president of Data Gap Consulting.

"From Twitter feeds to photo streams to RFID pings, the Big Data universe is rapidly expanding, providing unprecedented opportunities to understand the present and peer into the future. Tapping its potential while avoiding its pitfalls doesn't take magic; it takes a map. In *Too Big to Ignore*, Phil Simon offers businesses a comprehensive, clear-eyed, and enjoyable guide to the next data frontier."
—Chris Berdik, author of *Mind over Mind: The Surprising Power of Expectations*

"Business leaders are drowning in data, and the deluge has only just begun. In *Too Big to Ignore*, Simon delves into the world of Big Data, and makes the business case for capturing, structuring, analyzing, and visualizing the immense amount of information accessible to businesses. This book gives your organization the edge it needs to turn data into intelligence, and intelligence into action."
—Paul Roetzer, Founder & CEO, PR 20/20; author of *The Marketing Agency Blueprint*

"Phil Simon's *Too Big to Ignore* clearly demonstrates the increasing role and value of Big Data. His illustrative case studies and engaging style will dispel any doubts executives may have about how Big Data *is driving* success in today's economy."
—Adrian C. Ott, award-winning author of *The 24-Hour Customer*

Too Big
to Ignore

Wiley & SAS Business Series

The Wiley & SAS Business Series presents books that help senior-level managers with their critical management decisions.

Titles in the Wiley and SAS Business Series include:

Executive's Guide to Solvency II by David Buckham, Jason Wahl, and Stuart Rose

Fair Lending Compliance: Intelligence and Implications for Credit Risk Management by Clark R. Abrahams and Mingyuan Zhang

Foreign Currency Financial Reporting from Euros to Yen to Yuan: A Guide to Fundamental Concepts and Practical Applications by Robert Rowan

Human Capital Analytics: How to Harness the Potential of Your Organization's Greatest Asset by Gene Pease, Boyce Byerly, and Jac Fitz-enz

Information Revolution: Using the Information Evolution Model to Grow Your Business by Jim Davis, Gloria J. Miller, and Allan Russell

Manufacturing Best Practices: Optimizing Productivity and Product Quality by Bobby Hull

Marketing Automation: Practical Steps to More Effective Direct Marketing by Jeff LeSueur

Mastering Organizational Knowledge Flow: How to Make Knowledge Sharing Work by Frank Leistner

The New Know: Innovation Powered by Analytics by Thornton May

Performance Management: Integrating Strategy Execution, Methodologies, Risk, and Analytics by Gary Cokins

Retail Analytics: The Secret Weapon by Emmett Cox

Social Network Analysis in Telecommunications by Carlos Andre Reis Pinheiro

Statistical Thinking: Improving Business Performance, Second Edition by Roger W. Hoerl and Ronald D. Snee

Taming the Big Data Tidal Wave: Finding Opportunities in Huge Data Streams with Advanced Analytics by Bill Franks

The Value of Business Analytics: Identifying the Path to Profitability by Evan Stubbs

Visual Six Sigma: Making Data Analysis Lean by Ian Cox, Marie A. Gaudard, Philip J. Ramsey, Mia L. Stephens, and Leo Wright

Win with Advanced Business Analytics: Creating Business Value from Your Data by Jean Paul Isson and Jesse Harriott

For more information on any of the above titles, please visit www.wiley.com.

Too Big to Ignore

The Business Case for Big Data

Phil Simon

WILEY

Cover image: © Baris Simsek/iStockphoto
Cover design: John Wiley & Sons, Inc.

Other Books
by Phil Simon

Why New Systems Fail: An Insider's Guide to Successful IT Projects
The Next Wave of Technologies: Opportunities in Chaos
The New Small: How a New Breed of Small Businesses Is Harnessing the Power of Emerging Technologies
The Age of the Platform: How Amazon, Apple, Facebook, and Google Have Redefined Business
101 Lightbulb Moments in Data Management: Tales from the Data Roundtable (Editor)

The fact that we can now begin to actually look at the dynamics of social interactions and how they play out, and are not just limited to reasoning about averages like market indices is for me simply astonishing. To be able to see the details of variations in the market and the beginnings of political revolutions, to predict them, and even control them, is definitely a case of Promethean fire. Big Data can be used for good or bad, but either way it brings us to interesting times. We're going to reinvent what it means to have a human society.

—Sandy Pentland, Professor, MIT

Knowledge is good.

—Motto of fictitious Faber College, *Animal House*

Contents

List of Tables and Figures

Preface

Errors using inadequate data are much less than those using no data at all.

—Charles Babbage

It's about 7:30 a.m. on October 26, 2011, and I'm driving on The Strip in Las Vegas, Nevada. No, I'm not about to play craps or see Celine Dion. (While very talented, she's just not my particular brand of vodka.) I'm going for a more professional reason. Starting sometime in mid-2011, I started hearing more and more about something called *Big Data*. On that October morning, I was invited to IBM's Information on Demand (IOD) conference. It was high time that I learned more about this new phenomenon, and there's only so much you can do in front of a computer.

Beyond my insatiable quest for knowledge on all matters technology, truth be told, I went to IOD for a bunch of other reasons. First, it was convenient: The Strip is a mere fifteen minutes from my home. Second, the price was right: I was able to snake my way in for free. It turns out that, since I write for a few high-profile sites, some people think of me as a member of the media. (Funny how I never would have expected that ten years ago, but far be it from me to look a gift horse in the mouth.) Third, it was a good networking opportunity and my fourth book, *The Age of the Platform*, had just been published. I am familiar enough with the book business to know that authors have to get out there if they want to generate a buzz and move copies. These were all valid reasons to hop in my car, but for me there was an extra treat. I had the opportunity to meet and listen firsthand to the conference's two keynote speakers: Michael Lewis (one of my favorite writers) and a man by the name of Billy Beane.

For his part, Lewis wasn't at IOD to promote his latest opus like I was. On the contrary, he was there to speak about his 2003 book *Moneyball: The Art of Winning an Unfair Game*. The book had been enjoying a huge commercial resurgence as of late, thanks in no small part to the recent film of the same name starring some guy named Brad Pitt. I hadn't read *Moneyball* in some years, but I remember breezing through it. Lewis's writing style is nothing if not engaging. (He even made subprime mortgages and synthetic collateralized debt obligations [CDOs] interesting in *The Big Short*.)

I've always been a bit of a stats geek, and *Moneyball* instantly hit a nerve with me. It told the story of Beane, the general manager (GM) of the budget-challenged Oakland A's. Despite his team's financial limitations, he consistently won more games than most other mid-market teams—and even franchises like the New York Yankees that effectively printed their own money. The obvious question was how? Beane bucked convention and routinely ignored the advice of long-time baseball scouts, often earning their derision in the process. Instead, Beane predicated his management style on a rather obscure, statistics-laden field called *sabermetrics*. He signed free agents who he believed were undervalued by other teams. That is, he sought to exploit market inefficiencies.

One of Beane's favorite bargains: a relatively cheap player with a high on-base percentage (OBP).[*] In a nutshell, Beane's simple and irrefutable logic could be summarized as follows: players more likely to get on base are more likely to score runs. By extension, higher-scoring teams tend to win more games than their lower-scoring counterparts. But Beane didn't stop there. He was also partial to players (again, only at the right price) who didn't swing at the first pitch. Beane liked hitters who consistently made opposing pitchers work deep into the count. These patient batters were more likely to make opposing pitches tired—and then give *everyone* on the A's better pitches to hit. (Again, more runs would result, as would more wins.)

---

[*] For those of you not familiar with the term, *OBP* represents the true measure of how often a batter reaches base. It includes hits, walks, and times hit by a pitch. Beane also sought out those with high on-base plus slugging percentages. OPS equals the sum of a player's OBP and slugging percentage (total bases divided by at bats).

Figure P.1 Michael Lewis and Billy Beane with Katty Kay at IBM Information on Demand 2011[1]
Source: Todd Watson

Back then, evaluating players based on unorthodox stats like these was considered heresy in traditional baseball circles. And that resistance was not just among baseball outsiders. In the late 1990s and early 2000s, a conflict within the A's organization was growing between Beane and his most visible employee: manager Art Howe. A former infielder with three teams over twelve years, Howe for one wasn't on board with Beane's unconventional program, to put it mildly. As Lewis tells it in *Moneyball*, Howe was nothing if not old school. He certainly didn't need some newfangled, stat-obsessed GM telling him the X's and O's of baseball.

Oakland's internal conflict couldn't persist; a GM and manager have to be on the same page in all sports, and baseball is no exception. Rather than fire Howe outright (with the A's eating his $1.5 million salary), Beane got creative, as he is wont to do. He cajoled the New York Mets into taking him off their hands, not that the Mets needed much convincing. The team soon signed its new leader to a then-bawdy four-year, $9.4 million contract. After all, Howe had won a more-than-respectable 53 percent of his games with the small-market A's and *he just looks managerial*. The man has a great jaw. Imagine what Howe could do for a team with a big bankroll like the Mets?

Howe's tenure with the Mets was ignominious. The team won only 42 percent of its games on Howe's watch. After two seasons, the Mets realized what Beane knew long ago: Howe and his managerial jaw were much better in theory than in practice. In September 2004, the Mets parted ways with their manager.

While Beane may have been the first GM to embrace sabermetrics, he soon had company. His success bred many disciples in the baseball world and beyond. Count among them Theo Epstein, currently the President of Baseball Operations for the Chicago Cubs. In his previous role as GM of the Boston Red Sox, Epstein even hired Bill James, the godfather of sabermetrics. And it worked. Epstein won two World Series for the Sox, breaking the franchise's 86-year drought. Houston Rockets's GM Daryl Morey is bringing *Moneyball* concepts to the NBA. As a November 2012 *Sports Illustrated* article points out, the MBA grad takes a radically different approach to player acquisition and development compared to his peers.[2]

And then there's the curious case of Kevin Kelley, the head football coach at the Pulaski Academy, a high school in Little Rock, Arkansas. Kelley isn't your average coach. The man "stopped punting in 2005 after reading an academic study on the statistical consequences of going for the first down versus handing possession to the other team."[3] Coach Kelley simply refuses to punt. Ever. Even if it's fourth and 20 from his own ten-yard line. But it gets even better. Ever the contrarian, after Pulaski scores, Kelley has his kicker routinely try on-side kicks to try to get the ball right back. In one game, Kelley's team scored twenty-nine points before the opponent even touched the football![4] The results? The Bruins have won multiple state championships using their coach's unconventional style.

So why were Lewis and Beane the keynote speakers at IOD, a corporate information technology (IT) conference? Because, as *Moneyball* demonstrates so compellingly, today new sources of data are being used across many different fields in very unconventional and innovative ways to produce astounding results—and a swath of people, industries, and established organizations are finally starting to realize it.

This book explains why Big Data is a big deal. For example, residents in Boston, Massachusetts, are automatically reporting potholes and road hazards via their smartphones. Progressive Insurance tracks real-time customer driving patterns and uses that information to offer rates truly commensurate with individual safety. HR departments are using new sources of information to make better hiring decisions. Google accurately predicts local flu outbreaks based on thousands of user search queries. Amazon provides remarkably insightful, relevant, and timely product recommendations to its hundreds of millions of customers. Quantcast lets companies target precise audiences and key demographics throughout the Web. NASA runs contests via gamification site TopCoder, awarding prizes to those with the most innovative and cost-effective solutions to its problems. Explorys offers penetrating and previously unknown insights into health care behavior.

How do these organizations and municipalities do it? Technology is certainly a big part, but in each case the answer lies deeper than that. Individuals at these organizations have realized that they don't have to be statistician Nate Silver to reap massive benefits from today's new and emerging types of data. And each of these organizations has embraced Big Data, allowing them to make astute and otherwise impossible observations, actions, and predictions.

It's time to start thinking big.

This book is about an unassailably important trend: Big Data, the massive amounts, new types, and multifaceted sources of information streaming at us faster than ever. Never before have we seen data with the volume, velocity, and variety of today. Big Data is no temporary blip of a fad. In fact, it is only going to intensify in the coming years, and its ramifications for the future of business are impossible to overstate.

Put differently, Big Data is becoming too big to ignore. And that sentence, in a nutshell, summarizes this book.

Phil Simon
Henderson, NV
March 2013

NOTES

1. Watson, Todd, "Information on Demand 2011: A Data-Driven Conversation with Michael Lewis & Billy Beane," October 26, 2011, http://turbotodd.wordpress .com/2011/10/26/information-on-demand-2011-a-data-driven-conversation-with-michael-lewis-billy-beane/, retrieved December 11, 2012.

2. Ballard, Chris, "Lin's Jumper, GM Morey's Hidden Talents, More Notes from Houston," November 30, 2012, http://sportsillustrated.cnn.com/2012/writers/ chris_ballard/11/30/houston-rockets-jeremy-lin-james-harden-daryl-morey/index .html, retrieved December 11, 2012.

3. Easterbrook, Gregg, "New Annual Feature! State of High School Nation," November 15, 2007, http://sports.espn.go.com/espn/page2/story?page=easterbrook/071113, retrieved December 11, 2012.

4. Wertheim, Jon, "Down 29-0 Before Touching the Ball," September 15, 2012, http:// sportsillustrated.cnn.com/2011/writers/scorecasting/09/15/kelley.pulaski/index .html, retrieved December 11, 2012.

Acknowledgments

Kudos to the Wiley team of Tim Burgard, Shelly Sessoms, Karen Gill, Johnna VanHoose Dinse, Chris Gage, and Stacey Rivera for making this book possible so quickly. You all were a "big" help.

I am grateful to smart cookies Charlie Lougheed, Jim McKeown, Jason Crusan, Jag Duggal, Jim Kelly, Clinton Bonner, William McKnight, Scott Kahler, and Seth Grimes for their time and expertise. Talking to these folks made research fun. A tip of the hat to Hope Nicora, Andy Havens, Adrian Ott, Brad Feld, Chris Berdik, Terri Griffith, Jim Harris, Dalton Cervo, Jill Dyché, Todd Hamilton, Tony Fisher, Ellen French, Dick and Bonnie Denby, Kristen Eckstein, Bob Charette, Andrew Botwin, Thor and Keri Sandell, Clair Byrd, Jay and Heather Etchings, Karlena Kuder, Luke "Heisenberg" Fletcher, Michael, Penelope, and Chloe DeAngelo, Shawn Graham, Chad Roberts, Sarah Terry, Jeff Lee, Mark Cenicola, Brenda Blakely, Colin Hickey, Bruce Webster, Alan Berkson, Michael West, John Spatola, Marc Paolella, Angela Bowman, and Brian and Heather Morgan and their three adorable kids.

Next up are the usual suspects: my longtime Carnegie Mellon friends Scott Berkun, David Sandberg, Michael Viola, Joe Mirza, and Chris McGee.

My heroes from Rush (Geddy, Alex, and Neil), Dream Theater (Jordan, John, John, Mike, and James), Marillion (h, Steve, Ian, Mark, and Pete), and Porcupine Tree (Steven, Colin, Gavin, John, and Richard) have given me many years of creative inspiration through their music. Keep on keepin' on!

Vince Gillian, Aaron Paul, Bryan Cranston, Dean Norris, Anna Gunn, Betsy Brandy, RJ Mitte, and the rest of the cast and team of *Breaking Bad* make me want to do great work.

Next up: my parents. I'm not here without you.

Introduction: This Ain't Your Father's Data

Throughout history, in one field after another, science has made huge progress in precisely the areas where we can measure things—and lagged where we can't.

—Samuel Arbesman

C ar insurance isn't a terribly sexy or dynamic business. For decades, it has essentially remained unchanged. Nor is it an egalitarian enterprise: while a pauper and a millionaire pay the same price for a stamp ($0.45 in the United States as of this writing), the car insurance world works differently. Some people just pay higher rates than others, and those rates have at least initially very little to do with whether one is a "safe" driver, whatever that means. Historically, many if not most car insurance policies were written based on very few independent variables: age, gender, zip code, previous speeding tickets and traffic violations, documented accidents, and type of car. As I found out more than twenty years ago, a newly licensed, seventeen-year-old guy in New Jersey who drives a sports car has to pay a boatload in car insurance for the privilege—even if he rarely drives above the speed limit, always obeys traffic signals, and has nary an accident on his record. Like just about every kid my age, I wasn't happy about my rates. After all, I was an "above average" driver, or at least I liked to think so. Why should I have to pay such exorbitant fees?

Of course, we all can't be above average; it's statically impossible. Truth be told, I'm sure that back then I occasionally didn't come to a complete stop at every red light. While I've never been arrested for DUI, to this day I don't always obey the speed limit. (Shhh . . . don't tell anyone.) When I'm driving faster than the law says I should, I sometimes think of the famous George Stigler picture of Milton Friedman taken in the mid-twentieth-century. Friedman was paying a speeding ticket with, paradoxically, a big smile on this face. Why such joy? Because Friedman was an economist and, as such, he was rational to a fault. In his view of the world, the time that he regularly saved by exceeding the speed limit was worth more to him than the risk and fine of getting caught. To people like Friedman and me, speeding is only a simple expected value calculation: Friedman sped because the rewards outweighed the risks. When a cop pulled him over, he was glad to pay the fine. But I digress.

So why do most car insurance companies base their quotes and rates on relatively simple variables? The answer isn't complicated, especially when you consider the age of these companies. Allstate opened its doors in 1931. GEICO was founded in 1936, and the Progressive Casualty Insurance Company set up shop only one year later. Think about it: seventy-five years ago, those primitive models represented the best that car insurance companies could do. While each has no doubt tweaked its models since then, old habits die hard, as we saw with Art Howe and Billy Beane in the Preface. For real change to happen, somebody needs to upset the applecart. In this way, car insurance is like baseball.

BETTER CAR INSURANCE THROUGH DATA

The similarities between the ostensibly unrelated fields of baseball and car insurance don't end there. Much like the baseball revolution pioneered by Billy Beane, car insurance today is undergoing a fundamental transformation. Just ask Joseph Tucci. As the CEO at data storage behemoth EMC Corporation, he knows a thing or thirty about data. On October 3,

2012, Tucci spoke with Cory Johnson of Bloomberg Television at an Intel Capital event in Huntington Beach, California. Tucci talked about the state of technology, specifically the impact of Big Data and cloud computing on his company—and others.[1] At one point during the interview, Tucci talked about advances in GPS, mapping, mobile technologies, and telemetry, the net result of which is revolutionizing many businesses, including car insurance. No longer are rates based upon a small, primitive set of independent variables. Car insurance companies can now get much more granular in their pricing. Advances in technology are letting them answer previously unknown questions like these:

- Which drivers routinely exceed the speed limit and run red lights?
- Which drivers routinely drive dangerously slow?
- Which drivers are becoming less safe—even if they have received no tickets or citations? That is, who used to generally obey traffic signals but don't anymore?
- Which drivers send text messages while driving? (This is a big no-no. In fact, texting while driving [TWD] is actually considerably more dangerous than DUI.[2] As of this writing, fourteen states have banned it.)
- Who's driving in a safer manner than six months ago?
- Does a man with two cars (a sports car and a station wagon) drive each differently?
- Which drivers and cars swerve at night? (This could be a manifestation of drunk driving.)
- Which drivers checked into a bar using FourSquare or Facebook and drove their own cars home (as opposed to taking a cab or riding with a designated driver)?

Thanks to these new and improved technologies and the data they generate, insurers are effectively retiring their decades-old, five-variable underwriting models. In their place, they are implementing more contemporary, accurate, dynamic, and data-driven pricing models. For instance, in 2011, Progressive rolled out Snapshot, its Pay As You Drive (PAYD) program.[3] PAYD allows customers to voluntarily install a tracking device in their cars that transmits data to

Progressive and possibly qualifies them for rate discounts. From the company's site:

> How often you make hard brakes, how many miles you drive each day, and how often you drive between midnight and 4 a.m. can all impact your potential savings. You'll get a Snapshot device in the mail. Just plug it into your car and drive like you normally do. You can go online to see your latest driving details and projected discount.

Is Progressive the only, well, progressive insurance company? Not at all. Others are recognizing the power of new technologies and Big Data. As Liane Yvkoff writes on CNET, "State Farm subscribers self-report mileage and GMAC uses OnStar vehicle diagnostics reports. Allstate's Drive Wise goes one step further and uses a similar device to track mileage, braking, and speeds over 80 mph, but only in Illinois."[4]

So what does this mean to the average driver? Consider two fictional people, both of whom hold car insurance policies with Progressive and opt in to PAYD:

- Steve, a twenty-one-year-old New Jersey resident who drives a 2012, tricked-out, cherry red Corvette
- Betty, a forty-nine-year-old grandmother in Lincoln, Nebraska, who drives a used Volvo station wagon

All else being equal, which driver pays the higher car insurance premium? In 1994, the answer was obvious: Steve. In the near future, however, the answer will be much less certain: *it will depend on the data.* That is, vastly different driver profiles and demographic information will mean less and less to car insurance companies. Traditional levers like those will be increasingly supplemented with data on drivers' individual patterns. What if Steve's flashy Corvette belies the fact that he always obeys traffic signals, yields to pedestrians, and never speeds? He is the embodiment of safety. Conversely, despite her stereotypical profile, Betty drives like a maniac while texting like a teenager.

In this new world, what happens at rate renewal time for each driver? Based upon the preceding information, Progressive happily discounts Steve's previous insurance by 60 percent but triples Betty's renewal rate. In each case, the new rate reflects new—and far superior—data that Progressive has collected on each driver.

Surprised by his good fortune, Steve happily renews with Progressive, but Betty is irate. She calls the company's 1-800 number and lets loose. When the Progressive rep stands her ground, Betty decides to take her business elsewhere. Unfortunately for Betty, she is in for a rude awakening. Allstate, GEICO, and other insurance companies have access to the same information as Progressive. All companies strongly suspect that Betty is actually a high-risk driver; her age and Volvo only tell part of her story—and not the most relevant part. As such, Allstate and GEICO quote her a policy similar to Progressive's.

Now, Betty isn't happy about having to pay more for her car insurance. However, Betty *should* in fact pay more than safer drivers like Steve. In other words, simple, five-variable pricing models no longer represent the best that car insurance companies can do. They now possess the data to make better business decisions.

Big Data is changing car insurance and, as we'll see throughout this book, other industries as well. The revolution is just getting started.

POTHOLES AND GENERAL ROAD HAZARDS

Let's stay on the road for a minute and discuss the fascinating world of potholes. Yes, potholes. Historically, state and municipal governments have had a pretty tough time identifying these pesky devils. Responsible agencies and departments would often scour the roads in search of potholes and general road hazards, a truly reactive practice. Alternatively, they would rely upon annoyed citizens to call them in, typically offering fairly generic locations like "on Main Street, not too far from the 7-Eleven." In other words, there was no good automatic way to report potholes to the proper authorities. As a result, many hazards remained unreported for significant periods of time, no doubt causing car damage and earning the ire of many a taxpayer. Many people agree with the quote from acerbic comedian Dennis Miller, "The states can't pave [expletive deleted] roads."

Why has the public sector handled potholes and road hazards this way? For the same reason that car insurance companies relied upon

very few basic variables when quoting insurance rates to their customers: in each case, it was the best that they could do at the time.

At some point in the past few years, Thomas M. Menino (Boston's
longest-serving mayor) realized that it was no longer 1950. Perhaps
he was hobnobbing with some techies from MIT at dinner one night.
Whatever his motivation, he decided that there just had to be a better, more cost-effective way to maintain and fix the city's roads. Maybe
smartphones could help the city take a more proactive approach to road
maintenance. To that end, in July 2012, the Mayor's Office of New Urban
Mechanics launched a new project called Street Bump, an app that

> allows drivers to automatically report the road hazards to
> the city as soon as they hear that unfortunate "thud," with
> their smartphones doing all the work.
>
> The app's developers say their work has already sparked
> interest from other cities in the U.S., Europe, Africa and
> elsewhere that are imagining other ways to harness the
> technology.
>
> Before they even start their trip, drivers using Street
> Bump fire up the app, then set their smartphones either
> on the dashboard or in a cup holder. The app takes care
> of the rest, using the phone's accelerometer—a motion-
> detector—to sense when a bump is hit. GPS records the
> location, and the phone transmits it to a remote server
> hosted by Amazon Inc.'s Web services division.[5]

But that's not the end of the story. It turned out that the first version of the app reported far too many false positives (i.e., phantom potholes). This finding no doubt gave ammunition to the many naysayers
who believe that technology will never be able to do what people can
and that things are just fine as they are, thank you. Street Bump 1.0
"collected lots of data but couldn't differentiate between potholes and
other bumps."[6] After all, your smartphone or cell phone isn't inert; it
moves in the car naturally because the car is moving. And what about
the scores of people whose phones "move" because they check their
messages at a stoplight?

To their credit, Menino and his motley crew weren't entirely dis-
couraged by this initial setback. In their gut, they knew that they were

on to something. The idea and potential of the Street Bump app were worth pursuing and refining, even if the first version was a bit lacking. Plus, they have plenty of examples from which to learn. It's not like the iPad, iPod, and iPhone haven't evolved over time.

Enter InnoCentive Inc., a Massachusetts-based firm that specializes in open innovation and crowdsourcing. (We'll return to these concepts in Chapters 4 and 5.) The City of Boston contracted InnoCentive to improve Street Bump and reduce the number of false positives. The company accepted the challenge and essentially turned it into a contest, a process sometimes called *gamification*. InnoCentive offered a network of 400,000 experts a share of $25,000 in prize money donated by Liberty Mutual.

Almost immediately, the ideas to improve Street Bump poured in from unexpected places. Ultimately, the best suggestions came from

- A group of hackers in Somerville, Massachusetts, that promotes community education and research
- The head of the mathematics department at Grand Valley State University in Allendale, Michigan
- An anonymous software engineer

The result: Street Bump 2.0 is hardly perfect, but it represents a colossal improvement over its predecessor. As of this writing, the Street Bump website reports that 115,333 bumps have been detected. What's more, it's a quantum leap over the manual, antiquated method of reporting potholes no doubt still being used by countless public works departments throughout the country and the world. And future versions of Street Bump will only get better. Specifically, they may include early earthquake detection capability and different uses for police departments.

Street Bump is not the only example of an organization embracing Big Data, new technologies, and, arguably most important, an entirely new mind-set. With the app, the City of Boston was acting less like a government agency and more like, well, a progressive business. It was downright refreshing to see.

Crowdsourcing roadside maintenance isn't just cool. Increasingly, projects like Street Bump are resulting in substantial savings. And the public sector isn't alone here. As we've already seen with examples like Major League Baseball (MLB) and car insurance, Big Data is transforming many industries and functions within organizations. Chapter 5 will provide three in-depth case studies of organizations leading the Big Data revolution.

RECRUITING AND RETENTION

In many organizations, Human Resources (HR) remains the redhead-ed stepchild. Typically seen as the organization's police department, HR rarely commands the internal respect that most SVPs and Chief People Officers believe it does. I've seen companies place poor performers in HR because they couldn't cut it in other departments. However, I've never seen the reverse occur (e.g., "Steve was horrible in HR, so we put him in Finance."). For all of their claims about being "strategic partners," many HR departments spend the majority of their time on administrative matters like processing new hire paperwork and open enrollment. While rarely called *Personnel* anymore (except on *Mad Men*), many HR departments are anachronistic: they operate now in much the same way as they did four decades ago.

My own theory about the current, sad state of HR is as follows: As a general rule, HR folks tend not to make decisions based upon data. In this way, HR is unique. Employees rely almost exclusively on their gut instincts and corporate policy. What if employees in other departments routinely made important decisions sans relevant information? Absent data, the folks in marketing, sales, product, and finance wouldn't command a great deal of respect either. W. Edwards Deming once said, "In God we trust, all others must bring data." Someone forgot to tell this to the folks in HR, and the entire function suffers as a result.

I wrote a book on botched IT projects and system implementations, many of which involved HR and payroll applications. Years of consulting on these types of engagements have convinced me that most employees in HR just don't think like employees in other departments. Most HR people don't seek out data in making business decisions or even use the data available to them. In fact, far too many HR folks actively try to *avoid* data at all costs. (I've seen HR directors manipulate data to justify their decision to recruit at Ivy League schools, despite the fact that trying to hire Harvard and Yale alumni didn't make the slightest bit of financial sense.) And it's this lack of data—and, in that vein, a data mind-set—that has long undermined HR as a function. As we'll see throughout this book, however, ignoring data (big or small) doesn't make it go away. Pretending that it doesn't exist doesn't make it so. In fact, Big Data can be extremely useful, even for HR.

As the *Wall Street Journal* recently reported,[7] progressive and data-oriented HR departments are turning to Big Data to solve a long-vexing problem: how to hire better employees and retain them. It turns out that traditional personality tests, interviews, and other HR standbys aren't terribly good at predicting which employees are worth hiring—and which are not. Companies like Evolv "utiliz[e] Big Data predictive analytics and machine learning to optimize the performance of global hourly workforces. The solution identifies improvement areas, then systematically implements changes to core operational business processes, driving increased employee retention, productivity, and engagement. Evolv delivers millions of dollars in operational savings on average for each client, and guarantees its impact on operating profitability."[8]

Millions in savings? Aren't these just lofty claims from a start-up eager to cash in on the Big Data buzz? Actually, no. Consider some of the specific results generated by Evolv's software, as shown in Table I.1.

The lesson here is that Big Data can significantly impact each area of a business: its benefits can touch every department within an organization. Put differently, Big Data is too big to ignore.

Table I.1 Big Data Improves Recruiting and Retention

Employee Problem	Big Data Solution
Compensation	Caesars casino found that increasing pay within certain limits had no impact on turnover.
Attrition	Xerox found that experience was overrated for call-center positions. What's more, overly inquisitive employees tended to leave soon after receiving training.
Sick Time	Richfield Management tests applicants for opinions on drugs and alcohol. The company found that those who partake in "extracurricular" activities are more prone to get into accidents.

HOW BIG IS BIG? THE SIZE OF BIG DATA

How big is the Big Data market? IT research firm Gartner believes that Big Data will create $28 billion in worldwide spending in 2012, a number that will rise "to $34 billion in 2013. Most of that spending will involve upgrading 'traditional solutions' to handle the flood of data entering organizations from a variety of sources, including clickstream traffic, social networks, sensors, and customer interactions; the firm believes that a mere $4.3 billion in sales will come from 'new Big Data functionality.'"[9] For its part, consulting firm Deloitte expects massive Big Data growth, although precisely "estimating the market size is challenging."[10]

High-level projections from top-tier consulting firms are all fine and dandy, but most people won't be able to get their arms around abstract numbers like these. The question remains: just how big exactly is Big Data? You might as well ask, "How big is the Internet?"* We can't precisely answer these questions; we can only guess. What's more, Big Data got bigger in the time that it took me to write that sentence. The general answer is that Big Data is really big—and getting bigger all the time. Just look at these 2011 statistics on videos from website monitoring company Pingdom:

- **1 trillion**: The number of video playbacks on YouTube
- **140**: The number of YouTube video playbacks per person on Earth
- **48**: Hours video uploaded to YouTube every minute
- **82.5**: Percentage of the U.S. Internet audience that viewed video online
- **201.4 billion**: Number of videos viewed online per month (October 2011)
- **88.3 billion**: Videos viewed per month on Google sites, including YouTube (October 2011)
- **43**: Percentage share of all worldwide video views delivered by Google sites, including YouTube[11]

---

* For a stunning infographic on "A Day in the Life of the Internet," see www.mashable.com/2012/03/06/one-day-internet-data-traffic.

Figure I.1 The Internet in One Minute
Source: Image courtesy of Domo; www.domo.com

If those numbers seems abstract, look at the infographic in Figure I.1 to see what happens on the Internet every minute of every day.

As of 2009, estimates put the amount of data on the entire World Wide Web at roughly to 500 *exabytes*.[12] (An exabyte equals one million terabytes.) Research from the University of California, San Diego, reports that in 2008, Americans consumed 3.6 *zettabytes* of information,[13] a number that no doubt increased in subsequent years. (A zettabyte is equal to 1 billion terabytes.) You get my drift: Big Data is really big—and it's constantly expanding. Cisco estimates that, in 2016, 130 exabytes of data will travel through the Internet each year.[14]

WHY NOW? EXPLAINING THE BIG DATA REVOLUTION

We are at the beginning of an exciting time in the enterprise IT world. CIOs surveyed place Big Data at or near the top of their highest priorities for 2013 and beyond.[15] Right now, Big Data is just beginning. It is in the nascent stages of Gartner Research's oft-used Hype Cycle.[16] Without question, some people believe that the squeeze from Big Data will not be worth its juice.

For its part, the global management consulting firm McKinsey has boldly called Big Data "the next frontier for innovation, competition, and productivity."[17] You'll get no argument from me, but reading that statement should give you pause. Why now? After all, something as big as the Big Data Revolution doesn't just happen overnight. It takes time. Nor does a single, discrete event give rise to a trend this, well, big. Rather, Big Data represents more of an evolution than a Eureka moment. So what are some of the most important reasons for the advent and explosion of Big Data? This is not intended to be a comprehensive list. In the interest of brevity, here are the most vital factors:

- The always-on consumer
- The plummeting of technology costs
- The rise of data science
- Google and Infonomics
- The platform economy
- The 11/12 watershed: Sandy and politics
- Social Media and other factors

Let's explore each one.

The Always-On Consumer

I wasn't around in the early 1800s, but I can't help but think that most people were pretty patient back then. While I'm oversimplifying here, the Internet has made many citizens of industrialized countries pretty impetuous. It seems that most of us have too little idle time, far too many choices, and way too many things going on. Consider the following questions:

- Consumers who can watch a Netflix streaming video on their smartphones and tablets without buffering anywhere in the country are more likely to do so—and consume more data in the process. What would be the effect on Netflix if that same video constantly froze, like it often does on current airplane Wi-Fi connections?
- What if people had to wait six hours for their two-minute videos to upload to YouTube?
- What's the first thing that most people do when their airplane touches down (present company included)?
- Are most people going to remember to tweet something when they go back on the grid?

The answers to these questions should be obvious. As we'll see throughout this book, Big Data is largely consumer driven and consumer oriented. Moreover, the levels of data consumption we see today were simply impossible ten years ago—even if services like YouTube, Facebook, and Twitter had existed. Yes, data storage costs were just too high back then, but how many consumers really thought about that? In other words, the Big Data Revolution did not exclusively hinge upon lower corporate data storage prices. That was a necessary but insufficient condition, as was the arrival of the web. Neither immediately or directly triggered Big Data. Rather, Big Data was truly born when consumer technologies such as cell phones (and then smartphones), cloud computing, and broadband connections reached critical mass. Absent these improvements, innovations, and advents, we would not be hearing about Big Data. In its own way, each made generating, storing, and accessing data faster, easier, and more convenient for the masses. The always-on consumer represents arguably the biggest reason that the current Data Deluge is happening now. (Chapter 8 will have much more to say about the adjacent possible.)

The Plummeting of Technology Costs

For years now, consumers have been able to stay connected to the web from anywhere. In the process, they have consumed and generated unfathomable amounts of content and data. Many if not most consumers aren't aware of the precipitous drop in data storage costs—and others don't give it a second thought. Still, it's hard to overstate the impact of this on Big Data. If data storage costs had remained at 2000 levels, our world would be dramatically different. We would consume and generate far less data. Sites like YouTube may not exist—and they certainly wouldn't be nearly as popular.

We know from recent history that even small, non-zero fees represent a source of considerable economic friction. Tiny fees can have a disproportionately deterring effect on commercial behavior. In his 2009 book *Free: The Future of a Radical Price*, Chris Anderson writes about an Amazon promotion for free shipping on book orders of $25 (EU) or more across Europe. (In effect, this promotion would incentivize customers to order a second book. Most books cost less than $25.) Because of a programming error, though, Amazon inadvertently charged its French customers a nominal shipping fee of 1 franc (about 20 cents). The token charge ultimately yielded disproportionate and extremely telling results: significantly lower sales in France relative to other European countries. When Amazon fixed the error, French customers behaved like the rest of their European brethren.[*] The bottom line: price matters.

Back in June 2009, Anderson wrote a *Wired* piece "Tech Is Too Cheap to Meter,"[18] and those words today ring truer now than they did nearly four years ago. As I write this, I can buy a one terabyte (TB) external hard drive on eBay for $79. Fifteen years ago, I could expect to pay much, much more for such a device—if I could even find one. It's simple economics, really. If data storage costs had not dropped to the same extent, people would not be consuming and generating so much data (i.e., Big Data would not have happened). Just look at the carrier data usage rates among those with "all you

---

[*] Interesting postscript to the story: Amazon was sued for violating an obscure 1981 French law prohibiting such a promotion. A few years later, France joined the EU and that law disappeared.

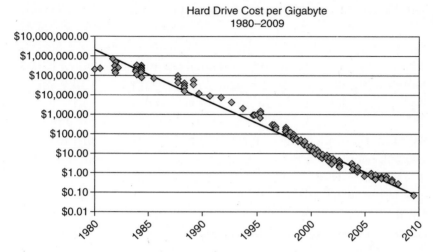

Figure I.2 The Drop in Data Storage Costs
Source: Matthew Komorowski

can eat" plans compared to those with strict data limits. Guess which folks use more data?

Whether online or off, data storage costs today are orders of magnitude cheaper than they were 30 years ago.

Figure I.2 is just the visual representation of Kryder's Law: magnetic disk areal storage density is increasing incredibly quickly, at a pace much faster than oft-cited Moore's Law. What's more, there's no end in sight to this trend—and data storage costs are not the only critical expenses to plummet over the past five years with respect to Big Data. Technologies like near field communication (NFC), radio-frequency identification (RFID), nanotechnology, and sensors have matured and become more commercially viable and affordable. To varying extents, each has allowed organizations to collect more data. Chapter 4 will have much more to say on these topics.

The Rise of Data Science

Five years ago, if you had asked 100 random people to tell you about a hot new field, I very much doubt that you would have heard any mention of the terms *data* and *science*. Since that time, though, the term *data scientist** has quietly begun to enter the business vernacular—and today it's white hot. In October 2010, *Harvard Business Review* called it the "sexiest job of the 21st century."[19] The reasons are simple: Big Data is blowing up, and supply and demand of practitioners is out of whack. More specifically, demand for data scientists far exceeds its available supply. Management consulting McKinsey predicts a severe "shortage of talent necessary for organizations to take advantage of Big Data. By 2018, the United States alone could face a shortage of 140,000 to 190,000 people with deep analytical skills . . . with the know-how to use the analysis of Big Data to make effective decisions."[20] As far as demand goes, myriad organizations are looking to leverage Big Data, but to do that they need plenty of help—and there aren't that many experienced data scientists out there. As a result, data scientists can pretty much write their own tickets these days.

But just what does a data scientist *do*, actually? While still evolving, data science encompasses a diverse set of fields, including math, statistics, data engineering, pattern recognition and learning, advanced computing, visualization, uncertainty modeling, data warehousing, and high-performance computing (HPC). While some overlap exists between the modern data scientist and a traditional statistician, they are not one and the same. By tapping into these varied disciplines, data scientists are able to extract meaning from data in innovative ways. Not only can they answer the questions that currently vex organizations, they can find better ones to ask.

As is the case with Big Data, there's no one generally accepted definition of the term. I happen to find IBM's definition of the *data scientist* complete and thought provoking:

> What sets the data scientist apart is strong business acumen, coupled with the ability to communicate findings to both business and IT leaders in a way that can influence how an organization approaches a business challenge. Good data scientists will not just address business problems. They will pick *the right problems* that have the most value to the organization. [Emphasis mine.]

---

* D.J. Patil and Jeff Hammerbacher coined the term *data science* in 2008. At the time, they were the leads of data and analytics efforts at LinkedIn and Facebook, respectively.

> The data scientist role has been described as "part analyst, part artist." Anjul Bhambhri, vice president of Big Data products at IBM, says, "A data scientist is somebody who is inquisitive, who can stare at data and spot trends. It's almost like a Renaissance individual who really wants to learn and bring change to an organization."
>
> Whereas a traditional data analyst may look only at data from a single source—a CRM system, for example—a data scientist will most likely explore and examine data from multiple disparate sources. The data scientist will sift through all incoming data with the goal of discovering a previously hidden insight, which in turn can provide a competitive advantage or address a pressing business problem. A data scientist does not simply collect and report on data, but also looks at it from many angles, determines what it means, then recommends ways to apply the data.[21]

I particularly like Bhambhri's insight that a data scientist is part analyst, part artist. The job entails—in fact, *requires*—a high degree of human judgment, especially with respect to selecting and defining the problem. That is, it's downright misleading to suggest that data scientists are slaves to computers, automation, and data.

It turns out that data science need not be the exclusive purview of data scientists. Companies such as Datahero, Infogram, and Statwing are trying to make analytics accessible even to laypersons.[22] Today, there are even data science dog-and-pony shows. For instance, in May 2012, I attended Greenplum's second annual Data Science Summit[23] while performing some of the preliminary research for this book. (Impressed by what I saw, I wrote a piece for *Huffington Post* titled "Big Data Goes Mainstream."[24]) I left that conference convinced that data science is here to stay. If anything, it's only going to get bigger.

Google and Infonomics

It's been a gradual process, but we've reached a point at which most progressive thinkers, leaders, and organizations acknowledge the fact that data is in fact a business asset—perhaps their *greatest* asset. In this regard, Google has been a watershed. The company has made tens of billions of dollars by serving up relevant ads exactly when its users were looking to buy something. While the company keeps the secret sauce of its search algorithm under tight wraps, at its core Google software runs on widespread and contextual *data*. Take that away, and it's hard to imagine Google as we know it. But Google embodies a much larger trend: more companies are finally recognizing that their success hinges upon how well they understand their users and customers.* In other words, it's all about the data.

In the late 1990s, Gartner's Douglas Laney[25] conducted extensive research on the value of information and its management. Laney certainly wasn't the first person to contend that information is valuable, but he went much further than most pundits had. He believed that information met the definition of a formal business asset and should be treated as such. He coined the term *Infonomics* (a portmanteau of *information* and *economics*) to describe the study and emergent discipline of quantifying, managing, and leveraging information. Its principles can be stated as follows:

- Information is an asset with value that can be quantified.
- Information should be accounted for and managed as an asset.
- Information's value should be used for budgeting IT and business initiatives.
- The realized value of information should be maximized.

To be sure, *Infonomics* remains an obscure term, in no small part due to the proprietary nature of Laney's research. Regardless of its popularity as a proper or recognized field, many people and companies have been unknowingly practicing Infonomics for decades. Case in point: Billy Beane.

On a typical corporate balance sheet, you'll find assets like cash and cash equivalents, short-term investments, receivables, inventory, and prepaid expenses. I have yet to see one, however, that lists an "information" bucket. Laney would like to see that change, and he has developed formal information asset valuation models. He even opened the nonprofit Center for Infonomics in 2010. Whether explicitly

---

* Amazon is another excellent example here.

quantified on a balance sheet or not, companies like Google and Facebook prove that data is exceptionally valuable.

If, like most learned folks, you believe that information is a business asset, then by definition Big Data inheres potentially enormous value. If you believe that data is a problem to be minimized, good luck surviving.

The Platform Economy

Without plugging my previous book too much here, it's imperative to at least briefly mention the role that platforms have played in the Big Data Revolution. Companies like Amazon, Apple, Facebook, and Google have all contributed to—and benefited from—the data avalanche in many ways. (There are some potentially nefarious effects to this trend, but that's a subject for Chapter 7.) More than the Gang of Four, other companies like LinkedIn, Twitter, and Salesforce.com have embraced platform thinking.

The impact of platforms on Big Data is hard to overstate. For instance, as smart as Mark Zuckerberg is, the idea of a social network preceded him. Early social networks like Classmates.com, MySpace, and Friendster all had transformative potential. For different reasons, however, those sites did not evolve into true platforms, effectively limiting their growth. From technical perspectives, they could not support anything near one billion users—or even a fraction of that number. For its part, in 2002 Friendster was extremely clunky. Despite its frequent problems, the site sported more than 3 million users soon after its launch. Friendster could only get so big. Back then no one wanted to visit a site that was down half of the time. The same is true now.

Give Zuckerberg credit for understanding how ubiquitous social networks and platforms could become, at least as they continued to offer a compelling user experience and rarely went down. Like Jeff Bezos, Larry Page, and Sergei Brin, Zuckerberg understood the impact of network effects on platforms. Put simply, bigger and wider platforms can support more users—and more users mean more data.

Many people forget that Apple's first iPhone launched in 2007 without the AppStore. The AppStore officially "opened" in July 2008 as an update to iTunes. In this sense, the original iPhone acted more like a traditional cell phone than the portable computer it ultimately became. As anyone who has paid attention over the past four years knows, the AppStore was nothing less than a game-changer. The expression "there's an app for that" entered the vernacular as developers from around the globe hurried to build an astonishing array of games, productivity tools, and so on.

Opening an AppStore only gets a company—even Apple—so far. Without the requisite tools to build many interesting apps (and some truly awful ones), developers would not have spent so much time and effort on them. As a result, apps would not have taken off—at least as quickly and to the same extent that they did. Application programming interfaces (APIs) and software development kits (SDKs) gave developers the tools to populate the AppStore with myriad offerings, and other companies like Google, Samsung, Microsoft, Facebook, and RIM followed Apple's lead. The result: further growth of Big Data.

The 11/12 Watershed: Sandy and Politics

We may look back at early November 2012 as the period in which Big Data entered the zeitgeist. In that short period, two watershed events took place that may well have ushered in the era of Big Data.

Before Halloween, meteorologists at the National Weather Service (NWS) had been keeping their eye on a bunch of clouds in the Caribbean. Those clouds appeared to be heading toward the Northeastern United States. Nearly a week later, a NWS computer model predicted that the Caribbean weather system would morph into a "superstorm" after taking a "once-in-a-century" sharp turn into New Jersey.[26] Ultimately, Hurricane Sandy wrecked an estimated $50 billion of damage on the country,[27] making it the second-worst natural disaster behind Katrina. While computer models and data couldn't *prevent* Sandy and its carnage, the ability of NWS to predict such a rare event allowed millions to prepare, minimized its damage, and saved lives.

Just a few days later, author and statistician Nate Silver came under fire from many conservatives. Silver's crime? He boldly asserted that Barack Obama had established himself as more than a 70 percent favorite to win the Presidential election[28] when many reputable polls at the time put the incumbent and Republican nominee Mitt Romney in essentially a dead heat. Toward the end of the campaign, Silver increased his confidence level to more than 90 percent. Outrage, claims of political bias, and mockery came from many old-school pundits. They questioned the wisdom in trusting the methods of a 34-year-old stats geek over tried-and-true polls. (The parallels between Silver and Billy Beane are obvious.)

Well, you know how this story turned out. Obama beat Romney by a comfortable margin. The wunderkind correctly predicted all 50 states,[29] and Silver's critics suddenly fell silent. The methodology behind his predictions isn't terribly important here,* but it has shown to be incredibly accurate. And Silver is no one-trick pony. His track record at predicting past elections is astonishing. In 2008, Silver predicted 49 of the 50 states in the presidential election. Then in 2010 Silver correctly forecasted:

- 92 percent of U.S. Senate races. (He missed Alaska, Nevada, and Colorado.)
- 95 percent of governor races. (He missed Illinois and Florida.)

Sales of Silver's recently released book *The Signal and the Noise: Why So Many Predictions Fail—but Some Don't* exploded. We'll come back to the 2012 presidential election and the use of Big Data later in the book. For now, suffice it to say that the highly public nature of these two events served as a data wake-up call of sorts.

Social Media and Other Factors

I don't want to devote too much space to it here, but I'd be remiss if I didn't mention the impact of social media on Big Data. LinkedIn, Twitter, Facebook, and other sites are driving a great deal of the Big Data revolution. And let's not forget about enormous advances in data capturing technologies such as RFID and sensors, discussed in more detail in Chapter 4.

---

* If you're curious, go to http://fivethirtyeight.blogs.nytimes.com/methodology.

On a broader and more philosophical level, as a society, the past few years seem to have proven that we have a nearly insatiable demand to generate and consume data. Perhaps it's something in our DNA, but much of this may have to do with the price of data consumption—often near zero. In the infamous words of American writer Steward Brand, "On the one hand information wants to be expensive, because it's so valuable. The right information in the right place just changes your life. On the other hand, information wants to be free, because the cost of getting it out is getting lower and lower all the time. So you have these two fighting against each other."

Finally, the Big Data revolution has arrived because of economic need. (Chapter 8 will have a great deal more to say about this.) Aside from the Oakland A's and the City of Boston, this book will introduce many people and institutions using data and available technologies to innovate, reduce costs, and reach new customers.

CENTRAL THESIS OF BOOK

It's easy for cynics and naysayers to dismiss Big Data as just another fad or the latest technology jargon. You don't have to look too hard to find an old-school CIO who considers Big Data hooey. And Big Data is not alone in this regard. Plenty of executives still view social media as nothing more than a waste of time, with every minute spent on "The Twitter" representing a minute better spent elsewhere. And then there are the naysayers who don't buy into the cloud either. In their view, the squeeze just isn't worth the juice.

All of this is to be expected. To be fair, in the world of technology, many companies, services, products, and vendors arrive with enormous hype only to quickly disappear—as do their acolytes. (Microsoft's Zune and Windows Me, and Sony's MiniDisc, Pressplay, and MusicNet, are just a few of tech's many misses. The dot-com bust need not be rehashed here.) This is the nature of the tech beast. Because of the high failure rates or ephemeral nature of the next shiny new things, any new technology or application initially faces far more laggards than early adopters—even the technologies that ultimately prove successful and important. This is doubly true in the enterprise,

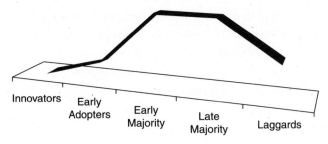

Innovators Early Adopters Early Majority Late Majority Laggards

Figure I.3 The Technology Adoption Life Cycle (TALC)

where conservative CIOs understandably don't want to bet the future of their organizations (and often their own careers) on a technology that may be a flash in the pan. And Big Data is certainly no exception to this rule. As I write this book, most organizations have yet to embrace it. Many CIOs believe or hope that it just goes away—at least until they retire, that is.

In this way, Big Data is just part of the Technology Adoption Life Cycle (TALC). TALC depicts the adoption of new technologies by group. In a nutshell, few people and organizations implement new technologies right after their introduction. This is represented graphically in Figure I.3.

For progressive organizations of all sizes, however, Big Data is anything but bunk. On the contrary, it represents an enormous opportunity for one simple reason: when done right, Big Data can yield superior information and unparalleled insights into a range of behaviors and even predict a few. With that information, everyone—employees, departments, organizations, scientists, and politicians—can make vastly better decisions.

When most of us make decisions, we tend to use heuristics and rules of thumb—not data. While this may be understandable in our personal lives, it's less so in our professional ones. As many books and studies have repeatedly shown, human beings are not terribly adroit at making good (read: rational) personal and business decisions. Economists like Daniel Kahneman, Dan Ariel, Steven Levitt, Stephen Dubner, and others have written books and done remarkable studies that effectively prove our generally poor decision-making abilities. In fact, behavioral economics has become quite the hot field primarily because it attempts to explain what traditional economic theory cannot. Human beings are not entirely rational, even when presented with complete information. Against that backdrop, is it remotely surprising that we are even more deficient when presented with unprecedented amounts of incomplete data?

PLAN OF ATTACK

Today, organizations no longer operate in a world in which only traditional data types and sources matter. That ship has long sailed. The fact that many organizations choose to ignore other forms and sources of data doesn't make them any less important.

The timing of Big Data could not be more propitious. Big Data and its attendant tools allow organizations to interpret previously unimaginable amounts and types of data, and the most progressive organizations are harnessing significant value in the process. Yes, there is a signal to go along with that noise. Big Data allows organizations to find the potential gold in the petabytes of tweets, texts, Facebook likes, blog posts and related comments, podcasts, photos, videos, and the like.

At a high level, *Too Big to Ignore: The Business Case for Big Data* makes a compelling business case for Big Data. Chapter 1, "Data 101 and the Data Deluge," provides the requisite background on Big Data and defines key terms, such as structured versus unstructured and semi-structured data. Chapter 2, "Demystifying Big Data," goes deeper. Much like *cloud computing* and *Web 2.0*, definitions of Big Data run the gamut. The chapter examines the major characteristics of Big Data. Chapter 3, "The Elements of Persuasion: Big Data Techniques," examines the specific techniques people are using to understand Big Data.

Chapter 4, "Big Data Solutions," moves us from theory to practice. We live in a world rife with data not easily represented in—much less effectively analyzed by—old standbys. To make Big Data come alive, new tools are needed, and this chapter introduces some of the most prevalent ones. Chapter 5, "Case Studies: The Big Rewards of Big Data," looks in depth at several organizations in different industries that have successfully deployed these tools.

Chapter 6, "Taking the Big Plunge," offers some advice on getting started with Big Data. Chapter 7, "Big Data: Big Issues and Big Problems," looks at the flip side of Big Data. We'll see that it's not all puppy dogs and ice cream. With Big Data, there is big danger. The book concludes with Chapter 8, "Looking Forward: The Future of Big Data." I'll offer some predictions about where Big Data is going and why it will cease to be a luxury in the coming years.

WHO SHOULD READ THIS BOOK?

Too Big to Ignore is about the increasingly important topic of Big Data. It makes the business case that there's tremendous value to be gleaned from the volume, variety, and velocity of information currently streaming at us. The book has no one intended audience, and many groups of people will benefit from reading it, including:

- CEOs, CIOs, and senior leaders who want to understand the fuss about Big Data
- Employees at consulting firms and software vendors who want to educate their current and prospective clients about the sea change that is Big Data
- Professors, school deans, and other academics who want to prepare their students about to enter the Big Data world
- Other people generally interested in Big Data and what they can do with it

Those looking for a technical guide on how to implement specific Big Data applications should look elsewhere. This is *not* a tactical, how-to book.

SUMMARY

For a variety of reasons, we are in the midst of a revolution of sorts. The Data Deluge has arrived, and it's only betting bigger. Car insurance, government, and recruiting are just three areas being transformed by Big Data. Organizations of all sorts are embracing it as we speak. And we're just getting started.

With the requisite foundation firmly in place, Chapter 1 looks at Big Data in a historical context. It examines how enterprise data has evolved in the Computer and Internet ages, with a particular emphasis on new data types and sources.

NOTES

1. Tucci, Joseph, "EMC CEO Says Big Data to Transform Every Industry," October 3, 2012, www.bloomberg.com/video/emc-ceo-says-big-data-to-transform-every-industry-XZ6adCHaTp~448vjZG97Zw.html, retrieved December 11, 2012.

2. LeBeau, Philip, "Texting and Driving Worse Than Drinking and Driving," June 25, 2009, www.cnbc.com/id/31545004/Texting_And_Driving_Worse_Than_Drinking_and_Driving, retrieved December 11, 2012.

3. "Snapshot Common Questions," www.progressive.com/auto/snapshot-common-questions.aspx, retrieved December 11, 2012.

4. Yvkoff, Liane, "Gadget Helps Progressive Offer Insurance Discount." March 21, 2011, http://reviews.cnet.com/8301-13746_7-20045433-48.html, retrieved December 11, 2012.

5. "'Street Bump' App Detects Potholes, Alerts Boston City Officials," July 20, 2012, www.foxnews.com/tech/2012/07/20/treet-bump-app-detects-potholes-alerts-boston-city-officials/, retrieved December 11, 2012.

6. Ngowi, Rodrique, "App Detects Potholes, Alerts Boston City Officials," July 20, 2012, www.boston.com/business/technology/articles/2012/07/20/app_detects_potholes_alerts_boston_city_officials/, retrieved December 11, 2012.

7. Walker, Joseph, "Meet the New Boss: Big Data Companies Trade In Hunch-Based Hiring for Computer Modeling," September 20, 2012, http://online.wsj.com/article/SB10000872396390443890304578006252019616768.html, retrieved December 11, 2012.

8. www.evolvondemand.com/home/about.php, retrieved December 11, 2012.

9. Kolakowski, Nick, "Big Data Spending Will Hit $28 Billion in 2012: Gartner," October 17, 2012, http://slashdot.org/topic/bi/big-data-spending-will-hit-28-billion-in-2012-gartner/, retrieved December 11, 2012.

10. "Billions and Billions: Big Data Becomes a Big Deal," 2012, www.deloitte.com/view/en_GX/global/industries/technology-media-telecommunications/tmt-predictions-2012/technology/70763e14447a4310VgnVCM1000001a56f00aRCRD.htm, retrieved December 11, 2012.

11. "Internet 2011 in Numbers," January 17, 2012, http://royal.pingdom.com/2012/01/17/internet-2011-in-numbers/, retrieved December 11, 2012.

12. Wray, Richard, "Internet Data Heads for 500bn Gigabytes," May 18, 2009, www.guardian.co.uk/business/2009/may/18/digital-content-expansion, retrieved December 11, 2012.

13. Wu, Suzanne, "How Much Information Is There in the World?" February 10, 2011, http://news.usc.edu/#!/article/29360/How-Much-Information-Is-There-in-the-World, retrieved December 11, 2012.

14. Fitchard, Kevin, "Despite Critics, Cisco Stands by Its Data Deluge," February 14, 2012, http://gigaom.com/2012/02/14/despite-critics-cisco-stands-by-its-data-deluge/, retrieved December 11, 2012.

15. Kolakowski, Nick, "CIOs See Big Data as Big Deal by 2013: Survey," May 10, 2012, http://slashdot.org/topic/bi/cios-see-big-data-as-big-deal/, retrieved December 11, 2012.

16. "Research Methodologies, Hype Cycles," copyright 2012, www.gartner.com/technology/research/methodologies/hype-cycle.jsp, retrieved December 11, 2012.

17. Manyika, James; Chui, Michael; Brown, Brad; Bughin, Jacques; Dobbs, Richard; Roxburgh, Charles; Hung Byers, Angela, "Big Data: The Next Frontier for Innovation, Competition, and Productivity," May 2011, www.mckinsey.com/insights/mgi/research/technology_and_innovation/big_data_the_next_frontier_for_innovation, retrieved December 11, 2012.

18. Anderson, Chris, "Tech Is Too Cheap to Meter: It's Time to Manage for Abundance, Not Scarcity," June 22, 2009, www.wired.com/techbiz/it/magazine/17-07/mf_freer?currentPage=all, retrieved December 11, 2012.

19. Davenport, Thomas H.; Patil, D.J., "Data Scientist: The Sexiest Job of the 21st Century," October 2012, http://hbr.org/2012/10/data-scientist-the-sexiest-job-of-the-21st-century/, retrieved December 11, 2012.

20. Manyika, James; Chui, Michael; Brown, Brad; Bughin, Jacques; Dobbs, Richard; Roxburgh, Charles; Hung Byers, Angela, "Big data: The next frontier for innovation, competition, and productivity," May 2011, www.mckinsey.com/insights/mgi/research/technology_and_innovation/big_data_the_next_frontier_for_innovation, retrieved December 11, 2012.

21. "What Is Data Scientist?," www-01.ibm.com/software/data/infosphere/data-scientist/, retrieved December 11, 2012.

22. Harris, Derrick, "5 Trends That Are Changing How We Do Big Data," November 3, 2012, http://gigaom.com/data/5-trends-that-are-changing-how-we-do-big-data/, retrieved December 11, 2012.

23. www.greenplum.com/datasciencesummit, retrieved December 11, 2012.

24. Simon, Phil, "Big Data Goes Mainstream," May 24, 2012, www.huffingtonpost.com/phil-simon/big-data-goes-mainstream_b_1541079.html, retrieved December 11, 2012.

25. www.gartner.com/AnalystBiography?authorId=40872, retrieved December 11, 2012.

26. Borenstein, Seth, "Predicting Presidents, Storms and Life by Computer," November 12, 2012, www.weather.com/news/nate-silver-predicting-presidents-storms-20121111, retrieved December 11, 2012.

27. Craft, Matthew, "Hurricane Sandy's Economic Damage Could Reach $50 Billion, Equecat Estimates," November 1, 2012, www.huffingtonpost.com/2012/11/01/hurricane-sandy-economic-damage_n_2057850.html, retrieved December 11, 2012.

28. Blodget, Henry, "Nate Silver: Obama's Odds of Winning Are Now Back Over 70%," October 25, 2012, www.businessinsider.com/who-will-be-president-2012, retrieved December 11, 2012.

29. Wu, Joyce, "The Nate Silver Effect," November 12, 2012, http://cornellsun.com/section/opinion/content/2012/11/12/nate-silver-effect, retrieved December 11, 2012.

CHAPTER 1

Data 101 and the Data Deluge

Any enterprise CEO really ought to be able to ask a question that involves connecting data across the organization, be able to run a company effectively, and especially to be able to respond to unexpected events. Most organizations are missing this ability to connect all the data together.

—Tim Berners Lee

oday, data surrounds us at all times. We are living in what some have called *the Data Deluge*.[1] *Everything* is data. There's even data about data, hence the term *metadata*. And data is anything but static; it's becoming bigger and more dynamic all the time. The notion of data is somewhat different and much more nuanced today than it was a decade ago, and it's certainly much larger.

Powerful statements like these might give many readers pause, scare some others, and conjure up images of *The Matrix*. That's understandable, but the sooner that executives and industry leaders realize this, the quicker they'll be able to harness the power of Big Data and see its benefits. As a starting point, we must explore the very concept of data in greater depth—and a little history is in order. If we want to understand where we are now and where we are going, we have to know how we got here.

This chapter discusses the evolution of data in the enterprise. It provides an overview of the types of data that organizations have at their disposal today. It answers questions like these: How did we arrive at the Big Data world? What does this new world look like? We have to answer questions like these before we can move up the food chain. Ultimately, we'll get to the big question: how can Big Data enable superior decision-making?

THE BEGINNINGS: STRUCTURED DATA

Make no mistake: corporate data existed well before anyone ever turned on a proper computer. The notion of data didn't even arrive years later, when primitive accounting systems became commercially viable. So why weren't as many people talking about data thirty years ago? Simple: because very little of it was easily (read: electronically) available.

Before computers became standard fixtures in offices, many companies paid employees via manual checks; bookkeepers manually kept accounting ledgers. The need for public companies to report their earnings on quarterly and annual bases did not start with the modern computer. Of course, thirty years ago, organizations struggled with this type of reporting because they lacked the automated systems that we take for granted today. While calculators helped, the actual precursor to proper enterprise systems was VisiCalc. Dan Bricklin invented the first spreadsheet program in the mid-1970s, and Bob Frankston subsequently refined it.

In the mid-1980s, user-facing or front-end applications like manufacturing resource planning (MRP) and enterprise resource planning (ERP) systems began to make inroads. At a high level, these systems had one goal: to automate standard business processes. To achieve this

Table 1.1 Simple Example of Structured Customer Master Data

CustomerID	CustomerName	ZipCode	ContactName
1001	Bally's	89109	Jon Anderson
1002	Bellagio	89109	Geddy Lee
1003	Wynn Casino	89109	Mike Mangini
1004	Borgata	08401	Steve Hogarth
1005	Caesar's Palace	89109	Brian Morgan

goal, enormous mainframe databases supported these systems. For the most part, these systems could only process *structured data* (i.e., "orderly" information relating to customers, employees, products, vendors, and the like). A simple example of this type of data is presented in Table 1.1.

Now a master customer table can only get so big. After all, even Amazon.com "only" serves 300 or 400 million customers—although its current internal systems can support many more times that number. Tables get much longer (not wider) when they contain *transactional* data like employee paychecks, journal entries, or sales. For instance, consider Table 1.2.

In Table 1.2, we see that many customers make multiple purchases from a company. For instance, I am an Amazon customer, and I buy at least one book, DVD, or CD per week. I have no doubt that each sale represents an individual record in a very long Amazon database table somewhere. (Amazon uses this data for two reasons: [1] process my payments; and [2] learn more about my purchasing habits and recommend products that, more often than not, I consider buying.)

Table 1.2 Simple Example of Transactional Sales Data

OrderNbr	CustomerID	ProductID	OrderDate	ShipDate
119988	1001	2112	1/3/13	1/6/13
119989	1002	1234	1/6/13	1/11/13
119990	1001	2112	1/6/13	1/9/13
119991	1004	778	1/6/13	1/12/13
119992	1004	999	1/7/13	1/15/13

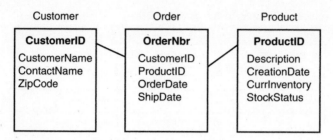

Figure 1.1 Entity Relationship Diagram (ERD)

Things are orderly under a *relational data model*. All data is stored in proper tables, and each table is typically joined with at least one other. Each table is its own entity. An *Entity Relationship Diagram* (ERD) visually represents the relationships between and among tables. A simple example of an ERD is shown in Figure 1.1.

Note that the ERD in Figure 1.1 is nothing like what you'd find behind the scenes in most large organizations. It's common for enterprise systems to contain *thousands* of individual tables (including some customized ones), although not every table in a commercial off the shelf (COTS) system contains data. Also, querying data from multiple tables requires JOIN statements. While you can theoretically query as many data sources and tables as you like (as long as they are properly joined), queries with a high number of huge tables tend to take a great deal of time to complete.[*] Queries improperly or inefficiently written can wreak havoc across an entire enterprise.

Throughout the 1990s and early 2000s, more and more organizations deployed systems built upon this relational data model. They uprooted their legacy mainframe systems and supplanted them with contemporary enterprise applications. Importantly, these applications were powered by orderly and expensive relational databases like Oracle, SQL Server, and others. What's more, organizations typically converted their legacy data to these new systems by following a process called *ETL* (extract, transform, and load).[**]

---

[*] Trust me. I've written tens of thousands of queries in my day.

[**] We'll see in Chapter 4 that ETL isn't really beneficial in a world of Hadoop and NoSQL because much data is far less structured these days.

Like their predecessors, ERP and CRM systems excelled at handling structured data, performing essential business functions like paying vendors and employees, and providing standard reports. With these systems, employees could enter, edit, and retrieve essential enterprise information. Corporate intranets, wikis, and knowledge bases represented early attempts to capture unstructured data, but most of this data was internal (read: generated by employees, not external entities). For the most part, intranets have not displaced e-mail as the *de facto* killer app inside many large corporations.

When asked about data, most people still only think of the structured kind mentioned in this section. "The relational model has dominated the data management industry since the 1980s," writes blogger Jim Harris on the Data Roundtable. That model "foster(s) the long-held belief that data has to be structured before it can be used, and that data should be managed following ACID (atomicity, consistency, isolation, durability) principles, structured primarily as tables and accessed using structured query language (SQL)."[2] Harris is spot-on. The relational data model is still very important, but it is no longer the only game in town. It all depends on the type and source of data in question.

Even in a Big Data world, transactional and structured data and the relational databases behind them are far from irrelevant. But organizations need to start leveraging new data sources and solutions.

STRUCTURE THIS! WEB 2.0 AND THE ARRIVAL OF BIG DATA

While business information is as old as capitalism itself, the widespread use of corporate data is a relatively recent development. The last section demonstrated how, in the 1980s and 1990s, relational databases, ERP and CRM applications, business automation, and computers all helped popularize the contemporary notion of data. Over the past few decades, organizations have begun gradually spending more time, money, and effort managing their data, but these efforts have tended to be mostly internal in nature. That is, organizations have focused on what the data generated by their own hands.

In or around 2005, that started to change as we entered Web 2.0—aka *the social web*. As a direct result, the volume, variety, and velocity of data rose exponentially, especially consumer-driven data that is, for the most part, *external* to the enterprise. The usual suspects include the rise of nascent social networks like Classmates.com, MySpace, Friendster, and then a little Harvard-specific site named The Facebook. Photo sharing began to go mainstream through sites like Flickr, eventually gobbled up by Yahoo! Blogging started to take off—as did micro-blogging sites like Twitter a few years later. More and more people began walking around with increasingly powerful smartphones that could record videos. Enter the citizen journalist. Sites like YouTube made video sharing easy and extremely popular, prompting Google to pay $1.65 billion for the company in 2007. Collectively, these sites, services, and advancements led to proliferation of unstructured data, semi-structured data, and metadata—the majority of which was external to the enterprise.

To be sure, many organizations have seen their structured and transactional data grow in velocity and volume. As recently as 2005, *Information Management* magazine estimated the largest data warehouse in the world at 100 terabytes (TB) in size. As of September 2011, Walmart, the world's largest retailer, logged "one million customer transactions per hour and fed information into databases estimated at 2.5 petabytes in size."[3] (I'll save you from having to do the math. This is 25 times as big.) For their part, today companies like Amazon, Apple, and Google are generating, storing, and accessing much more data now than they did in 2005. This makes sense. As Facebook adds more users and features, Apple customers download more songs and apps, Google indexes more web pages, and Amazon sells more stuff, each generates more data.

However, it's essential to note that Web 2.0 did not increase internal IM demands at every organization. Consider a medium-sized regional hospital for a moment. (I've consulted at many in my career.) Let's say that, on a typical day, it receives 200 new patients. For all of its transformative power, the Internet did not cause that hospital's daily patients to quadruple. Hospitals only contain so many beds. Think of a hospital as an anti-Facebook, because it faces fairly strict limits with respect to scale. Hospitals don't benefit from network effects. (Of course, they can always expand their physical space, put in more beds, hire more employees, and the like. These activities will increase the amount of data the hospitals generate, but let's keep it simple in this example.)

Unstructured Data

We know from Tables 1.1 and 1.2 that structured data is relational, orderly, consistent, and easily stored in spreadsheets and database tables. Unstructured data is its inverse. It's big, nonrelational, messy, text laden, and not easily represented in traditional tables. And unstructured data represents most of what we call *Big Data*. According to ClaraBridge, a leader in sentiment and text analytics software, "Unstructured information accounts for more than 80 percent of all data in organizations."[4] By some estimates, unstructured data is growing ten to fifty times faster than its structured counterpart.

While everyone agrees on the growth of data, there's plenty of disagreement on the precise terminology we should be using. Some believe that unstructured data is in fact a contradiction in terms.[5] And then there's Curt Monash, Ph.D., a leading analyst of and strategic advisor to the software industry. He defines *poly-structured data* as "data with a structure that can be exploited to provide most of the benefits of a highly structured database (e.g., a tabular/relational one) but cannot be described in the concise, consistent form such highly structured systems require."[6] Debating the technical merits of different definitions isn't terribly important for our purposes. This book uses the term *unstructured data* in lieu of *poly-structured data*. It's just simpler, and it suits our purposes just fine.

Semi-Structured Data

The rise of the Internet and the web has led not only to a proliferation of structured and unstructured data. We've also seen dramatic increases in two other types of data: semi-structured data and metadata. Let's start with the former.

As its name implies, semi-structured data contains characteristics of both its structured and unstructured counterparts. Examples include

- Extensible Markup Language (XML) and other markup languages

- E-mail
- Electronic Data Interchange (EDI), a particular set of standards for computer-to-computer exchange of information

Many people are using semi-structured data whether they realize it or not. And the same holds true for metadata, discussed next.

Metadata

The information about the package is just as important as the package itself.

Fred Smith, Founder and CEO of FedEx, 1978

Now let's move on to metadata, a term that is increasingly entering the business vernacular. As the quote indicates, people like Fred Smith grasped its importance thirty-five years ago. The term *metadata* means, quite simply, data about data.

We are often creating and using metadata whether we realize it or not. For instance, my favorite band is Rush, the Canadian power trio still churning out amazing music after nearly forty years. While I usually just enjoy the music at concerts, sing along, and air drum,* I occasionally take pictures. Let's say that when I get home, I upload them to Flickr, a popular photo-sharing site. (Flickr is one of myriad companies that extensively use tags and metadata. Many stock photo sites like iStockphoto and Shutterstock rely heavily upon metadata to make their content easily searchable. In fact, I can't think of a single major photo site that doesn't use tags.)

So I can view these photos online, but what if I want other Rush fans to find them? What to do? For starters, I can create an album titled *Rush 2012 Las Vegas Photos*. That's not a bad starting point, but what if someone wanted to see only recent pictures of the band's insanely talented drummer Neil Peart? After all, he's not in all of my pictures, and it seems silly to make people hunt and peck. The web has evolved, and so has search. No bother; Flickr has me covered. The site encourages me to tag pictures with as many descriptive labels as I like, even offering suggestions based upon similar photos

---

*To see what I mean, Google "Rush Car Commercial Fly By Night 2012."

and albums. In the end, my photos are more findable throughout the site for everyone, not just me. For instance, a user searching for "Las Vegas concerts" or "rock drummers" may well come across a photo of Peart in action in Las Vegas, whether she was initially looking for Rush or not.

In this example, the tags are examples of metadata: they serve to describe the actual data (in this case, the photo and its "contents"). But these photos contain metadata whether I choose to tag them or not. When I upload each photo to Flickr, the site captures each photo's time and date and my username. Flickr also knows the size of the photo's file (its number of KBs or MBs). This is more metadata. And it gets better. Perhaps the photo contains a date stamp and GPS information from my camera or smartphone. Let's say that I'm lazy. I upload my Rush photos in mid-2013 and tag them incorrectly as "Cleveland, Ohio." Flickr "knows" that these photos were actually taken in November 2012 in Las Vegas and kindly makes some recommendations to me to improve the accuracy of my tags and description.[*] In the future, maybe Flickr will add facial recognition software so I won't have to tag anyone anymore. The site will "learn" that my future Rush photos will differ from those of a country-music-loving, conservative Republican who adores radio show host Rush Limbaugh. (For more on how tagging works and why it's so important, check out *Everything Is Miscellaneous: The Power of the New Digital Disorder* by David Weinberger.)

Because of its extensive metadata, Flickr can quickly make natural associations among existing photos for its users. For instance, Flickr knows that one man's "car" is another's "automobile." It also knows that maroon and mauve are just different shades of red and purple, respectively. This knowledge allows Flickr to provide more accurate and granular search results (see Figure 1.2).

If I want to find photos taken of Neil Peart from 6/01/2012 to 10/01/2012 in HD only with the tag of "Clockwork Angels" (the band's most recent studio album), I can easily perform that search. (Whether I'll see any results is another matter; the more specific the criteria, the

---

[*] The site uses Exif data (short for Exchangeable Image File), a standard format for storing interchange information in digital photography image files using JPEG compression.

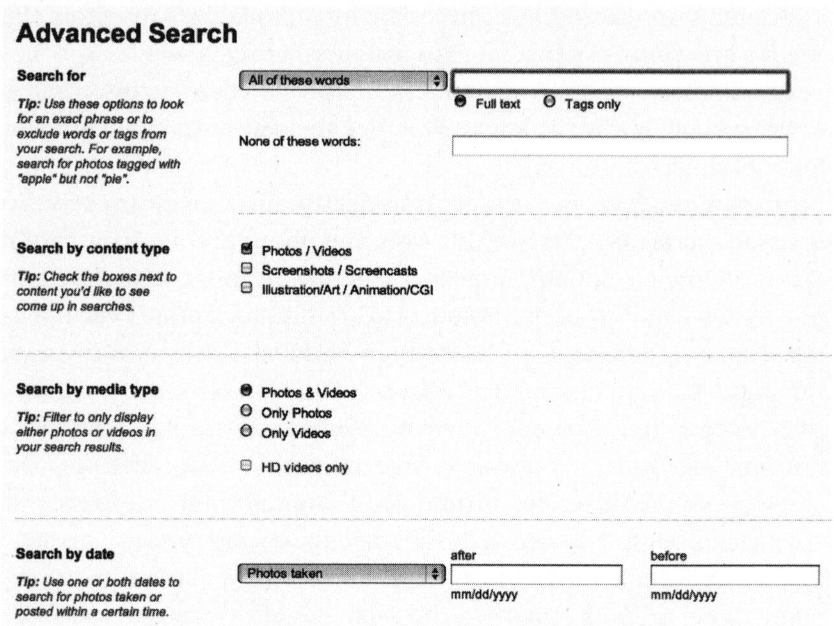

Advanced Search

Search for

Tip: Use these options to look for an exact phrase or to exclude words or tags from your search. For example, search for photos tagged with "apple" but not "pie".

| All of these words | ⬍ |

○ Full text   ○ Tags only

None of these words:

Search by content type

Tip: Check the boxes next to content you'd like to see come up in searches.

☑ Photos / Videos
☐ Screenshots / Screencasts
☐ Illustration/Art / Animation/CGI

Search by media type

Tip: Filter to only display either photos or videos in your search results.

◉ Photos & Videos
○ Only Photos
○ Only Videos

☐ HD videos only

Search by date

Tip: Use one or both dates to search for photos taken or posted within a certain time.

| Photos taken | ⬍ |

after
mm/dd/yyyy

before
mm/dd/yyyy

Figure 1.2 Flickr Search Options
Source: Flickr.com

less likely that I'll see any results.) The larger point is that, without metadata, searches like these just aren't possible.

Smartphones with GPS functionality make tagging location easier than ever—and just wait until augmented reality comes to your smartphone. If not the final frontier, the next logical step in tagging is facial recognition. To this end, in June 2012, Facebook acquired facial recognition start-up Face.com for an undisclosed sum (rumored to be north of $100 million). The Tel Aviv, Israel-based start-up "offers application programming interfaces (APIs) for third-party developers to incorporate Face.com's facial-recognition software into their applications. The company has released two Facebook applications: Photo Finder, which lets people find untagged pictures of themselves and their Facebook friends, and Photo Tagger, which lets people automatically bulk-tag photos on Facebook."[7]

So from a data perspective, what does all of this mean? Several things. First, even an individual photo has plenty of metadata associated with it—and that data is stored somewhere. Think about the billions of photos online, and you start to appreciate the amount of data involved in their storage and retrieval. Second, photos today are more complex because they capture more data than ever—and this trend is only intensifying.

Let's get back to my Rush example. If I look at my concert pictures from last night, I'm sure that I'll find one with poor focus. Right now, there's not much that I can do about it; Photoshop can only do so much. But soon there might be hope for fuzzy pictures, thanks to the folks at the start-up Lytro. Through light field technology, Lytro's cameras ultimately "allow users to change the focus of a picture after the picture is taken."[8] Plenoptic cameras such as Lytro's represent "a new type of camera that dramatically changes photography for the first time since the 1800s. [It's] not too far away from those 3D moving photographs in the *Harry Potter* movies."[9]

THE COMPOSITION OF DATA: THEN AND NOW

Over the past decade, many organizations have continued to generate roughly the same amount of internal, structured, and transactional data as they did before the arrival of Web 2.0. For instance, quite a few haven't seen appreciable changes in the same number of employee and vendor checks cut. They book roughly the same number of sales and generate a more or less stable number of financial transactions. The "data world" *inside* of the organization in many cases has not changed significantly. However, this is in stark contrast to the data world outside—and *around*—the enterprise. It could not be more different. Consider Figure 1.3.

As Figure 1.3 shows, there is now much more external and unstructured data than its structured counterpart—and has been for a long time. At the same time, the amount of structured, transactional data has grown exponentially as well. The ostensible paradox can be explained quite simply: while the amount of structured data has grown fast, the amount of unstructured data has grown much faster. Analytics-as-a-service pioneer 1010data "now hosts more than 5 trillion—yes, trillion with a "t"—records for its customers."[10] Despite statistics like this, most data today is of the unstructured variety.

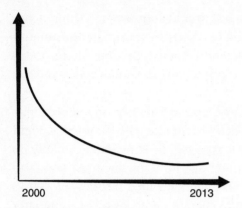

Figure 1.3 The Ratio of Structured to Unstructured Data

As mentioned before, unstructured data has always existed, even though few people thought of it as "data." So other than the terminology, what's different now? First, as mentioned earlier, there's just more unstructured data today than at any point in the past. Second, much of this unstructured data is digitized and available nearly *instantly*—especially if its owners want it to be.* Delays have evaporated in many cases, although many organizations cannot access real-time data. Be that as it may, by and large, today unstructured data doesn't need to be transcribed, scanned into computers, or read by document storage systems. *Data is born digital*—or at least it can be. (There are still plenty of hospitals and doctors' offices that refuse to embrace the digital world and electronic medical records.)

Consider books, newspapers, and magazines for a moment—all good examples of unstructured data (both 20 years ago and now). For centuries, they were released only in physical formats. With the rise of the Internet, this is no longer the case. Most magazines and newspapers (sites) are available electronically, and print media has been dying for some time now. Most proper books (including this one) are available both in traditional and electronic formats. There is no time lag. In fact, some e-books and Kindle singles are *only* available electronically.

---

* Even this isn't entirely true, as Julian Assange has proven.

THE CURRENT STATE OF THE DATA UNION

Unstructured data is more prevalent and bigger than ever. This does not change the fact that relatively few organizations have done very much with it. For the most part, organizations lamentably have turned a deaf ear to this kind of information—and continue to do so to this day. They have essentially ignored the gigantic amounts of unstructured or semi-structured data now generated by always-connected consumers and citizens. They treat data as a four-letter word.

It's not hard to understand this reluctance. To this day, many organizations struggle managing just their own transactional and structured data. Specific problems include the lack of master data, poor data quality and integrity, and no semblance of data governance. Far too many employees operate in a vacuum; they don't consider the implications of their actions on others, especially with regard to information management (IM). Creating business rules and running audit reports can only do so much. Based upon my nearly fifteen years of working in different IM capacities across the globe, I'd categorize most organizations' related efforts as shown in Figure 1.4.

For every organization currently managing its data very well, many more are doing a poor job. Call it *data dysfunction*, and I'm far from the only one who has noticed this disturbing fact. As for why this is the case, the reasons vary, but I asked my friend Tony Fisher for his take on the matter. Fisher is the founder of DataFlux and the author

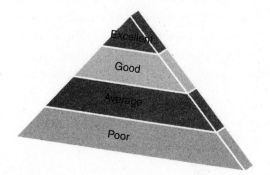

Figure 1.4 The Organizational Data Management Pyramid

of *The Data Asset: How Smart Companies Govern Their Data for Business Success.* Fisher told me

> The problem with data management in most organizations today is that they manage their data to support the needs of a specific application. While this may be beneficial in the context of any one application, it falls woefully short in supporting the needs of the entire enterprise. With more sources of data—and more variety of data and larger volumes of data, organizations will continue to struggle if they don't adopt a more contemporary and holistic mind-set. They need to reorient themselves, aligning their data management practices with an *organizational* strategy instead of an application strategy.[11]

In other words, each department in an organization tends to emphasize its own data management and application needs. While this may seem to make sense for each department, on a broader level, this approach ultimately results in a great deal of organizational dysfunction. Many employees, departments, teams, groups, and organizations operate at a suboptimal level. Sadly, they often make routine and even strategic decisions without complete or accurate information. For instance, how can a VP of Sales make accurate sales forecasts when his organization lacks accurate master customer data? How can an HR Director make optimal recruiting decisions without knowing where her company's best and brightest come from? They can't—at least easily.

Far too many organizations struggle just trying to manage their structured data. (These are the ones too busy to even dabble with the other kinds of data discussed earlier in his chapter.) The results can be seen at individual employee levels. Because of poor data management, many employees continue to spend far too much time attempting to answer what should be relatively simple and straightforward business questions. Examples include

- **HR:** How many employees work here? Which skills do our employees have? Which ones are they lacking?
- **Payroll:** Are employees being paid accurately?
- **Finance and Accounting:** Which departments are exceeding their budgets?

- **Sales:** How many products do we sell? Which ones are selling better than others? Which customers are buying from us? How many customers in New York have bought from us in the past year?
- **Supply Chain:** What are our current inventory levels of key products and parts? When can we expect them to be replenished? Will we have enough inventory to meet current and future demand?
- **Marketing:** What's our company's market share? How has that changed from last year or last quarter?

For organizations with cultures that have embraced information-based decision-making, answers to questions like these can be derived quickly.

THE ENTERPRISE AND THE BRAVE NEW BIG DATA WORLD

The questions at the end of the previous section represent vast simplifications of many employees' jobs. I am certainly not implying that the entire responsibilities of employees and departments can be reduced a few bullet points. The previous synopses only serve to illustrate the fact that bad data is downright confounding. Poor data management precludes many organizations and their employees from effectively blocking and tackling. Many cannot easily produce accurate financial reports, lists of customers, and the like. As a result, at these data-challenged companies, accurately answering broader and mission-critical questions like, "How do we sell more products?" is extremely difficult, if not impossible.

On occasion, executives will try to address big-picture items like these by contracting external agencies or perhaps bringing in external consultants. As one of these folks, let me be blunt: we aren't magicians. While we hopefully bring unique perspectives, useful methodologies, and valuable skills to the table, we ultimately face the same data limitations as everyday employees.

The pernicious effects of bad data have plagued organizations for decades, not to mention consultants like me. Inconsistent, duplicate, and incomplete data mystifies everyone. At a minimum, data issues complicate the answering of both simple and more involved business questions. At worst, they make it impossible to address key issues.

Now let's move to the other end of the spectrum. Consider the relatively few organizations that manage their data exceptionally well (Figure 1.4). I have found that, all else being equal, employees in companies at the top of the pyramid are more productive than those at the bottom. The former group can focus more of its energies on answering bigger, broader questions. They don't have to routinely massage or second-guess organizational data. For instance, it's easier for the head of HR to develop an effective succession plan when the organization knows exactly which employees have which skills. With impeccable customer and sales data, it's more feasible for the chief marketing officer (CMO) to optimize her company's marketing spend.

Today, "simple" and traditional business questions still matter, as do their answers. The advent of Twitter and YouTube certainly did not obviate the need for organizations to effectively manage their structured and transactional data. In fact, doing so remains critical to running a successful enterprise. At the same time, though, Web 2.0 is a game-changer. We're not in Kansas anymore. It is no longer sufficient for organizations to focus exclusively on collecting, analyzing, and managing "table-friendly" data. Twitter, YouTube, Facebook, and their ilk only mean that, for any organization, structured data now only tells part of the story. Texts, tweets, social review sites like Yelp and Angie's List, Facebook likes, Google +1s, photos, blog posts, and viral videos collectively represent a new and important breed of cat. This data cannot be easily (if at all) stored, retrieved, and analyzed via standalone employee databases, large database tables, or often even traditional data warehouses.

The Data Disconnect

Today many organizations suffer a disconnect between new forms of data and old tools that handled, well, old types of data. Many employees cannot even begin to answer critical business questions made more complicated by the Big Data explosion. Examples include

- How do our customers feel about our products or customer service?

- What products would our customers consider buying?
- When is the best time of the year to launch a new product?
- What are people publicly saying about our latest commercial or brand?

Why the disconnect? Several reasons come to mind. First, let's discuss the elephant in the room. Many businesspeople don't think of tweets, blog posts, and Pinterest pins as "data" in the conventional sense, much less potentially valuable data. Why should they waste their time with such nonsense, especially when they continue to struggle with "real" data? Fewer than half of organizations currently collect and analyze data from social media, according to a recent IBM survey.[12] To quote from *Cool Hand Luke*, "Some men you just can't reach."

At least there's some good news: not everyone is in denial over Big Data. Some organizations and employees do get it—and this book will introduce you to many of them. Count among them the U.S. federal government. In March 2012, it formally recognized the power of—and need for—Big Data tools and programs.[13]

But there's no magic "Big Data switch." Simply recognizing that Big Data matters does not mean that organizations can *immediately* take advantage of it, at least in any meaningful way. Many early Big Data zealots suffer from a different problem: they lack the requisite tools to effectively handle Big Data. When it comes to unstructured data, standard reports, ad hoc queries, and even many powerful data warehouses and business intelligence (BI) applications just don't cut it. They were simply not built to house, retrieve, and interpret Big Data. While these old stalwarts are far from dated, they cannot accommodate the vast technological changes of the past seven years—and the data generated by these changes. To paraphrase The Who, the old boss isn't the same as the new boss.

Big Tools and Big Opportunities

As the Chinese say, there is opportunity in chaos. While relatively recent, the rise of Big Data has hardly gone unnoticed. New applications and technologies allow organizations to take advantage of Big Data.

Equipped with these tools, organizations are deepening their understanding of essential business questions.

But, as we'll see in this book, Big Data can do much, much more than answer even complex, predefined questions. Predictive analytics and sentiment analysis are not only providing insights into existing problems, but addressing unforeseen ones. In effect, they are suggesting new and important questions, as well as their answers. Through Big Data, organizations are identifying issues, trends, problems, and opportunities that human beings simply cannot.

Unlocking the full power of Big Data is neither a weekend project nor a hackathon. To be successful here, organizations need to do far more than purchase an expensive new application and hire a team of consultants to deploy it. (In fact, Hadoop, one of today's most popular Big Data tools, is available for free download to anyone who wants it.) Rather, to succeed at Big Data, CXOs need to do several things:

- Recognize that the world has changed—and isn't changing back.
- Disavow themselves of antiquated mind-sets.
- Realize that Big Data represents a big opportunity.
- Understand that existing tools like relational databases are insufficient to handle the explosion of unstructured data.
- Embrace new and Big Data–specific tools—and encourage employees to utilize and experiment with them.

The following chapter will make the compelling business case for organizations to embrace Big Data.

SUMMARY

This chapter has described the evolution of enterprise data and the arrival of the Data Deluge. It has distinguished among the different types of data: structured, semi-structured, and unstructured. With respect to managing their structured data, most organizations in 2013 are doing only passable jobs at best. This squeaking by has rarely come quickly and easily Today, there's a great deal more unstructured data than its structured equivalent (although there's still plenty of the latter).

It's high time for organizations to do more with data beyond just keeping the lights on. There's a big opportunity with Big Data, but what exactly is it? Answering that question is the purpose of the next chapter. It characterizes Big Data.

NOTES

1. "The Data Deluge," February 25, 2012, www.economist.com/node/15579717, retrieved December 11, 2012.
2. Harris, Jim, "Data Management: The Next Generation," October 24, 2012, www.dataroundtable.com/?p=11582, retrieved December 11, 2012.
3. Rogers, Shawn, "Big Data Is Scaling BI and Analytics," September 1, 2011, www.information-management.com/issues/21_5/big-data-is-scaling-bi-and-analytics-10021093-1.html, retrieved December 11, 2012.
4. Grimes, Seth, "Unstructured Data and the 80 Percent Rule," copyright 2011, http://clarabridge.com/default.aspx?tabid=137&ModuleID=635&ArticleID=551, retrieved December 11, 2012.
5. Pascal, Fabian, "'Unstructured Data': Why This Popular Term Is Really a Contradiction," September 19, 2012, www.allanalytics.com/author.asp?section_id=2386&doc_id=250980, retrieved December 11, 2012.
6. "What to Do About 'Unstructured Data,'" May 15, 2011, www.dbms2.com/2011/05/15/what-to-do-about-unstructured-data/, retrieved December 11, 2012.
7. Reisinger, Don, "Facebook Acquires Face.com for Undisclosed Sum," June 18, 2012, http://news.cnet.com/8301-1023_3-57455287-93/facebook-acquires-face.com-for-undisclosed-sum/, retrieved December 11, 2012.
8. Couts, Andrew, "Lytro: The Camera That Could Change Photography Forever," June 22, 2011, www.digitaltrends.com/photography/lytro-the-camera-that-could-change-photography-forever/, retrieved December 11, 2012.
9. Lacy, Sarah, "Lytro Launches to Transform Photography with $50M in Venture Funds (TCTV)," June 21, 2011, http://techcrunch.com/2011/06/21/lytro-launches-to-transform-photography-with-50m-in-venture-funds-tctv/, retrieved December 11, 2012.
10. Harris, Derrick, "Like Your Data Big? How About 5 *Trillion* Records?," January 4, 2012, http://gigaom.com/cloud/like-your-data-big-how-about-5-trillion-records/, retrieved December 11, 2012.
11. Personal conversation with Fisher, October 25, 2012.
12. Cohan, Peter, "Big Blue's Bet on Big Data," November 1, 2012, www.forbes.com/sites/petercohan/2012/11/01/big-blues-bet-on-big-data, retrieved December 11, 2012.
13. Kalil, Tom, "Big Data Is a Big Deal," March 29, 2012, www.whitehouse.gov/blog/2012/03/29/big-data-big-deal, retrieved December 11, 2012.

CHAPTER 2

Demystifying Big Data

I know it when I see it.

—Supreme Court Justice Potter Stewart on his
threshold test for possible obscenity.
Concurring opinion, *Jacobellis v. Ohio* (1964)

The previous quote comes from perhaps the most famous of all U.S. Supreme Court cases. Stewart's line "I know it when I see it" long ago entered the vernacular, at least in the United States. It's been applied to myriad different scenarios. Those seven words illustrate a number of things, not the least of which is the difficulty that even really smart people have in defining ostensibly simple terms.

Fast forward nearly fifty years, and many learned folks are having the same issue with respect to Big Data. Just what the heck is it, anyway? Much like the term *cloud computing*, you can search in vain for weeks for the "perfect" definition of Big Data. Douglas Laney (then with the META group, now with Gartner) fired the first shot in late 2001. Laney wrote about the growth challenges and opportunities facing organizations with respect to increasing amounts of data.[1]

Years before the term *Big Data* was *de rigueur*, Laney defined three primary dimensions of the Data Deluge:

- **Volume:** the increasing amount of data
- **Variety:** the increasing range of data types and sources
- **Velocity:** the increasing speed of data

Laney's three *v*'s stuck, and today most people familiar with Big Data have heard of them. That's a far cry from saying, however, that everyone agrees on the proper definition of Big Data. Just about every major tech vendor and consulting firm has a vested interest in pushing its own agenda. To this end, many companies and thought leaders have developed their own definitions of Big Data. A few have even tried to introduce additional *v*'s like *veracity* (from IBM[2]) and *variability* (from Forrester Research[3]). Among the *technorati*, arguments abound, and it often gets pretty catty.

Let's save some time: the perfect definition of Big Data doesn't exist. Who can say with absolute certainty that one definition of the term is objectively better than all the others? Rather than searching for that phantom definition, this chapter describes the characteristics and demystifies the term.

CHARACTERISTICS OF BIG DATA

Providing a simple and concise definition of Big Data is a considerable challenge. After all, it's a big topic. Less difficult, though, is describing the major characteristics of Big Data. Let's go.

Big Data Is Already Here

Big Data is not some pie-in-the-sky, futuristic notion like flying cars. Nor is it a phenomenon largely in its infancy, such as the semantic web. Whether your particular organization currently does anything with Big Data is moot; it doesn't change the fact that it has already arrived. Amazon, Apple, Facebook, Google, Yahoo!, Facebook, LinkedIn, American Airlines, IBM, Twitter, and scores of other companies currently use Big Data and related applications. While it's not a perfect

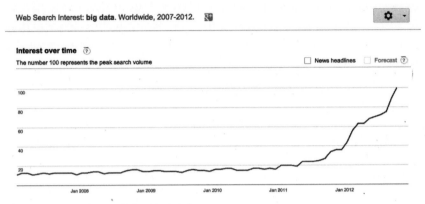

Figure 2.1 Google Trends for Big Data[4]
Source: Google

barometer or visualization, look at Figure 2.1 on news stories about Big Data captured by Google Trends.

As Figure 2.1 shows, interest in Big Data has skyrocketed over the past few years, and Google only sees this trend continuing for the fore-seeable future. And this is not just about Google searches or new buzz-words from consulting firms and software vendors. As I write these words, the United States has just reelected Barack Obama. Pundits called it the election of Big Data.[5] "This election will be remembered for the role that Big Data played behind the scenes, at every step," says Tarun Wadhwa, a research fellow at Singularity University studying digital identification systems and their impact on governance. "Obama won by identifying potential supporters and driving voter turnout in swing states."[6]

Two days after the election, *Time Magazine* ran a fascinating account of how Obama's team of sophisticated number crunchers identified key trends, performed extensive A/B testing, and made critical decisions. Ultimately, these actions helped the Obama campaign raise more than $1 billion and win the election.[7] New political rock stars were anoint-ed, like Jim Messina, Obama's campaign manager. From the article, "The 'scientists' created regular briefings on their work for the Presi-dent and top aides in the White House's Roosevelt Room, but public details were in short supply as the campaign guarded what it believed to be its biggest institutional advantage over Mitt Romney's campaign: *its data*." [Emphasis mine.] In fact, the Democrats' technology and data advantage may extend to 2016 and beyond. On the Business Insider site, Grace Wyler writes, "Nowhere were the GOP's shortcomings more apparent than in the realm of data gathering and microtargeting, an increasingly important field of electioneering that provides campaigns with crucial insights into the nature of the electorate."[8]

In a word, *wow*. I'll be shocked if at least one book isn't published soon about the role that Big Data played in the election—and the impact that it will have on future elections. I don't see Big Data playing a smaller role in the 2014 and 2016 elections.

But Big Data goes way beyond politics and has for some time now. Few industries are more old school than wine, but Big Data is even making inroads there. Centuries-old winemakers like Gallo are launching new varietals based upon advanced analytics and data culled from social networks.[9] Also on the wine front, data-driven companies like Fruition Sciences are using sensors to optimize grapevine quality and minimize wasted water.[10] Laboratory and clinical scientists are collaborating and reaching conclusions from the same pool of (big) data—a process called *translational research*.[11] The impact on medical research and drug discovery is potentially enormous. UPS regularly mines truck delivery data to optimize new routing methods and reduce expenses.[12] Even pizza joints are getting in on the Big Data action.[13] Each of these fields has been traditionally a "data-free zone."

I could go on, but you get my drift: Big Data is already having an impact in many areas of business and society. Chapter 5 will provide three compelling case studies of organizations already on the Big Data train.

Big Data Is Extremely Fragmented

On February 28, 1983, *M*A*S*H* said good-bye. The series finale, titled "Goodbye, Farewell, and Amen," became the most watched television broadcast in the history of television. An estimated 125 million viewers tuned in.[14] While that number was unprecedented, back then consumer habits were fairly homogenous. That is, large numbers of us would buy the same records, read the same materials (books, magazines, and newspapers), go to the same movies, and watch the same shows. For instance, in the 1950s, a very large percentage of U.S. households routinely watched *I Love Lucy*. No, society wasn't uniform, but the Long Tail hadn't arrived yet. Relatively speaking, many of us consumed few different types of content.

That was then, and this is now. Compared to that era, today is Bizarro World. Hollywood hits still exist, and we still see best-selling books and albums. Relatively speaking, however, we consume many different types of content. Returning to TV, in 2011 the most popular show in the country (and, in fact, the world) was the forensic crime show *CSI*, but beneath its ratings something very different was going on. Sure, the show sports roughly 63 million viewers, but not among the 310 million citizens of the United States. Those 63 million come from more than *three billion* people across the globe.[15] Authors like Seth Godin have written extensively about why the effectiveness of mass marketing has waned so precipitously. *There is no mass market anymore.* Today, there's only one remaining commercial way to reach the masses every year: The Super Bowl.* For that reason, the average price for a 30-second ad for the 2012 game was a record-breaking $3.5 million.[16]

Today, it's a far cry from the 1980s, much less the 1950s. We long ago escaped the tyranny of a three-television-network world. People don't confine their viewing to whatever shows are on ABC, CBS, and NBC. On the contrary, the Long Tail remains alive and well fifteen years after its arrival. We watch an ever-increasing number of niche shows and movies—and can even create our own programs via YouTube. Many of us haven't listened to an FM or AM radio station in years. Today, we build our own customized radio stations on sites like Pandora. We read the blogs we like where we like. In mid-October 2012, *Newsweek* announced that it was discontinuing its print edition after 80 years. So how does all of this tie back to Big Data?

At a high level, we are no doubt generating and consuming more data—*and different types of data*—than ever. Not surprisingly, most of us only concern ourselves with the content relevant to us. (While I can

---

*The Olympics takes place every four years but, because of its duration, it cannot command the same number of eyeballs—at least in a concentrated period of time.

talk your ear off about golf, tennis, the English progressive rock band Marillion, and technology, my knowledge of contemporary pop music and classic literature is laughable, and I know very little about reality TV.) Relative to the world's entire body of content, very little actually matters to each of us individually. We don't concern ourselves with the vast majority of books, movies, websites, etc., out there. For instance, more than seven in ten tweets are ignored—and that's among the microscopic percentage of people we follow on Twitter.[17] Someone with 3,000 "friends" on Facebook is still subject to Dunbar's Number, meaning that each of us can really only keep track of 150 people in any meaningful way.[18] (I laugh when I see individuals who follow 80,000 others on Twitter. Really?) For every YouTube video that goes viral, I suspect that tens of thousands only register a handful of views. (YouTube is a vintage Long Tail site.) After all, users upload more and more video content to the site every minute.[19] Most blog posts aren't read, and only a small percentage receives comments. Why? No one can possibly keep up with it all. Our ability to generate data far exceeds our ability to digest it. Data is just too big today.

In a sense, nothing has changed from the 1950s in that all of us still pick and choose what and how much we'll consume. The difference today is that there's much more choice by orders of magnitude. That is, relatively few of us watch a show "just because it's on TV" or read the newspaper because there's nothing else available.

None of the noisy statistics and facts just mentioned changes one simple truth: there's still a signal in this noise, even if that signal is weak and difficult to find. As we'll see in the next two chapters, Big Data tools allow that noise to be reduced; they strengthen that signal. Dismissing social media as junk specifically, and all forms of unstructured data generally, entirely misses the point. There's gold in the streets, even if it's surrounded by litter. With the right tools, organizations can find the gold in Big Data and do something with it.

Big Data Is Not an Elixir

For years, organizations have been searching in vain for that technology silver bullet, the one thing that would solve all their problems. Untold billions have been spent on new applications and related implementations, development efforts, consultants, systems, and methodologies. Let me be crystal clear here: Big Data is not an elixir in business, politics, government, or anything else. Think of Big Data as just one club in the bag, although an increasingly critical one. While potentially very powerful, it obviates neither the need for—nor the importance of—traditional data management. Don't expect Big Data to resurrect a dying business, reverse the effects of incompetent management, or fix a broken corporate culture. A November 2011 *Forbes* article cited a recent survey of chief marketing executives. Among the survey's key findings, " . . . more than 60 percent of knowledge workers at large enterprises say their organizations lack the processes and the skills to use information effectively for decision making."[20]

So Big Data has no magical powers. Recalcitrant employees unwilling to make decisions based upon data won't suddenly do that because their employer got Big Data religion. What's more, by itself, Big Data guarantees nothing; embracing it only increases the chances of success in any given area. Plenty of organizations have been extremely profitable without doing anything Big Data related, and it's hard to imagine a day in which *every* company will get on board the Big Data train. Let's say that two organizations (A and B) are identical save for one thing: A effectively uses Big Data, while B does not. All else being equal, I'll bet on A over B any day of the week and twice on Sunday.

Small Data Extends Big Data

It's critical for any enterprise to effectively manage its internal, structured data—aka, its *Small Data*. (Note, however, that Small Data is often quite big. It's only "small" in comparison to Big Data. Many organizations store petabytes of structured, transactional data. Some database tables contain *tens of billions* of records.) Distinctions and definitions aside, the need to diligently manage Small Data is universal; it transcends organizational type, industry, and size.

Now, let's not oversimplify matters here. Data management is a continuum, not a binary, and no group manages its own internal data without incident. However, I'm hard-pressed to think of any successful organization that routinely struggles with what is effectively basic blocking and tackling. I am sure that these companies exist—(i.e., those that are making a killing despite their truly messy enterprise data and related internal practices). I can't help but wonder, though, how much better they would do if they took data management and governance seriously. In the end, these organizations succeed despite their internal data management practices, not because of them. And this success is usually ephemeral.

What's the Big Data implication of all of this? All else being equal, parties that manage Small Data well will benefit more from Big Data than those that don't. Well-managed organizations don't waste time and resources manually cobbling together things like master customer, product, and employee lists. Employees at these companies merely click a mouse a few times or, better yet, receive these reports automatically. These organizations don't need *weeks* to balance their books. As a result, they are often able to quickly understand their market share, sales, current liabilities, levels of risk, and the like. They can spot emerging trends. What's more, they can more easily tie Small Data to Big Data, reaping greater rewards in the process.

> It's wonderful to know what your customers are saying about your company and its products and services on blogs or Twitter, but that benefit is tempered when you don't even know who your customers are.

At a high level, then, Small Data serves an important *descriptive* purpose: businesses can use it to determine what's currently happening across a number of different areas—that is, they can understand the status quo. Still, this is just the tip of the iceberg. Data can do so much more, especially as a predictive tool. Data can help organizations spot nascent trends (both positive and negative), even if the precise reason driving a particular trend isn't entirely clear.

The same can be said about metadata: it extends Big Data. Accurate metadata makes *all* types of data more meaningful—big and small, structured and unstructured, internal and external.

Big Data Is a Complement, Not a Substitute

While enormously powerful, Big Data can only do so much. At a high level, Big Data does not usurp the role of transactional and structured data and systems. Without question, Big Data can help organizations understand their customers better or make superior hiring decisions. However, Big Data cannot perform many essential organizational functions. For instance, Hadoop won't generate an accurate P&L statement, trial balance, or aging receivables report. And hopefully, you're not using Google's Big Data tools to try to figure out how many employees work at your company. (Beyond its limitations, it's also important to recognize the problems and issues associated with Big Data, topics covered more fully in Chapter 7.)

If I can use a golf analogy, think of Big Data as a driver. If swung right, one can hit a ball 300 yards with it, but you sure wouldn't want to putt with it. No one hits a putter off the tee, and there's a reason for that. If you want to shoot a low score, you'll probably have to do well with both clubs. To finish off the golf analogy, organizations adroit with both Small and Big Data are more likely to find themselves wearing green jackets. Alternatively, think of Small Data as checkers and Big Data as chess. If you can't grasp the former, it's unlikely that you'll be very good at the latter.

Big Data Can Yield Better Predictions

Generally speaking, it isn't terribly difficult for employees to spot trends, especially when they possess the right tools. However, there's an important caveat to this statement. For a bevy of reasons, most people still try to identify trends based largely upon historical Small Data. For instance, most companies can predict their sales and profits for the next quarter and year, at least within a reasonable range and barring some type of calamity. (Of course, even ostensibly small deviations from these estimates can result in substantial stock price fluctuations for publicly traded companies.) For their part, retailers know that each year they'll have to augment their staff with temps during Thanksgiving and Christmas, a process known as holiday hire.

Now, better predictions and more accurate forecasts should not be confused with *perfect* predictions and forecasts. Those who expect Big Data to predict the future with certainty will ultimately be disappointed. Big Data isn't chemistry or algebra. Certitude evades us; Big Data only serves to reduce it.

Big Data Giveth—and Big Data Taketh Away

Reed Hastings did much more than just make renting DVDs more convenient and put Blockbuster out of business. Hastings did something truly special and rare: he built a company that millions of people actually *loved*. Few people really care about the inner technical workings of Netflix, but behind the scenes it utilizes Big Data, collaborative filtering technology, and crowdsourcing to build a powerful entertainment recommendation engine.

> Collaborative filtering technology powers recommendation engines. It groups movies, books, CDs, and other products based upon crowdsourcing and common characteristics (read: metadata). For instance, people who like *Scarface* will probably enjoy *The Godfather* and anything by Martin Scorsese. Chapter 4 will have much more to say about collaborative filtering.

For now, consider the following Netflix statistics as reported by GigaOM on June 14, 2012:

- More than 25 million users
- About 30 million plays per day (and Netflix tracks every time its customers rewind, fast-forward, and pause a movie streamed over its site)
- More than 2 billion hours of streaming video watched during the last three months of 2011 alone
- About 4 million ratings per day
- About 3 million searches per day
- 75 percent of current customers select movies based on recommendations, a number the company wants to make even higher[21]

The size of these numbers is impressive, but Netflix doesn't just count how many times movies like *Memento* are watched, when online viewers stop watching them, and so on. Hastings understands the importance of metadata. The company tracks user geo-location and device information, purchases extensive external metadata from third parties such as Nielsen, and integrates as much user social media data from Facebook and Twitter.[22] For videos streamed via its website, Netflix knows the time of the day and week that its customers watched different programs and movies. For instance, the company knows that its customers watch more TV shows during the week and more movies during the weekend.

One could make the argument that much of Netflix's success emanated from its effective use of Big Data. As Hastings discovered in the summer of 2011, however, Big Data can be a sword as well as a shield. Over a public and painful two-month period, Netflix lost more than half of its market value. The company rebranded and repriced its DVD-by-mail service (Qwikster), an ill-conceived move that "alienated customers and drove away investors."[23] Many erstwhile Netflix customers and advocates quickly switched camps, becoming vociferous detractors and taking their frustration to Twitter, Facebook, and other social media channels. "Netflix sucks" videos appeared on YouTube.[24] By the time the bleeding stopped, the company had lost more than 800,000 customers and enormous goodwill.[25] According to some estimates, Twitter alone was responsible for more than 10 percent of the decline in the Netflix stock price. After a halfhearted Hastings's apology,[26] Netflix reversed course and nixed Qwikster. As of this writing, the stock has partially recovered, and many users have returned.[27]

From a Big Data standpoint, the Netflix fiasco is particularly instructive. Even in a Twitter-free world, it's likely that Netflix still would have suffered from its gaffe. That is, Twitter didn't "cause" Netflix to lose half of its value. If anything, Twitter and Facebook served as accelerants. Fundamentally, Qwikster was a bad business decision, and social media sites only intensified the anti-Netflix momentum. For our purposes, Big Data made a bad situation much worse for Netflix. The lesson here: those who only see the upsides of Big Data would do well to keep that in mind. Perhaps Big Data is the ultimate frenemy.

Big Data Is Neither Omniscient Nor Precise

In a sense, Big Data changes nothing. While it may increase our ability to spot trends, it certainly will not let us consistently and accurately predict the future. Even in a Big Data world, we will still have to live with varying degrees of uncertainty. This is true despite—or perhaps because of—the veritable sea of data out there.

The notion that we can only see some events hindsight is the premise behind *Black Swan*, the 2007 bestseller by Lebanese polymath Nassim Nicholas Taleb. In the book, Taleb explains why we often miss events that should have been completely obvious to us in hindsight. Examples of black swans include 9/11, bestselling books that hit upon a national nerve, and the valuation of individual and groups of stocks. For instance, not that long ago, online grocer WebVan was once famously "worth" $1.2 billion during the height of the dot-com bubble.[28] In hindsight, that entire period was the acme of irrational exuberance.

Perhaps the most salient recent example of a black swan is the subprime housing meltdown and subsequent Great Recession. Here, Taleb's background is particularly instructive. Taleb was no academic—at least, not entirely. For years before the market imploded, he put his Black Swan Theory into practice in the stock market. That is, he walked the talk. Taleb was so convinced that the mortgage bubble would explode that he based his entire investment strategy on it, ultimately making a fortune when most investment bankers were losing their shirts. While rare, Taleb's contrarian beliefs weren't completely flying under the radar ten years ago. Malcolm Gladwell wrote an article on Taleb and his investment philosophy in 2002 for *The New Yorker*,[29] five years before *Black Swan* was published.

Nor was Taleb alone in raising a red flag about the housing market years ago. While comparatively few, others also predicted the financial turmoil that erupted in 2008. (Predicting that it *would* happen is hardly the same as predicting precisely *when* it would happen.) In *The Big Short: Inside the Doomsday Machine*, Michael Lewis introduces us to some of these colorful characters, including Dr. Michael Burry, a one-eyed neurologist with Asperger's syndrome. Convinced of the irrationality of the stock market, Burry started a blog, more as a hobby than anything else. He quickly and unexpectedly gained a devoted following and received several offers to manage a good deal of others' money. Eventually, Burry left neurology and started Scion Capital. He bet heavily against subprime mortgages. While Lehman Brothers and Bear Stearns were collapsing, Burry was on his way to earning a personal profit of $100 million and more than $700 million for Scion investors.[30]

Were there signals to the debacle? Of course, but the consequences were still nothing short of devastating. The larger point: even in a Big Data world, plenty of activity (both disturbing and surprisingly good) will continue to lie beneath the surface. Plenty of things will remain virtually undetected by people and parties that ought to know better.

Big Data Is Generally Wide, Not Long

Go into any table in a relational database management system (RDBMS), an application that stores structured enterprise data that techies like me often call *the back end*. You'll almost always see structured data with many rows and relatively few columns. For instance, let's consider a table with employee information. In the table, you'll find key fields like employee number, first name, last name, social security number (hopefully not the same as the employee number), and tax information. Occasionally vendors will update their software to include new fields, like employee e-mail address. For the most part, though, new fields or columns are added infrequently. Contrast that with new rows. They are constantly added for one simple reason: companies hire employees on a regular basis. Each new employee represents a row in the employee table. For this reason, tables in ERP and CRM systems tend to be long, not wide. (I have worked with employee timekeeping tables in excess of 35 million records. Even those aren't terribly big, especially by today's standards.)

Big Data is very different for technical storage and retrieval reasons that are well beyond the scope of this book.* Suffice it to say that Big Data has given rise to a new breed of databases that have very little to do with "rows" and Structured Query Language.

> ● SQL is a special-purpose programming language designed for managing data in relational database management systems (RDBMSs). While enormously powerful, traditional SQL doesn't typically handle large amounts of unstructured data very well.

---

* If you're curious about the technical reasons, see www.tinyurl.com/mcknight-columnar.

Columnar databases (discussed in more detail in Chapter 4) are the antitheses of their row-based counterparts. Because they are more wide than long, they are arguably better suited for Big Data. We'll come back to that, though.

Big Data Is Dynamic and Largely Unpredictable

Why did Facebook agree to buy Instagram in April 2012 for more than $1 billion in cash and stock? The reason sure wasn't accretive. Not only did Instagram lack profits; it lacked any proper revenue. Was Instagram "the best" or even the only photo-sharing app? Had it pioneered amazing technology that Facebook couldn't replicate? Again, the answers are no. So what was Mark Zuckerberg thinking?

It was all about the app's popularity and existing user base. Instagram had become the *de facto* standard for mobile photo sharing. Before the acquisition, Instagram "had reached nearly 30 million registered users before it launched an Android app, a turbo-charging event for the company."[31]

And Instagram was not the only app to suddenly burst onto the scene. Even über-smart Steve Jobs could never have predicted that *Angry Birds* would have been downloaded more than one billion times.[32] If venture capitalists (VCs) are so smart, why didn't they make a deal with Pebble Watch CEO Eric Migicovsky *before* his product raised more than $10 million on Kickstarter?[33] His company's initial goal: a mere $100,000.

The main point is that today business is inherently unpredictable and, thanks to the rapid change engendered by technology, more unpredictable than ever. Much like YouTube videos or Internet memes, today apps can quickly go viral. New sites like Pinterest are taking off in very little time—and generating new data sources. Existing sites, companies, and web services suddenly spike, and generate even more data. Social commerce sites like The Fancy and Fab.com don't even attempt to predict sales of any given product. There's no central planner at Etsy. The CEOs of these companies don't even know all the products they'll be selling or featuring next month, never mind next year. There may be wisdom in crowds, but no one knows for certain what that wisdom will be.

Big Data Is Largely Consumer Driven

In my previous two books, I've written about the consumerization of IT. It's nothing less than a game-changer and certainly warrants a mention here. In a nutshell, this isn't 1995 anymore. Back then, the majority of people used technology exclusively at their desktops while working. Sure, there were tech aficionados like yours truly, but we were the exceptions to the rule.

Now that smartphones are becoming pervasive and e-readers and tablets are getting there, technology is *everywhere*—and not just for adults. Slate reports, "Two San Antonio, Texas schools have joined others in Houston and Austin in requiring students to wear cards with radio-frequency identification (RFID) chips embedded in them, allowing administrators to track their whereabouts on campus."[34] Pebble Watch (mentioned in the previous section) is yet another example of wearable technology.

Ubiquitous technology means that many IT departments are in effect throwing in the towel. They have given up trying to mandate the devices their own employees can and can't use while on the clock, a movement termed *bring your own device* (BYOD). Think that this is just a private sector trend? Think again. Count federal agencies in the mix as well.[35]

One of the consequences of the consumerization of IT is that we are *constantly* generating, accessing, and consuming data. Big Data is a direct consequence of ubiquitous technology and near-constant connectivity. A company may block access to Facebook, Twitter, or other "unproductive" sites on its network via a service like Websense, but that means almost nothing anymore. Employees simply take out their smartphones and go to these forbidden sites. This is BYOD in action. I don't know of any enterprise that can entirely prevent its employees from pinning photos on Pinterest, watching YouTube videos, updating Facebook, or tweeting. And venting over your boss during lunch is small potatoes compared to the increasing trend of employee data theft. "Personally owned mobile devices are increasingly being used to access employers' systems and cloud-hosted data, both via browser-based and native mobile applications," said John Yeoh, research analyst at Cloud Security Alliance. "This, without a doubt, is a tremendous concern for enterprises worldwide."[36]

Enterprises still generate and consume quite a bit of data but, unlike twenty years ago, they are not the only game in town. Consumers are anything but passive bystanders these days; the term *citizen journalist* developed for a reason. I'd argue that consumers are driving Big Data more than traditional organizations, although the latter can stand to reap most Big Data benefits.

Big Data Is External and "Unmanageable" in the Traditional Sense

Data governance, master data management (MDM), quality, and stewardship all fall under the general umbrella of *data management*, an intentionally broad and fairly generic term. Data management implies that organizations actively manage *their* data (i.e., data that exists within their own internal systems, applications, and databases). What's more, an organization's employees for the most part generate, access, and ultimately control this data. This is true even if a company "rents" its applications. For example, perhaps it uses a SaaS customer relationship management (CRM) application such as Salesforce.com. For this reason, a company can go live with its new application in a relatively short period of time, especially compared with traditional on-premise applications requiring hardware purchases, configurations, and probably customizations. Note, however, that such an application will have limited use if it's loaded with suspect, duplicate, or incomplete information.

Now, to be sure, an organization can manually import external data into its existing systems or automatically build a bridge. Companies like Twitter encourage the latter via making their application programming interfaces (APIs) open for others. However, it would be misleading to think about "managing" Big Data, at least as organizations have traditionally tried to manage Small Data. For instance, adding a duplicate employee, vendor, product, or customer into an enterprise system can cause some thorny problems. I can't think of any enterprise system that doesn't provide at least some safeguards against this type of thing. If Jeanette in HR somehow adds a duplicate record for Jordan, an existing employee, at some point the organization will have to purge one record and consolidate the information concurrently split between two different employee numbers. (In point of fact, the organization may use an MDM solution to further minimize the chance that this occurs in the first place.) The same thing can be said for a duplicate customer, vendor, or product code. (Duplicate paychecks, sales, and invoices often cause major data management headaches.) Small Data needs to be actively managed and kept as pure as possible.

Contrast the need for a master record—and, more generally, "data perfection"—with Big Data. I might tweet the same 140 characters five times about my dissatisfaction with my cable company, Cox Communications. Employees at Cox can ignore my tweets, but they can't delete or manage them, at least in the traditional sense. (No one can delete my tweets but Twitter and me; and besides me, only Google can yank my videos from YouTube.) Rather, the fact that I've vented over Twitter about the same issue multiple times should signal to Cox's customer service department that I'm not a happy camper—and someone should step in. In fact, I might be angrier than a customer who has tweeted only once or not at all.

Big Data Is Inherently Incomplete

Yes, Big Data is enormous, but don't for a minute think that there's such a thing as a "complete" set of data anywhere. Far from it. Even mighty Google cannot index the entire web—and not for want of trying. Although Google's mission is "to organize the world's information and make it universally accessible and useful," it will never *completely* succeed. Standard search engines can only index the Surface Web, not the much larger Deep Web. The former is just the tip of the iceberg.

So we know that Google's algorithm lacks many sources of information and content, but what percentage of data is Google missing? Phrased a bit differently, what percentage of all content on the Internet is on the Surface Web—and, by extension, not available to search engines? While impossible to precisely quantify, some estimates put that number at 96 percent.[37] Figure 2.2 provides more estimates about what even the best search engines cannot index.

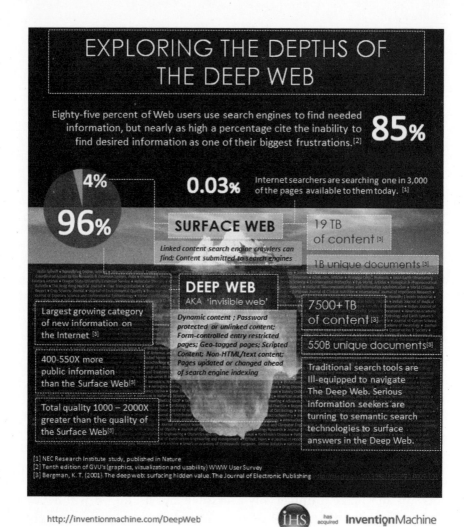

Figure 2.2 The Deep Web*
Source: Invention Machine

And it's not as if search engines like Google can index even the entire Surface Web. An incredible amount of web traffic eludes even the world's best search engines. Imagine how much more powerful Google would be if its software could crawl and index currently hidden content like

---

* Also called the Deepnet, the Invisible Web, the Undernet, or the hidden Web.

- Text and instant messages.
- Dynamic or scripted content.
- Unlinked content (i.e., pages to which other pages do not link). This omission can prevent web crawling programs from accessing the content.
- Password-protected websites.
- Videos specifically hidden from the search engines, a feature extremely easy to do on sites like Vimeo.
- Content in private e-mails. (While Google can mine text in Gmail, that information only serves to provide more relevant ads. You can't Google "Who e-mailed Phil in Spanish today?")
- Absent some type of hack, proprietary and private corporate information, networks, and intranets.
- Absent some type of hack, personal health and financial information.
- Physical documents not put online.
- Uncensored photos that StreetView *could* collect except for laws prohibiting the company from doing so (e.g., the European Union).[38]
- Content on closed, personal social networks managed through Yammer, Ning, and others.
- Content on private and membership-based sites such as Lexis-Nexis.
- Content on sites behind pay walls like the *Wall Street Journal* and *New York Times*.

And let's not forget another 800-pound gorilla. Much to Google's chagrin, Facebook's data lies behind a walled garden—and this is anything but an accident. (Of course, Facebook will open that garden to advertisers who are willing to pay for information, although COO Sheryl Sandberg insists that, like Google, her company does not sell or rent uniquely identifiable user information to anyone or any company.[39]) While it hasn't always taken privacy seriously as a company, Facebook has always done one thing exceptionally well: kept its vast trove of user-provided information away from Google, something that annoys CEO Larry Page.

Bottom line: nothing even remotely close to a single repository or amalgamation of Big Data exists. I'm no sorcerer, but it's hard to see such a data store coming in the foreseeable future. While an organization may—and should—manage customer master data in one central place, it cannot do the same with respect to Big Data. For potent Big Data solutions discussed in Chapter 4 to handle photos, analyze videos,[40] and the like, one precondition must be met: the data must be accessible in the first place.

Big Overlap: Big Data, Business Intelligence, and Data Mining

Business intelligence (BI) has been with us for a while. By way of background, IBM researcher Hans Peter Luhn originally used the term *business intelligence* in a 1958 article, defining it as "the ability to apprehend the interrelationships of presented facts in such a way as to guide action towards a desired goal."[41]

More than three decades later, BI applications finally rose to prominence. During the mid-1990s, many organizations finally implemented expensive CRM and ERP systems like Oracle, PeopleSoft, Siebel, and SAP. Post-implementation, a fundamental and important problem remained: while those vendors' relational database applications excelled at getting data *into* systems, they weren't designed to get that same data *out*. Many end users found that vendor-provided standard reports and ad hoc query tools just didn't cut it. Organizations found that they needed separate, more powerful applications to interpret and analyze the massive amounts of data now available to them on customers, employees, financial transactions, and the like. Early BI vendors like Hyperion, MicroStrategy, and Canadian giant Cognos (acquired by IBM in January 2008[42]) provided such functionality.

Some people view Big Data as merely another name for business intelligence. It's not. To be sure, the two concepts are not completely different and even share the same ultimate business objective: to derive value from information. The key difference between Big Data and traditional BI applications boils down to *the type of data* that each is equipped to handle. Traditional BI tools cannot effectively handle largely unstructured and semi-structured information that comprises Big Data. That is, at a high level, most BI applications allow organizations to make sense out of their structured data. For their part, most prominent Big Data solutions are designed to handle all types of data, including unstructured and semi-structured data. This does not mean that one set of tools is inherently "better" than the other. To be sure, online analytical processing (OLAP) cubes loaded with sales data can provide extremely valuable insights into customer behavior. Just don't try to load those same cubes with photos, videos, blog posts, call detail records (CDRs), and tweets and then expect them to spit out meaningful results. Conversely, Big Data solutions can handle structured data as well, as we'll see in Chapter 4. Hybrid solutions are currently being developed and improved. The goal here: to allow organizations to theoretically manage *every* type and source of data in one place. Be that as it may, most organizations won't be replacing their best-of-breed BI applications anytime soon.

At this point, it's fair to ask about the relationship between Big Data and data mining, the latter of which many organizations have used for years. Perhaps the most famous data mining case study involves Harrah's Entertainment and came from the *Harvard Business Review*.* CEO Gary Loveman wrote about how, in the early 2000s, Harrah's used sophisticated data mining techniques to target current and would-be customers very effectively.[43] (Some would argue *too* effectively, like the folks at Gamblers Anonymous. Many gambling addicts were trying to quit, only to be lured back to the tables by remarkably enticing offers in the mail.)

For reasons that will become more apparent in Chapter 4, things are a little bit different now. That is, traditional data mining tools have largely attempted to harness value from large amounts of Small Data—and mostly the structured kind at that. They have largely ignored unstructured and semi-structured information, an increasing part of what we now call *Big Data*. (Big Data even 15 years ago just wasn't as big, and it certainly wasn't nearly as important as it is in 2013.) Put differently, historically people have used data mining software on much smaller, more

---

* See http://hbr.org/product/gary-loveman-and-harrah-s-entertainment/an/OB45-PDF-ENG.

orderly datasets than the unstructured ones of today. Now, at the time, those datasets were considered very large. (It's all relative, right?) In a similar vein, the best computers of 2002 came with then-unprecedented power and speed. In each case, things have changed.

So what is the impact of Big Data on data mining? Data mining tools are expanding and evolving because, quite simply, data itself has expanded and evolved. Big Data is forcing many longstanding data mining solutions to either adapt or perish. For example, IBM's Intelligent Miner, Microsoft's Analysis Services, and SAS's Enterprise Miner all become less and less relevant if they can only handle a decreasing percentage of available data (i.e., the structured kind). This goes double if other applications can effectively handle Big Data. As we'll see in Chapter 4, newer solutions like Hadoop, columnar databases, and NoSQL can more quickly and efficiently handle all—*or at least many more*—types, sources, and amounts of data (especially compared to RDBMs). As Big Data moves to the right of the Technology Adoption Life Cycle, the popularity of these newer Big Data solutions will only increase—especially the less expensive open-source variety.

Perhaps we'll begin hearing more about *Data Mining 2.0* (yes, the term is already out there[44]). New data mining solutions must incorporate very different types of data—and lots of it. They will allow users to find more and different patterns in increasingly larger datasets. They will help people understand more about what's actually going on and why. Ultimately, expect better predictions.

Big Data Is Democratic

There's another big difference between Big Data and early BI efforts. Early BI efforts were almost exclusively the purview of fairly large enterprises. As any CIO will tell you, predecessors to cloud computing like application service providers (ASPs) in 2000 certainly weren't cheap. Further, relatively few small companies purchased and implemented BI software. Financial firms were often notable exceptions to this rule in large part because the stakes were so high. A 30-employee hedge fund with $1 billion under management might decide that the benefits of BI more than covered its not inconsiderable costs.

Of course, current-day BI solutions are nothing like their expensive mid-1990s counterparts. (What technology has remained constant?) Today, the cloud has taken hold, and BI/Big Data start-ups like SiSense, Birst, iJento, and Pentaho are taking affordable BI to the masses. Each has raised millions of dollars in VC funding.

By contrast, Big Data finds itself born into a much more open, cost-effective era. The prevalence of free and open-source software like Hadoop and NoSQL (discussed extensively in Chapter 4), open APIs and datasets, and the like, only collectively underscore the fact that Big Data is inherently more democratic than many embryonic technologies over the past twenty years. It's important to note, however, that one shouldn't confuse free speech with free beer, as open-source folks like to say. (Showing off my Latin, *gratis* is not the same as *libre*.) Yes, open-source Big Data solutions like Hadoop may not require purchasing a formal license. However, this does not negate other related costs such as hardware (potentially), consulting, and employee training and salaries.

THE ANTI-DEFINITION: WHAT BIG DATA IS NOT

Having come full circle, now it's time to return to the quote at the beginning of the chapter. If you think of Big Data as you would obscenity or pornography, the term may well be best defined against its inverse (i.e., that which it is not). In that vein, consider the following definition of Big Data from *The Register*:[45]

> Big Data is any data that doesn't fit well into tables and that generally responds poorly to manipulation by Structured Query Language (SQL).

> [T]he most important feature of Big Data is its structure, with different classes of Big Data having very different structures.

With that definition, let's consider some examples. Data from a Twitter feed is Big Data, but the census isn't. Images, CDRs from telecoms companies, web logs, social data, and RFID output can all be Big Data. Lists of customers, employees, and products are not. At a high level, Big Data doesn't fit well into traditional database tables.

Is this "no SQL" definition a bit too technical for most folks? It sure is, and, while instructive, even that one is hardly perfect. I'm not the most technical person in the world, but it doesn't take a data scientist or rocket scientist to populate a spreadsheet, database table, or flat file with basic Twitter data and metadata. Such a table would include handle, time and date of tweet, tweet, and hashtags. As a general rule, though, traditional data management tools cannot truly harness the power of Big Data. Forget stalwarts like Microsoft Excel and Access; even expensive traditional relational databases just don't cut it.

While we're on the subject of tools, Big Data is about so much more than merely buying, downloading, and deploying a new application or program. Yes, Big Data requires new tools like Hadoop and sentiment analysis. But, more important, Big Data necessitates a new mind-set. Regardless of your own personal definition of the term, don't make the mistake of assuming that heretofore methods and applications are sufficient.

SUMMARY

This chapter demystified the term *Big Data* and described many of its characteristics. Among other things, we learned that Big Data differs from Small Data in terms of the tools required to access it, not to mention the types, sources, and amounts of data associated with it. Now that we have garnered a much more complete understanding of Big Data, it's time to go deeper. Chapters 3 and 4 examine the specific elements that comprise Big Data and look at some of the major solutions being used to operationalize it, respectively.

NOTES

1. Laney, Doug, "3D Data Management: Controlling Data Volume, Velocity, and Variety," February 6, 2001, http://blogs.gartner.com/doug-laney/files/2012/01/ad949-3D-Data-Management-Controlling-Data-Volume-Velocity-and-Variety.pdf, retrieved December 11, 2012.
2. "What Is Big Data?," www.-01.ibm.com/software/data/bigdata, retrieved December 11, 2012.
3. Gogia, Sanchit, "The Big Deal About Big Data for Customer Engagement," June 1, 2012, www.forrester.com/The+Big+Deal+About+Big+Data+For+Customer+Engagement/fulltext/-/E-RES72241, retrieved December 11, 2012.

4. www.google.com/trends/explore#q=big+data, retrieved December 11, 2012.

5. Talmadge, Candace, "Big Data May Transform Election Day Ground Game," November 3, 2012, www.politicususa.com/big-data-transform-election-day-ground-game.html, retrieved December 11, 2012.

6. Farr, Christina, "Election 2012 Is Big-Data Nerds' Gut Punch to Traditional Punditry," November 7, 2012, http://venturebeat.com/2012/11/07/big-data-brigade/, retrieved December 11, 2012.

7. Scherer, Michael, "Inside the Secret World of the Data Crunchers Who Helped Obama Win," November 7, 2012, http://swampland.time.com/2012/11/07/inside-the-secret-world-of-quants-and-data-crunchers-who-helped-obama-win/, retrieved December 11, 2012.

8. Wyler, Grace, "Republicans Have an Enormous Tech Problem, and It Could Kill Them in 2016," November 26, 2012, www.businessinsider.com/republicans-tech-data-orca-obama-election-2012-11#ixzz2CmC8qVLE, retrieved December 11, 2012.

9. Henschen, Doug, "How Gallo Brings Analytics into the Winemaking Craft," September 12, 2012, www.informationweek.com/global-cio/interviews/how-gallo-brings-analytics-into-the-wine/240006776, retrieved December 11, 2012.

10. O'Brien, Jeffrey M., "The Vine Nerds," October 21, 2012, www.wired.com/wired-science/2012/10/mf-fruition-sciences-winemakers/, retrieved December 11, 2012.

11. "Increasing Research Efficiency: Case Study for Big Data and Healthcare," October 18, 2012, www.brightplanet.com/2012/10/increasing-research-efficiency-case-study-for-big-data-and-healthcare/, retrieved December 11, 2012.

12. Brynjolfsson, Erik; McAffe, Andrew, "The Big Data Boom Is the Innovation Story of Our Time," November 21, 2011, www.theatlantic.com/business/archive/2011/11/the-big-data-boom-is-the-innovation-story-of-our-time/248215/, retrieved December 11, 2012.

13. Simon, Phil, "A Retail BI Case Study," August 2, 2012, www.philsimon.com/blog/emerging-tech/bi/a-retail-bi-case-study/, retrieved December 11, 2012.

14. Hyatt, Wesley, *Television's Top 100* (Jefferson, NC, and London: McFarland, 2012).

15. Bibel, Sara, "'CSI: Crime Scene Investigation' Is the Most-Watched Show in the World," June 14, 2012, http://tvbythenumbers.zap2it.com/2012/06/14/csi-crime-scene-investigation-is-the-most-watched-show-in-the-world-2/138212/, retrieved December 11, 2012.

16. Hipes, Patrick, "Top Super Bowl Ad Goes for $4 Million as NBC Inventory Sells Out," January 3, 2012, www.deadline.com/2012/01/top-super-bowl-ad-goes-for-4m-as-inventory-sells-out/, retrieved December 11, 2012.

17. Geere, Duncan, "It's Not Just You: 71 Percent of Tweets Are Ignored," October 11, 2010, www.wired.com/business/2010/10/its-not-just-you-71-percent-of-tweets-are-ignored/, retrieved December 11, 2012.

18. Laden, Greg, "What Is Dunbar's Number?," June 10, 2012, http://scienceblogs.com/gregladen/2012/06/10/what-is-dunbars-number/, retrieved December 11, 2012.

19. Jarboe, Greg, "60 Hours of Video Is Now Uploaded to YouTube Every Minute," February 2012, www.reelseo.com/60-hours-video-uploaded-to-youtube-minute/, retrieved December 11, 2012.

20. Spenner, Patrick, "Beware the Big Data Hype," November 9, 2011, www.forbes.com/sites/patrickspenner/2011/11/09/beware-the-big-data-hype/, retrieved December 11, 2012.

21. Harris, Derrick, "Netflix Analyzes *a Lot* of Data About Your Viewing Habits," June 14, 2012, http://gigaom.com/cloud/netflix-analyzes-a-lot-of-data-about-your-viewing-habits/, retrieved December.11, 2012.

22. Ibid.

23. Grover, Ronald; Nazareth, Rita; Edwards, Cliff, "Netflix Gets 57% Cheaper for Amazon-to-Google Acquirer: Real M&A," September 26, 2011, www.bloomberg.com/news/2011-09-26/netflix-proves-57-less-expensive-for-amazon-to-google-acquirers-real-m-a.html, retrieved December 11, 2012.

24. YouTube user "yourwiseguy," "Netflix Sucks!," July 15, 2011, www.youtube.com/watch?v=Sa6Iod9pr-8, retrieved December 11, 2012.

25. Wingfield, Nick; Stelter, Brian, "How Netflix Lost 800,000 Members, and Good Will," October 24, 2011, www.nytimes.com/2011/10/25/technology/netflix-lost-800000-members-with-price-rise-and-split-plan.html?pagewanted=all&_r=0, retrieved December 11, 2012.

26. Hastings, Reed, "An Explanation and Some Reflections," September 18, 2011, http://blog.netflix.com/2011/09/explanation-and-some-reflections.html, retrieved December 11, 2012.

27. Gilbert, Jason, "Netflix Users Returning, Subscriptions Rebounding As Customers Forgive 'Qwikster' Debacle," May 18, 2012, www.huffingtonpost.com/2012/05/18/netflix-users-subscriptions-rebound-qwikster_n_1527290.html, retrieved December 11, 2012.

28. Goldman, David, "10 Big Dot.Com Flops," March 10, 2010, http://money.cnn.com/galleries/2010/technology/1003/gallery.dot_com_busts/2.html, retrieved December 11, 2012.

29. Gladwell, Malcom, "Blowing Up How Nassim Talep Turned the Inevitability of Disaster into an Investment Strategy.," April 22 & 29, 2002, www.gladwell.com/2002/2002_04_29_a_blowingup.htm, retrieved December 11, 2012.

30. Lewis, Michael, "Betting on the Blind Side," April 2010, www.vanityfair.com/business/features/2010/04/wall-street-excerpt-201004, retrieved December 11, 2012.

31. Malik, Om, "Here Is Why Facebook Bought Instagram," April 9, 2012, http://gigaom.com/2012/04/09/here-is-why-did-facebook-bought-instagram/, retrieved December 11, 2012.

32. Kersey, Ben, "Angry Birds Reaches One Billion Downloads," May 9, 2012, www.slashgear.com/angry-birds-reaches-one-billion-downloads-09227363/, retrieved December 11, 2012.

33. "Pebble: E-Paper Watch for iPhone and Android," Launched April 11, 2012 Project fully funded May 18, 2012, www.kickstarter.com/projects/597507018/pebble-e-paper-watch-for-iphone-and-android, retrieved December 11, 2012.

34. Oremus, Will, "Texas Schools Are Forcing Kids to Wear RFID Chips. Is That a Privacy Invasion?," October 11, 2012, www.slate.com/blogs/future_tense/2012/10/11/rfid_tracking_texas_schools_force_kids_to_wear_electronic_chips.html, retrieved December 11, 2012.

35. "Bring Your Own Device," April 23, 2012, www.whitehouse.gov/digitalgov/bring-your-own-device, retrieved December 11, 2012.

36. Dale, Jonathan, "Data Loss, Insecure Networks Among Enterprises' Biggest Mobile Concerns," October 8, 2012, www.maas360.com/news/industry-news/2012/10/data-loss-insecure-networks-among-enterprises-biggest-mobile-concerns-800881059/, retrieved December 11, 2012.

37. Henry, Rebecca, "INFOGRAPHIC: Exploring the Deep Web with Semantic Search," September 18, 2012, http://inventionmachine.com/the-Invention-Machine-Blog/bid/90626/INFOGRAPHIC-Exploring-the-Deep-Web-with-Semantic-Search, retrieved December 11, 2012.

38. Blake, Heidi, "Google's EU Warning Over Street View Privacy," February 26, 2010, www.telegraph.co.uk/news/worldnews/europe/7322309/Googles-EU-warning-over-Street-View-privacy.html, retrieved December 11, 2012.

39. Goodwin, Danny, "Google to Talk Privacy Policy in Private with Congress," February 1, 2012, http://searchenginewatch.com/article/2143109/Google-to-Talk-Privacy-Policy-in-Private-with-Congress, retrieved December 11, 2012.

40. "Hadoop and Big Data," copyright 2012 Cloudera, Inc, www.cloudera.com/what-is-hadoop/hadoop-overview/, retrieved December 11, 2012.

41. IBM Journal of Research and Development, www.research.ibm.com/journal/rd/024/ibmrd0204H.pdf, retrieved December 11, 2012.

42. "IBM Completes Acquisition of Cognos," January 31, 2008, www.-03.ibm.com/press/us/en/pressrelease/23423.wss, retrieved December 11, 2012.

43. Loveman, Gary, "Diamonds in the Data Mine," May 2003, http://faculty.unlv.edu/wrewar_emba/WebContent/Loveman_DataMining.pdf, retrieved December 11, 2012.

44. Lee, Thomas, "Data Mining 2.0," October 11, 2009, www.startribune.com/business/63905422.html?refer=y, retrieved December 11, 2012.

45. Whitehorn, Mark, "Big Data Bites Back: How to Handle Those Unwieldy Digits When You Can't Just Cram It into Tables," August 27, 2012, www.theregister.co.uk/2012/08/27/how_did_big_data_get_so_big/, retrieved December 11, 2012.

CHAPTER **3**

The Elements of Persuasion: Big Data Techniques

Intuition becomes increasingly valuable in the new information society precisely because there is so much data.

—John Naisbitt

C hapter 2 helped us get comfortable with Big Data, at least at a conceptual level. At this point, we know a good deal about the general characteristics of Big Data—its DNA. But Big Data is a catchall, an umbrella classification that encompasses many fields and subfields. In this chapter, we drill down and explore those *specific* fields and subfields. What are the specific elements or fields that comprise Big Data? How can these fields help us make sense of Big Data? Answering these questions is the goal of this chapter.

In May 2011, management consulting firm McKinsey released a lengthy e-book titled *Big Data: The Next Frontier for Innovation, Competition, and Productivity*.[1] In it, the authors list many techniques for analyzing Big Data. While not a definitive list, the following tools can be used to operationalize Big Data:

> A/B testing, association rule learning, classification, cluster analysis, collaborative filtering, crowdsourcing, data fusion and integration, data mining, ensemble learning, genetic algorithms, machine learning, natural language processing (NLP), neural networks, pattern recognition, predictive modeling, regression, radio-frequency identification (RFID), sentiment analysis, signal processing, supervised and unsupervised learning, simulation, text analytics,[*] time series analysis, and visualization

Before continuing, it's important to note a few things here. First, some of these techniques have long preceded anything resembling Big Data. That is, Big Data didn't spawn regression analysis; that has roots dating back to the early nineteenth century. The U.S. federal government has been noodling with RFID for decades. On a personal level, I worked with A/B testing nearly fifteen years ago, well before Big Data entered the business vernacular. What's more, McKinsey's list of Big Data elements is so long because Big Data is, well, so big. Each technique can be effective, but don't for a minute think that all can be applied equally well across every type and source of data. For instance, a call center records conversations between its representatives and its customers. There's tremendous *potential* value to be gleaned from this data. However, the phone calls are not yet suited for regression or sentiment analysis. For the company to make heads or tails out of the thousands of MP3 files at its disposal, it will have to use text or speech analytics. Only then will that data be ready for stepwise, forward, or backward regression. (Of course, these intermediate steps may disappear as each technology improves.)

Finally, there are instances in which combinations of these tools can be used concurrently. To some extent, many of these technologies overlap. To be sure, there may be one industry "best practice" to tackle a particular issue. Big Data is far too big and dynamic, and its tools are far too numerous (see Chapter 4). For instance, one shouldn't assume

---

[*] While not in the McKinsey report, I'd put speech analytics in here as well.

the best methods and tools to analyze call detail records (CDRs) in 2006 have remained unchanged. That may well be the case, but foolish is the person who blindly makes that assumption without so much as a Google search. A few hours of research may save weeks' worth of time—and produce insights impossible to see by using antiquated methods and tools.

This chapter highlights five commonly used techniques for analyzing Big Data:

1. Statistical techniques and methods
2. Data visualization
3. Automation
4. Semantics
5. Predictive analytics

Note that this section is not intended to represent a comprehensive list of—and guide to—every conceivable Big Data technique. Each one discussed next could fill a separate tome.

THE BIG OVERVIEW

At a high level, Big Data allows organizations to do three key things:

1. Better (if not completely) understand the past (i.e., what has happened and why)
2. Better (if not completely) understand the present (i.e., what is happening and why)
3. Better (if not completely) understand the future (i.e., what *will* happen and why)

Note that the inverses of these are also critical to understand (i.e., what has *not* happened and why). Also, Big Data is no time machine: it cannot change the past, although we can use Big Data to learn a great deal about it. But even knowledge has its limits. We may not be able to completely alter the present just because we know more about what's going on. While they are certainly not panaceas, the techniques discussed in this chapter should help organizations significantly augment their ability to predict future trends.

As you read this chapter, keep the following in mind: Big Data only brightens the flashlight; it does not eliminate darkness. In other words, Big Data reduces uncertainty and increases the accuracy of our predictions. With Big Data, we can understand more, but we will not understand all.

STATISTICAL TECHNIQUES AND METHODS

For centuries, statisticians have been looking at scientific, economic, and medical data for a cauldron of reasons. Academics also love statistics. Read any article in an academic journal, and you'll more than likely find a note in the conclusion about the need for more research or more data. Wonks like these welcome Big Data with open arms. In a Big Data world, many of the techniques are still the same as they were twenty years ago, even if the software programs are different. However, the datasets and sources are much, much more robust. If you're a statistician, Big Data makes you one happy camper.

Note that many of the well-trodden Big Data techniques in this chapter may be able to accomplish each of the three objectives listed in the previous section, "The Big Overview." In other words, they aren't restricted to merely interpreting the past; they may well be able to do the same with the present while keeping an eye on the future. For instance, regression analysis, discussed in the next section, can do far more than shed light on historical events like last quarter's product sales or last year's cases of insurance fraud. If regression analysis is used properly and, critically, *with the right data*, it can help organizations increase the accuracy and reliability with which they make predictions.

Regression

This chapter and the next cover new uses, tools, and techniques to handle Big Data. Some programming languages like traditional SQL are clearly not ideal for datasets in the petabytes. By the same token, though, some tools and methods hold up very well. Count regression analysis among them (even though Big Data may require new software applications).

Table 3.1 Sample Regression Analyses

Dependent Variable	Potential Independent Variables
Product sales	Company marketing spend, seasonality, age of product, social media mentions, product reviews, number and price of competing products
Employee attrition	Unemployment rate, employee compensation, demand for certain skills (e.g., programming)
Vacancy rate (for an individual apartment complex)	Unemployment rate, advertising, interest rates, housing prices, supply of existing apartments

At a high level, regression analysis lets people understand the relationships among different variables in a given dataset. I'll simplify the discussion here for the sake of brevity. Through regression, one can attempt to explain dependent variables like product sales as a function of independent variables like marketing spend or age of product. Some simple samples are shown in Table 3.1.

Regression analysis has many valuable business uses and comes in various forms. When employed correctly, regression is an invaluable tool for understanding data—not just what's happening, but *why*. Like A/B testing, regression can take much of the guesswork out of decision-making and significantly increase our empirical understanding of events.

Let's say that, as part of your job, you have historically used regression analysis to examine and understand sales data. Recently, sales of some of your company's products have increased, and you'd like to know why this has happened. However, you're in the Big Data world now and, as such, you have more data—both in terms of types and amounts. While regression still allows you to isolate the independent variables causing sales to remain the same, you may need a new and more robust software program to handle Big Data.

Do not assume that traditional statistical methods cannot work on new types and sources of data, *especially if that data is transformed into more usable formats*. It depends. For instance, it's probably still advisable to use Bayesian methods to analyze data.* They can be

---

*Put simply, Bayes's theory provides insights on how to refine initial guesses in the presences of new data.

exceptionally potent, even if unstructured data needs to be converted into a more structured format first (using the solutions described in Chapter 4).

 It's more than likely that Big Data will require many organizations to augment their existing applications and techniques with new ones.

A/B Testing

Put simply, A/B testing (aka, *split* or *bucket testing*) compares different or refined variations of content against a baseline control.[2] A/B testing flies in the face of how many employees currently make decisions. To this day, many employees argue about what to do and how to do it. Many have traditionally relied upon things like the volume of their voices, their rank, logic, internal politics, and, if all else failed, intimidation. While not an elixir, A/B testing allows people to make data-oriented decisions. They employ a more scientific method.

Now, A/B testing is hardly new. Harrah's CEO Gary Loveman once famously said, "There are two ways to get fired from Harrah's: stealing from the company, or failing to include a proper control group in your business experiment."[*] On a personal level, fifteen years ago, I worked for credit card behemoth CapitalOne, a company that extensively used A/B testing. CapitalOne would constantly run tests, collect information, refine products based upon the results, and test some more. For instance, CapitalOne would send 5,000 credit card offers to two groups of customers, represented in Table 3.2.

Table 3.2 Simple CapitalOne A/B Test Example with Hypothetical Data

Group	Annual Percentage Rate (APR)	Annual Fee	Credit Card Limit	Response Rate
A	13.5%	$49	$4,000	2.6%
B	9.9%	$29	$7,000	3.2%[3]

---

[*] Note that a 0.6% difference may seem inconsequential. On a sufficiently large sample size, however, it may be quite significant. In fact, an ostensibly small difference can be tremendously important.

On the basis of tests like these, CapitalOne could determine optimal offers and terms for much larger groups of people—and concurrently maximize its profits. The company was extremely proficient and aggressive at segmenting its customers in this manner, a practice that continues to this day. In 2007, the company ran a reported 28,000 separate tests on current and prospective customers.[4] From its inception in 1995, CapitalOne ingrained data-driven management and decision-making into its business. For instance, in the credit card world, very little was left to chance; even letter and envelope fonts, colors, and verbiage were run through the A/B ringer.

A/B testing is increasingly moving beyond laboratories and into the realm of everyday business. Companies like CapitalOne are becoming less exceptional. A May 2012 *Wired* magazine article titled "Test Everything"[5] summarizes quite nicely the merits and contemporary usage of A/B testing. First and foremost, A/B testing allows people faced with making a decision to generate their own data. That is, organizations can proactively generate their own data; they need not exclusively and *reactively* rely upon data created by others. From the aforementioned *Wired* piece:

> "It [A/B testing] is your favorite copyeditor," says IGN co-founder Peer Schneider. "You can't have an argument with an A/B testing tool like Optimizely, when it shows that more people are reading your content because of the change. There's no arguing back."

Now, A/B testing may not be prudent for every organization, and certainly not for every product. The decision to go this route hinges upon a number of factors. Timing, culture, and sample sizes are just a few things to consider. If you go down this road, though, don't stop just because you don't like or understand what the data is telling you.

And don't think for one moment that A/B testing is the exclusive purview of big companies. Nothing could be further from the truth. Case in point: Eric Reis, author of the 2011 bestseller *The Lean Startup*. In the book, Reis advocates that start-ups remove as much of the guesswork as possible from their development efforts by utilizing A/B testing. But here's the rub: Reis actually eats his own dog food. In the following interview with Dan Blank of We Grow Media, he explains his uniquely quantitative approach to selecting the book's cover and title:

> Many of his tests were about the cover and the subtitle—the two things he thought would be most impactful, and two things that are traditionally hard to analyze to determine the best of each. He describes how he fought with his publisher over "horrendous" covers that were presented to him. He was thrilled to have empirical data to show them, based on what people reacted most favorably to—what actually drove book sales. In the end, they tested and tested until he found something that he liked, the publisher liked, and actually sold books.
>
> What's more, he shared the data on his experiments, and used this too to sell books. One idea that really sold a lot of books for him was offering people to see this data if you pre-ordered a book. So Eric offered people a chance to go behind the scenes to see the book marketing testing that he was doing on the site. Due to the nature of the book, testing ideas that work, this really resonated with his audience. All the data can still be accessed on his website, including experiments and trends among his book-buying customers.[6]

Reis conducted a number of experiments on his site, constantly refining his cover, title, and subtitle until he found the optimal one. The results of one such experiment are provided in Figure 3.1.

Lest you think that you have to be a statistician or web developer to get started with A/B testing, think again. Companies like Optimizely (mentioned earlier) make it easier than ever to apply a more math- and science-driven method to website design and, more generally, business decisions.

DATA VISUALIZATION

Data visualization has certainly come a long way. I remember when it used to mean throwing a little data into Microsoft Excel and then creating a pretty basic chart or graph. Today, that seems so 1996. Now

Experiment Details

back

Book Covers

	purple	red
Unique people in experiment	549	544
People who clicked through to checkout page	148 / 26.9%	121 / 22.2%
People who purchased a book	16 / 2.9%	10 / 1.8%
Average order value per person who purchased	$26.5	$26.2
People who shared	4 / 0.7%	8 / 1.4%
Total Shares	4	10
Average shares per person who shared	1.0	1.2
People who clicked on a share	0	13
Friends who bought a book	0	0 / 0.0%
Friends who shared	0	0 / 0.0%
Average number of shares for people who clicked on a share and then shared	-	-
Number of people who clicked on a share by Friends	0	0

Figure 3.1 Reis's Book Cover Experiment Data[7]
Source: Eric Reis

entire companies like Tableau Software and Visually[*] specialize in helping people and organizations better understand their data though creative and interactive visualizations, no matter how big their data may be.[8] Consider the representation of how we eat in Figure 3.2.

While not quite The Oscars, Tableau has won awards like "Best Overall in Data Visualization" by *DM Review* and "Best of 2005 for Data Analysis" by *PC Magazine*. It's not hard to understand why data visualization is becoming so important. You may be able to identify outliers or trends in a table with 100 records, but try 100 million. Even Rainman would struggle with such a task. Data visualization enables people to understand data and identify trends quickly and much more easily than by looking at raw data.

---

[*] Visually is a one-stop shop for the creation of data visualizations and infographics. The site brings together more than 35,000 "marketing gurus, data nerds, and design junkies based on shared interests."

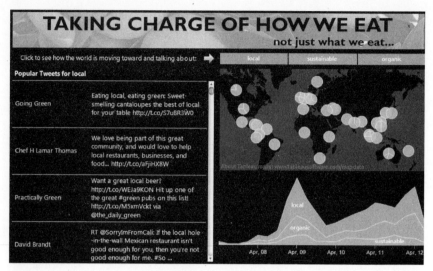

Figure 3.2 Tableau Interactive Data Visualization on How We Eat
Source: Tableau

Heat Maps

A special type of visualization is the heat map. In reality, they have been with us for decades, but many of us weren't aware of them until fairly recently. Why the explosion of heat maps?* Several reasons come to mind, including the rise of Big Data and attendant technologies. Not surprisingly, one interesting use of heat maps comes from a company that has for years embraced both Big Data and powerful technologies: Amazon.com. Specifically, according to a recent *Wired* article, Amazon introduced a heat map of the political books recently sold in the United States. The preponderance of red on the heat map indicates that conservative-themed books are outselling left-leaning ones coast to coast.** Amazon is quick to point out that the system isn't scientific. Rather:

> The map presents a rolling 30-day average of book-buying data and classifies them as red or blue depending on

---

* Some of the content in this section originally appeared on The Data Roundtable. See www.dataroundtable.com/?p=11254.

** To view the heat map, see www.amazon.com/gp/election-heatmap.

promotional materials and customer classifications. And there's no sliding scale. A book is either red or blue, so there's no nuance for centrists.[9]

"Just remember, books aren't votes," Amazon reminds us on its website. "So a map of book purchases may reflect curiosity as much as commitment."

Sure, the Amazon heat maps suffer from some significant limitations discussed in the *Wired* article. I'd also add a few more. First, an Amazon heat map doesn't reflect books sold in other locations—and this has important ramifications for attempting to forecast political trends. Consider that AARP members may not be terribly likely to buy books online, especially compared to Gen Xers and Millennials. Why might this matter? In short, because senior citizens consistently vote more than any other demographic in the United States. (This is a big reason that most politicians are afraid to even imply that cuts to Medicare and Social Security are required, but we can have that discussion over beers sometime.)

Second, book purchases don't "prove" political affiliations. For instance, books bought by John Q. Public may or may not ultimately be read by John Q. Public. John may give the book as a gift or choose not to read it altogether. Even if John does read it, we can't definitely say that he agrees with its content. (I've read several Ayn Rand books but don't fancy myself a libertarian.)

Despite the limitations of Amazon's heat maps, they can be of considerable value—as can other new forms of data. Nor does Jeff Bezos's company stop there. Amazon offers authors similar tools for understanding where their books are sold.

On a broader level, for every data and tech zealot like me, I have little doubt that many old-school professionals think that all this data is just plain hooey. My response: ignore new and exciting forms of data at your own peril.

Time Series Analysis

Let's say that I have run a local electronics store (Phil's Gadgets) for some time now. I don't have to be a rocket scientist to look at my sales data and see routine trends. Year after year, I notice that sales tend to rise around the time of Black Friday (the day after Thanksgiving). My customers buy holiday gifts for their loved ones. From a seasonal perspective, sales at my hypothetical electronics shop are probably pretty consistent. After all, timing matters. People buy more suntan lotion in the summer and more shovels in the winter. Summer and holiday movies tend to do better than movies released during relative dead periods—and the majority of movies make most of their money in the first weekend of their releases.

Each of these examples is a *time series,* formerly defined as "an ordered sequence of values of a variable at equally spaced time intervals."[10] Additional examples include certain industrial processes, stock prices, and other corporate business metrics.

Time series analysis accounts for the seasonality of certain types of data. Or, more technically, date-specific data points may have their own internal structure (such as autocorrelation, trend, or seasonal variation) that should be accounted for.[11] Going back to the Phil's Gadgets' example, I could use time series analysis to understand if there was something going on in my business (by virtue of my sales data) masked by the inherent seasonality of retail.

An observed time series can be decomposed into three components:

1. The trend (long-term direction)
2. The seasonal (systematic, calendar-related movements)
3. The irregular (unsystematic, short-term fluctuations)

Time series databases are optimized for handling data that is organized by time. Again, Tableau Software is one of the leaders in the field.[12]

AUTOMATION

Like data, automation is nothing new. The increasing power and prevalence of today's technologies has taken automation to an entirely new level. The collective effects of these changes are well beyond the scope of this book, but there can be no doubt that they have enabled Big Data—and made it much bigger.

Machine Learning and Intelligence

Machine learning has been with us for a long time. In 1959, computer gaming pioneer Arthur Samuel defined *machine learning* as a "field of study that gives computers the ability to learn without being explicitly programmed."[13] If you think that this sounds an awful lot like artificial intelligence, you're right.

Martin Hack knows a thing or two about machine learning. He's CEO of Skytree, a company that focuses on Big Data analytics with a machine-learning bent. In his words, "To use Big Data previously, people had to know what to ask for. Machine learning can help users delve deeper into the information. Previously, it's essentially a human writing a certain query that says 'look for somebody who is 35 and bought a BMW last year.' Machine learning would allow you to look for patterns that you wouldn't have even thought about before."[14]

Put differently, human beings can only find so many trends. The three *v*'s of Big Data discussed in Chapter 2 mean that even the brightest of us will likely miss key events and insights obscured in the vast forests of unstructured data. Machines can help us spot that which our eyes probably would have missed. For instance, consider credit cards. Every time someone makes a purchase with a Visa or American Express card, a computer is using predictive models based on past evidence to determine if it's really you or if it's fraud. More broadly, computer model predictions based on historical evidence represent "one of more positive trends we're going to see this century," says Tom Mitchell, head of the Machine Learning Department at Carnegie Mellon University. "We're just beginning."[15]

Current machine learning zealots include Twitter, Google, Facebook, website accelerator CloudFlare, popular news-browsing app Summly, and *Huffington Post* (HuffPo), a top-100 site on the web now owned by America Online (AOL). HuffPo generates a tremendous amount of content, in large part through the unpaid contributions from people lucky enough to write for it, including yours truly.* As of this writing, collectively those articles have generated more than 200 million comments. While a majority of them are legitimate responses to articles or Op-Ed pieces, a decent percentage comes from Internet

---

*For a list of my HuffPo pieces, go to http://tinyurl.com/huff-phil.

trolls, spammers, and generally angry people. And other comments contain profanity or other content that HuffPo finds objectionable. What to do?

HuffPo could hire a team of low-paid comment regulators that manually determines if every response is appropriate—or at least, doesn't violate its terms of service. But even a team of monkeys working around the clock couldn't approve so many comments, at least in a timely manner. Instead, HuffPo uses machine learning technology to automatically

- Approve what it believes to be legitimate comments
- Reject comments it considers spam or otherwise inappropriate
- Put in a queue the relatively few comments about which it is not sure

HuffPo saves a great deal of money through machine learning and natural language processing (discussed later in this chapter). But this is just the tip of the iceberg. Predictive software companies like Numenta are doing fascinating things. While in limited release as of this writing, Numenta's Grok processes "streams of real-time information from sensors, not the trillions of bytes of data that companies are amassing."[16] In theory, this would obviate the need for an organization to store, retrieve, and analyze its data. "This is the future of machine intelligence," says Numenta cofounder and neuroscientist Jeff Hawkins.

Sensors and Nanotechnology

Forget for a minute the new data sources of today and tomorrow and their impact on Big Data. Advances in sensors and nanotechnology are allowing vastly more data to be captured from *existing* data sources. Consider an airplane for a moment. Today relatively few people think of things like a 747 jet as a traditional data source. After all, most people just think of planes as a means to get from point A to point B. Fair enough, but I don't even want to think about a truly dataless flight. Current technology limitations do not allow airlines to capture as much data as they could but, like many things, this is changing. As Shawn Rogers writes in a September 2011 *Information Management* piece, "Boeing jet engines can produce 10 terabytes of operational information for every 30 minutes they turn. A four-engine jumbo jet can create 640 terabytes of data on just one Atlantic crossing; multiply that by the more than 25,000 flights flown each day, and you get an understanding of the impact that sensor and machine-produced data can make on a BI environment."[17]

It's hard to overstate the potential implications of more and better flight data on safety and cost. And air travel is just one of many ways in which sensors will be able to automatically collect stunning amounts of data in long-neglected areas. In the summer of 2008, the Project on Emerging Nanotechnologies estimated that nearly 1,000 manufacturer-identified nanotech products had been made publicly available, with three or four new ones hitting the market every week. Bottom line: we ain't seen nothin' yet.

RFID and NFC

In the past fifteen years, we have seen considerable advances in data capturing technology. Sensors and nanotechnology (described in the previous section) are just part of the story. Consider radio-frequency identification (RFID), a technology with roots in the 1940s and the Cold War as an espionage tool. These early RFID chips and enabled devices were prohibitively expensive. If they had remained so, companies wouldn't be slapping them on millions of their products—and schools in Texas wouldn't be slapping similar devices on hundreds of kids. What's more, they just couldn't gather as much data as they do today. RFID tags differ from sensors in that the former can only generate data from relatively short distances. That is, RFID and near field communication (NFC, discussed next) are specifically designed to handle close-proximity transactions.

The U.S. Department of Defense was an early proponent of RFID technology, as was mega-retailer Walmart. The latter fell in love with RFID more than decade ago and, as it typically does, forced its "partners" to fall in line. The company required its top-100 suppliers to tag pallets and cases of goods with (RFID) tags.[18] (It has since backed off.) Fast-forward to today, and RFID has not caught on as much as many had anticipated. It remains mostly a technology for tracking inventory, although 7-Eleven, Dairy Queen, credit card companies

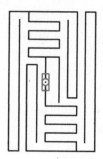

Figure 3.3 RFID Tag[19]
Source: "El Presidente," © 2008 Yodel Anecdotal, used under a Creative Commons Attribution 2.0 Generic license: http://creativecommons.org/licenses/by/2.0/legalcode

like MasterCard, and other organizations have experimented with RFID-enabled cell phones, loyalty programs, and mobile payments. A picture of an RFID tag is shown in Figure 3.3.

Some have called RFID a solution in search of a problem. As a standalone technology, it may face an uncertain future, especially given the growth of NFC. In point of fact, RFID may be unleashed when it is integrated with NFC.

Think of NFC and RFID as cousins, with NFC being the newer, more refined, and more powerful one.* In fact, current NFC technology even uses RFID standards. The digital security company Gemalto defines NFC as "a short-range wireless technology that enables the communication between devices over a distance of less than 10 cm."[20]

Like RFID, NFC enables quick, seamless transactions and tracks the data behind that transaction. Relative to RFID, however, NFC is much more robust. Its uses include a much wider variety of areas, including commerce, Bluetooth, Wi-Fi, and transportation. And for that reason, it is starting to take off. Some estimate that by 2014, an astonishing 50 percent of smartphones will include integrated NFC chips, essentially transforming them into *de facto* digital wallets.[21] Google is betting heavily on NFC.

While specific predictions are difficult to make about which technologies will ultimately emerge victorious, one thing is certain: more data will be available tomorrow than today—and from more sources.

---

* For more on the differences between the two, see http://tinyurl.com/nfc-vs-rfid.

And more and more of this data will be machine-generated (read: automated). Regardless of the specific technologies used, in a Big Data world, flying in a plane, buying a bus ticket, and connecting to a wireless network will automatically generate an increasing amount of data.

SEMANTICS

Unstructured and semi-structured data is, by its nature, largely text based. Even numbers are often surrounded by words, like an article on a company's stock. This section describes some of the tools that translate what is often a bunch of gobbledygook into meaningful information, the result of which can be utilized by many of the tools described in the next chapter.

Natural Language Processing

Electronic health records (EHRs) have been with us for quite some time. Some cite legitimate security concerns and thorny system issues as reasons that their adoption rate has been sluggish in the United States. Holding off on the veracity of these claims for a moment, there's little doubt that we would benefit from the widespread adoption of EHRs. Karen Bell, director of the Office of Health IT Adoption at the U.S. Department of Health and Human Services, said as much in an interview in September 2008. Bell noted that "health care . . . problem(s) could be solved, or at least drastically reduced, by electronic health records, which allow data to be easily shared among physicians, pharmacies, and hospitals. Such systems help coordinate a patient's care, eliminating duplicate testing and conflicting prescriptions, and ultimately cutting costs. But despite the benefits, only 15 to 18 percent of U.S. physicians have adopted electronic health records."[22]

EHRs don't happen overnight, even with government-provided subsidies like those announced by the Obama administration. Countries like Denmark with high EHR adoption rates didn't magically move from 0 to 100 percent. But even if EHR adoption hits 100 percent, is digitizing medical data the best that we can do here? Not even close. After the data is put into a usable and accessible format, we can get to the good stuff.

Consider Natural Language Processing (NLP), a technology that can produce readable summaries of chunks of text. Basic examples of NLP include social media, newspaper articles, and, as the Parliament of Canada and the European Union have done, translating governmental proceedings into all official languages. But this is just the tip of the iceberg. NLP can do much, much more, including deciphering doctors' notes and other unstructured information generated during patient visits. NLP can take EHRs to an entirely different level.

While turning unstructured data into something useful may not get your juices flowing, many people feel passionately about the subject. Count among them tech-savvy doctors like Jaan Sidorov and Kevin Pho, the web's top social media influencer in health care and medicine according to Klout. In an article on KevinMD (Pho's site), Sidorov cites statistics that an astonishing 80 percent of clinical documentation existing in health care today is unstructured. Yet that information is largely ignored, sometimes:

> . . . referred to as 'the text blob' and is buried within electronic health records (EHRs). The inherent problem with 'the text blob' is that locked within it lies an extraordinary amount of key clinical data—valuable information that can and should be leveraged to make more informed clinical decisions, to ultimately improve patient care and reduce healthcare costs. To date, however, because it consists of copious amounts of text, the healthcare industry has struggled to unlock meaning from 'the text blob' without intensive, manual analysis or has chosen to forego extracting the value completely.[23]

Sidorov goes on to tell the story of NLP-based applications that accurately read and analyze text from doctors' visits. In one instance, an application amazingly spotted diseases with an accuracy rate north of 90 percent based solely upon doctors' text-based descriptions—in other words, *before* any lab testing. NLP has a similar impact on medicine and the treatment of disease to Google Flu (see Figure 3.4 later in this chapter). Imagine trends discovered via NLP that allow doctors to proactively contact and treat their patients after they have exhibited similar symptoms—without having staff cobble through hundreds of patient records. And Google is hardly alone. Consider DataSift, a company that uses NLP to turn Twitter firehoses and other unstructured social data into structured, digestible, and valuable information. In mid-November 2012, the company received $15 million in venture funding.[24]

Examples like this prove that NLP can be both more effective and less expensive than traditional methods of disease detection.[*] Upon reading this, you should be asking yourself several questions:

- Isn't this similar to Speed Bump?
- Why aren't more health care organizations using NLP?
- When will Sidorov and Pho start the technology equivalents of medical Fight Clubs?

Text Analytics

Let's say that you're the CEO of Applebee's. You have heard some rumblings that more and more people are not pleased with their meals. Intrigued, you look at customer reviews on social review sites like Yelp. While not all negative, you see plenty of one-star ratings, especially as of late. In some reviews, you see more specific complaints about the service, the quality of the food, and the price. This could be potentially very valuable information, but there are more than 2,000 Applebee's restaurants in the world. On Yelp, there are more than 150 separate reviews alone for the Applebee's on 51 Curtner Avenue in San Jose, California.[25] You certainly can't read them all, much less try to make sense of them. What to do with all of that mostly unstructured data on Yelp? And what about other sites?

Enter text analytics: software in this field can help make sense of this highly unstructured data. After originally taking hold in brand management and enterprise search, as of late text analytics has started making inroads in other fields, such as e-commerce, financial services, and social media. At a high level, text analytics help organizations make sense of e-mails, legal or scientific documents, forum and blog posts, call center transcripts, and other forms of unstructured data, even if there is structured data in this sea of

---

[*] Modern NLP algorithms are based on machine learning, especially statistical machine learning.

unstructured data. For instance, a blog post may contain references to stock prices.

But how exactly can value be extracted from text? In short, the process is called *text analytics*, defined as an exciting new research area that attempts to solve "the information overload problem by using techniques from data mining, machine learning, NLP, information retrieval, and knowledge management. Text analytics involves the preprocessing of document collections (text categorization, information extraction, term extraction), the storage of the intermediate representations, the techniques to analyze these intermediate representations (distribution analysis, clustering, trend analysis, association rules, etc.) and visualization of the results."[26] At a high level, the process works as follows:

 TEXT ANALYTICS 101[27]

Text analytics adds semantic understanding to many elements or *features*, including:

- Named entities: people, companies, places, etc.
- Pattern-based entities: e-mail addresses, phone numbers, etc.
- Concepts: abstractions of entities.
- Facts and relationships.
- Concrete and abstract attributes (e.g., 10-year, expensive, comfortable).
- Subjectivity in the forms of opinions, sentiments, and emotions: attitudinal data.

Text analytics transforms Information Retrieval (IR) into Information Access (IA). At a high level, the process is as follows:

- Search terms become queries.
- Retrieved material is mined for larger-scale structure.
- Retrieved material is mined for features such as entities and topics or themes.
- Retrieved material is mined for smaller-scale structure such as facts and relationships.
- Results are presented intelligently, for instance, grouping on mined topics-themes.
- Extracted information may be visualized and explored.

In the main, text analytics automates what researchers, writers, scholars, and all the rest of us have been doing for years. Text analytics applies linguistic and/ or statistical techniques to extract concepts and patterns that can be applied to categorize and classify documents, audio, video, and images. It transforms un- structured information into data for application of traditional analysis techniques. Finally, it discerns meaning and relationships in large volumes of information computers previously could not process.

Seth Grimes is the leading industry analyst covering text analytics and the owner and principal consultant of Alta Plana Corporation. He also serves as the contributing editor at TechWeb's *InformationWeek*.

Sentiment Analysis

Analyzing text and turning it into searchable and accessible data is one thing. But collectively what does all this text actually mean? Answer- ing that question is the fundamental goal behind sentiment analysis: it allows people to more easily understand the patterns inherent in unstructured, text-laden data—and yes, it is *data*. Formally defined, sentiment analysis is

> a linguistic analysis technique where a body of text is exam-
> ined to characterize the tonality of the document. Though
> the method pre-dates modern technological tools, the use
> of sentiment analysis has accelerated in recent years with
> the development of large-scale computational infrastructure
> that can analyze large unstructured textual datasets.[28]

Because user-generated content is growing so fast, sentiment analy- sis enables many things, including effective social media monitoring. Companies can automatically characterize the overall feeling or mood of their customers as it relates to specific brands and products.

Sentiment analysis is not merely about identifying simple keywords from strings of text; it's more nuanced than that. At a high level, spe- cific combinations of words allow for more precise sentiment to be deter- mined. Analysis of unstructured text often shows that certain adjectives and adverbs convey the *degree* of a particular sentiment. For instance, the negative sentiment for a tweet containing "Product X sucks" isn't as strong as one with "Product X *really* sucks." Sentiment analysis can shed light on how people feel but, arguably more important, it can provide insights into the strength of their feelings and why people feel the way they do.

Sentiment can be derived from many different sources: e-mails, social media, and other text-laden data. Its implications are nothing less than far-reaching. Forget commerce for a moment. It could transform politics, making traditional polling obsolete—and plenty are taking notice. Large companies like IBM are using über-powerful computers like Watson to quantify social sentiment.[29] At the other end of the spectrum, start-ups can quickly process and interpret gigantic amounts of data. That is, cloud computing, the ability to scale horizontally across hundreds of servers, and new ultra-fast data persistence* and computation technologies are not the sole purview of billion-dollar corporations like IBM and Oracle.

Consider BrightContext, a start-up providing real-time sentiment analysis and game-style interactivity for Super Bowl–sized TV audiences. I asked CEO John Funge about how start-ups can utilize Big Data and new technologies. "Over the course of the last five years or so, the combination of robust new open-source technologies like NoSQL databases and Hadoop, the continued declines in processing and storage costs, and the flexibility [of] cloud computing have democratized the ability to leverage ultra-large datasets," Funge told me. "Basically, Big Data is truly now accessible to even the smallest of businesses. Systems that today cost $100K to build would have cost many millions just ten years ago—or would not have not been possible at all. It's pretty amazing—and very disruptive."[30]

BIG DATA AND THE GANG OF FOUR

To many folks, Big Data seems like a bit of an amorphous term. Chapter 2 defined Big Data and described its characteristics, but a few statistics are in order here. Consider the following Big Data numbers from Amazon, Apple, Facebook, and Google—aka *the Gang of Four*:

- **Amazon:** Excluding books, the company sells 160 million products on its website. Target sells merely 500,000. Amazon is

---

* A persistent data structure always preserves the previous version of itself when it is modified.

reported to have credit cards on file for 300 million customers. 300 million.

- **Apple:** In May 2012 the company passed 25 billion app downloads.[31]
- **Facebook:** As of this writing, more than one billion registered users share more than one billion pieces of content every day.[32]
- **Google:** As of two years ago, Google handled 34,000 searches per second.[33]

These numbers are nothing short of breathtaking. Because of the manner in which they manage their data, these companies can do simply amazing things. For instance, let's focus on Google. The company has "found that certain search terms are good indicators of flu activity. Google Flu Trends uses aggregated Google search data to estimate flu activity."[34]

And Google is hardly alone. While Facebook's rate of growth seems to be waning,[35] make no mistake: it's still growing. *Deceleration of growth* shouldn't be confused with deceleration. Beyond the Gang of Four, other companies are producing astonishing amounts of data. Let's look at some of Twitter's Big Data statistics. On the company's five-year anniversary, it posted the following mind-boggling numbers:

- **3 years, 2 months, and 1 day:** The time it took from the first tweet to the billionth tweet.
- **1 week:** The time it now takes for users to send a billion tweets.
- **50 million:** The average number of tweets people sent per day, one year ago.
- **140 million:** The average number of tweets people sent per day, in the past month.[36]
- **80:** Oddly, the percentage of all tweets in 2011 that involved Charlie Sheen.

OK, I'm making the last one up, but you get my drift.

A few things strike me about these numbers. First, this is a staggering amount of data. Second, all these companies keep their data somewhere. To varying extents, these companies and others are turning data into information and, ultimately, knowledge.* Third, Amazon, Apple, Facebook, Google, Twitter, and other successful organizations today don't view Big Data as an annoying problem; *they view it as a tremendous asset.* (See "Google and Infonomics" in the Introduction.)

What these companies do with that knowledge varies, but no one can doubt the potential of so much data—even if much of it is noise. If 90 percent of tweets are worthless, that doesn't change the fact that there may be considerable value in that other 10 percent. Those who recognize the inherent value of Big Data should start asking big questions. Will we continue to be comfortable with our data being sold to the highest bigger? We will ever want to take control of our data? Will people continue to use ad-supported platforms? Or, will private, ad-free platforms like app.net flourish?

A big revolt against Big Data doesn't appear imminent, although Chapter 7 looks at some of the downsides of the Data Deluge. For the time being, for-profit platforms like Amazon, Apple, Facebook, and Google will continue to generate a boatload of data. The continuation of the Data Deluge does not hinge upon the continued growth of open or "somewhat-open" platforms.

Those who think that consumers are going to be generating and using *less* data in the upcoming years are clearly living in an alternate reality. Today, many enterprises are realizing that they need to immediately take steps to ensure that they have the software, hardware, and human capabilities to handle vastly increasing amounts and types of data.

PREDICTIVE ANALYTICS

Let's say that you're sitting in front of your computer or tablet. You go to Google and you type in "how to wrte a bok" but you really meant to type "how to write a book." Because untold others have made the same mistake, Google takes you to your intended search results. Google's software predicts that you really meant the latter, not the former. Of course, you can still try to query "how to wrte a bok" if you like, although you probably won't get much back in the way of

---

* Opinions vary on these terms. For one take, see www.infogineering.net/data-information-knowledge.htm.

meaningful results. In fact, you didn't even need to finish typing "bok" and press Enter. If you enable Google's autocomplete option (or don't disable it, to be precise), its search engine will suggest results as soon as it recognizes a pattern, as shown in Figure 3.4.

And this is just one example of pattern recognition and prediction. We saw in the previous section that Google Flu aggregates search results by location to predict flu outbreaks throughout the world— and hopefully minimize the contagion. How does Google do this? The short answer is data. The longer answer is that Google uses a combination of IP addresses, search history, user-provided information, and GPS data. With this information, Google's algorithm not only knows what people are searching for, but *where* most of those searches are taking place.

While instructive as an example, Google doesn't have a monopoly on effectively using pattern recognition to predict what people really mean—or what will happen. Google just happens to be ubiquitous and extremely good at it. In fact, many organizations are finally recognizing the power of analytics. According to a joint SAS and Accenture survey, "45 percent of businesses increased their analytics spending in 2011, and even more—65 percent—planned to increase it" in 2012.[37]

The Holy Grail of Big Data is predictive analytics. *ComputerWorld* defines this as "the branch of data mining concerned with forecasting probabilities. The technique uses variables that can be measured to predict the future behavior of a person or other entity. Multiple predictors are combined into a predictive model. In predictive modeling, data

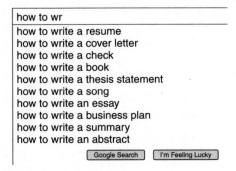

Figure 3.4 Google Autocomplete
Source: Google.com

is collected to create a statistical model, which is tweaked as additional data becomes available."[38]

Entire books have been written about business analytics. I won't attempt to summarize them here, except to say that predictive analytics has arrived in full swing and is becoming increasingly important. No, predictive analytics may never *completely* supplant gut feel and intuition—at least in our lifetimes. Of this much, however, I am sure: more and more business and societal policies and decisions will be based upon data, numbers, and analytics. Against that backdrop, this chapter closes with a look at several critical topics related to analytics and Big Data.

> ● The main point of this section can be stated as follows: despite phenomenal advances in capturing, storing, and analyzing data, making accurate predictions can still be challenging, even with Big Data. The effective use of Big Data doesn't guarantee complete certainty about the present, much less the future.

Two Key Laws of Big Data

All the Big Data techniques described in this chapter—and many of the ones that are not—allow organizations to take advantage of the Law of Large Numbers (LLN). Now, LLN is anything but new. In fact, it has roots back to the sixteenth century. There are many definitions, but, in a nutshell, LLN can be stated as follows:

> As the number of samples increases, the average of these samples is likely to reach the mean of the whole population.[39]

More colloquially, we can be more confident of our predictions with larger samples than we can be with smaller ones. For instance, let's go back to baseball.* A player hits twenty home runs for eight straight years and then suddenly hits fifty. All else being equal, how many is he likely to hit next year? That number should be much closer

---

*This law applies to all of us. For example, as an avid but pretty poor golfer, I consistently shoot in the mid-90s. I have never come close to breaking 80, and it's been a while since I've gone north of 110. Google "standard deviation" for more on this subject.

to 20 than 50—unless, of course, he's been taking steroids. (Case in point: Former Baltimore Orioles' "slugger" Brady Anderson. The legendary Hank Aaron never hit fifty dingers in a season, but Anderson did.) However, we can be much less confident in predicting what a rookie who hit twenty home runs will do next year. We just don't have the same baseline. As you may remember from your college days, statisticians call this phenomenon *regression toward the mean*.[40]

Text analysis and speech recognition software such as Apple's Siri and Dragon by Nuance depend largely on LLN to spot patterns. Their ability to interpret input, spot patterns, and ultimately *understand* these types of unstructured data increases in direct proportion to their number of observations or inputs. In other words, while not perfect, each improves with more data.

Another law helps us explain the relationship between Big Data and predictions: the Law of Diminishing Marginal Utility (LDMU). For example, if you're stuck in the desert, a glass of water provides enormous utility. The second provides less than the first, the third less than the second, and so on. In fact, the fiftieth glass might make you physically ill (i.e., negative utility).

Now, let's look at a more data-specific example of LDMU. When trying to analyze and ultimately solve any business problem, you may well start with zero data. You soon add 100,000 data points and, because you started with nothing, these are incredibly valuable. Now at least you can get your arms around the problem. You add the second 100,000 data points and, while helpful, they will probably only refine your previous understanding. That is, they help less than the first 100,000. The same can be said for the third 100,000. With a sufficiently large sample size, marginal data helps less and less.

As a direct result of LDMU and historically high data storage costs (at least compared to today), many organizations have limited the amount of data they store. Fortunately, this doesn't have to be the case anymore. The beauty of today's technologies (like those discussed in the next chapter) and the low cost of data storage (discussed in the Introduction) is that "marginally less valuable" data can be captured, stored, retrieved, and analyzed. To continue with our example, the tenth set of 100,000 data points might provide relatively little business value, but they still inhere *some* value. What's more, what if a new trend begins to manifest itself in that last set of 100,000? If you didn't have to worry about storage costs and system performance, wouldn't you rather have that data and not need it than need it and not have it? All else being equal, more data can yield more accurate predictions, as we'll see next.

Collaborative Filtering

What happens when you splice together LLN, powerful technology, crowdsourcing, metadata, and Big Data? As companies like Google, Facebook, Twitter, Netflix, Pandora, Apple, and Amazon have discovered, you wind up with collaborative filtering (CF). (See "Big Data Giveth—and Big Data Taketh Away" in Chapter 2.) CF allows companies to make remarkably accurate suggestions about their products and learn a great deal about their users and customers.

COLLABORATIVE FILTERING, OUTLIERS, AND PROGRESSIVE ROCK

We know from Chapter 1 that I am a slightly obsessive fan of Rush, for my money Canada's finest export. In iTunes, I rate their songs, along with those from other bands that I enjoy. I tend to like music from the 1970s and 1980s. As such, I listen to quite a bit of Genesis, Porcupine Tree, Marillion, Dream Theater, Pink Floyd, Yes, and other bands in the progressive rock genre. I rate many songs by these bands high as well, helping Apple learn about my listening habits. (I do the same with books on Amazon and movies on Netflix, but let's stick with music here.)

Now, multiply my ratings by the millions of people who use iTunes. Now, no two *individuals* may have precisely the same taste in music (or books, apps, movies, TV shows, or art, for that matter). Via its technology and massive troves of data, Apple learns a great deal about *group* listening habits. As a result, Apple will recommend relevant songs to me—and I just might buy a few.

But not everyone is as loyal as I am to one particular genre of music. Some people out there have odd (i.e., inconsistent) tastes. They like Rush, but they're also huge Beyoncé fans. (There's nothing wrong with Beyoncé or her music; it's just that most Rush fans don't listen to her.) These outliers give high marks to the latest Beyoncé album, as well as Rush's most recent release, *Clockwork Angels*. Won't this throw off Apple's rating systems that tend to associate Rush's music with some of the bands mentioned earlier?

Or what about those who just hate Rush? There are plenty of haters, including many of my own friends. I'll be the first to admit that Rush is an acquired taste. Plenty of people not only don't share my passion for Rush, but actively despise the band. Reasons include its cerebral lyrics, its 20-minute songs, its liberal use of odd time signatures, and Geddy Lee's voice. What if they intentionally rate Pink Floyd songs high but Rush songs low? What if Rush haters rate Rush songs high and intentionally suggest songs in a completely unrelated genre such as country or Gangsta Rap? Won't these actions make Apple's Rush-related recommendations less relevant?

In a word, no. Apple's recommendation technology effectively leverages LLN and extensive metadata about millions of songs. Large sample sizes are relatively impervious to true outliers and bad data. They can withstand some inaccurate entries, intentionally misleading ratings, and legitimate anomalies. The bigger the data, the more immune that large datasets are to relatively small amounts of "bad" data. In fact, collaborative filtering only works well with (relatively) Big Data.

This sidebar is based upon a post that I wrote for MIKE2.0. It is used with permission.[41]

LIMITATIONS OF BIG DATA

Before concluding this chapter, a few words of moderation are in order. Regression analysis, A/B testing, and other statistical and Big Data methods can be extremely powerful. As much as data and stats can help, however, they cannot solve every problem. Big Data certainly does not put an end to internal bickering about best courses of action. I have no doubt that many companies won't replace focus groups and traditional forms of market research anytime soon. In a May 25, 1998, *BusinessWeek* article, Steve Jobs said, "It's really hard to design products by focus groups. A lot of times, people don't know what they want until you show it to them." The larger question is: do you really want to crowdsource everything? There's something to be said for the vision of an individual, small team, or small company. Giving everyone a vote may well drive a product to mediocrity. That is, in an attempt to please everybody, you'll please nobody.

The use of Big Data in no way eliminates the need for sage human judgment. There's still some art to go with that science. But, without question, A/B testing allows people to increase the mix of science in that recipe. A/B testing relying upon the laws of statistics still applies, especially *statistical significance*. A site that gets 50,000 unique hits per day can reasonably chop its audience into two and, in the end, feel confident that the results of testing are accurate. Without getting all "statsy," if done right on large sample sizes, A/B testing means less of a chance of either Type I or Type II errors.* Now, if a site gets fifty unique visitors per day, the chances of seeing a "false positive" or failing to see a legitimate cause-effect relationship are considerably higher.

We shouldn't ignore the human side of Big Data. In my experience, data naysayers often discount data because, in large part, they're "not numbers' people" or they somehow think that they know what's happening and why—and what will happen. While some people will always find reasons to discredit that which they don't understand, Big Data can provide some pretty strong ammunition against skeptics. After all, what happens when website layout A, book cover A, or product description page A shows twice the level of engagement as its alternatives? Facts like those will cause many but not all skeptics to admit defeat. As Arthur Schopenhauer once said, "Every man takes the limits of his own field of vision for the limits of the world."

SUMMARY

This chapter provided an overview of the individual fields and subfields that comprise Big Data. It covered Big Data techniques like A/B testing, sentiment analysis, text analytics, automation, data visualization, and RFID.

The next chapter goes deeper. We know that unstructured data doesn't play nice with relational databases and that traditional SQL statements don't work well with Big Data. But what does? Chapter 4 looks at the exciting new tools and technologies that are, for the most part, much better suited for Big Data than traditional Small Data solutions.

---

* Type I errors incorrectly state that a relationship exists among variables when, in fact, no relationship exists. Type II errors fail to acknowledge that a true relationship exists among variables.

NOTES

1. www.mckinsey.com/~/media/McKinsey/dotcom/Insights%20and%20pubs/MGI/Research/Technology%20and%20Innovation/Big%20Data/Big_Data_The_next_frontier_for_innovation_epub.ashx.

2. Taylor, Dan, "Why A/B Testing Is Essential to Your Startup's Campaigns," August 4, 2012, http://thenextweb.com/entrepreneur/2012/08/04/why-ab-testing-is-essential-to-your-startups-campaigns, retrieved December 11, 2012.

3. Brynjolfsson, Erik; Scharge, Michael, "The New, Faster Face of Innovation," August 17, 2009, http://online.wsj.com/article/SB10001424052970204830304574130820184260340.html, retrieved December 11, 2012.

4. Jacobs, Ron, "How Direct Marketing Applies in a Multichannel Marketing World," January 3, 2011, www.slideshare.net/amdiaweb/how-direct-marketing-applies-in-a-multichannel-marketing-world, retrieved December 11, 2012.

5. Christian, Brian, "Test Everything: Notes on the A/B Revolution," May 9, 2012, www.wired.com/epicenter/2012/05/test-everything-notes-on-the-ab-revolution/, retrieved December 11, 2012.

6. Blank, Dan, "How to Become a Bestselling Author—Lessons from Eric Ries," October 28, 2011, http://wegrowmedia.com/how-to-become-a-bestselling-author-lessons-from-eric-ries/, retrieved December 11, 2012.

7. Reis, Eric. Experiments. http://lean.st/experimenter/experiments/20, retrieved December 11, 2012.

8. "Big Data Analysis," copyright 2003–2012 Tableau Software, www.tableausoftware.com/solutions/big-data-analysis, retrieved December 11, 2012.

9. www.wired.com/gadgetlab/2012/08/amazon-political-heat-map.

10. "Introduction to Time Series Analysis," www.itl.nist.gov/div898/handbook/pmc/section4/pmc4.htm, retrieved December 11, 2012.

11. Ibid.

12. "Time Series Analysis," copyright 2003–2012 Tableau Software, www.tableausoftware.com/solutions/time-series-analysis, retrieved December 11, 2012.

13. "01 and 02: Introduction, Regressing Analysis, and Gradient Descent," www.holehouse.org/mlclass/01_02_Introduction_regression_analysis_and_gr.html, retrieved December 11, 2012.

14. Samuels, Diana, "Skytree: Machine Learning Meets Big Data," February 23, 2012, www.bizjournals.com/sanjose/blog/2012/02/skytree-machine-learning-meets-big-data.html?page=all, retrieved December 11, 2012.

15. Borenstein, Seth, "2012 Is the Year of Nate Silver and the Prediction Geeks," November 11, 2012, www.huffingtonpost.com/2012/11/11/nate-silver-predictions_n_2114274.html?ir=Technology, retrieved December 11, 2012.

16. Hardy, Quentin, "Jeff Hawkins Develops a Brainy Big Data Company," November 28, 2012, http://bits.blogs.nytimes.com/2012/11/28/jeff-hawkins-develops-a-brainy-big-data-company/, retrieved December 11, 2012.

17. Rogers, Shawn, "Big Data Is Scaling BI and Analytics," September 1, 2011, www.information-management.com/issues/21_5/big-data-is-scaling-bi-and-analytics-10021093-1.html, retrieved December 11, 2012.

18. Malone, Matthew, "Did Wal-Mart Love RIFD to Death?," February 14, 2012, www.smartplanet.com/blog/pure-genius/did-wal-mart-love-rfid-to-death/7459, retrieved December 11, 2012.

19. Figure used via Creative Commons' license. See www.flickr.com/photos/hublera/2728064278, retrieved December 11, 2012.

20. "NFC Definition," See www.gemalto.com/nfc/definition.html, retrieved December 11, 2012.

21. Chandler, Nathan, "What's the Difference Between RFID and NFC?," March 7, 2012, http://electronics.howstuffworks.com/difference-between-rfid-and-nfc1.htm, retrieved December 11, 2012.

22. Singer, Emily, "What's Delaying Digital Health Records?," September 26, 2008, www.technologyreview.com/biotech/21428/#afteradbody, retrieved December 11, 2012.

23. Sidorov, MD, Jaan, "Natural Language Processing in EMRs Can Improve Disease Tracking," January 30, 2012, www.kevinmd.com/blog/2012/01/natural-language-processing-emrs-improve-disease-tracking.html, retrieved December 11, 2012.

24. Rao, Leena, "DataSift Raises $15M to Help Businesses Mine and Analyze Data," November 12, 2012, http://techcrunch.com/2012/11/12/datasift-raises-15m-to-help-businesses-mine-and-analyze-social-data/, retrieved December 11, 2012.

25. www.yelp.com/biz/applebees-san-jose, retrieved December 11, 2012.

26. www.ir.iit.edu/cikm2004/tutorials.html#T2, retrieved October 13, 2012.

27. Text Analytics Summit 2011 Workshop, given on May 17, 2011. Used with permission, retrieved December 11, 2012.

28. "Sentiment Analysis," copyright 2012 The Financial Times LTD, http://lexicon.ft.com/Term?term=sentiment-analysis, retrieved December 11, 2012.

29. "IBM Social Sentiment Index," www.ibm.com/analytics/us/en/conversations/social-sentiment.html, retrieved December 11, 2012.

30. Personal conversation with Funge, November 17, 2012.

31. Brian, Matt, "Apple Hits 25 Billion App Store Downloads," March 5, 2012, www.usatoday.com/tech/news/story/2012-03-05/apple-app-downloads/53372352/1, retrieved December 11, 2012.

32. Protalinski, Emil, "Facebook: 1 Billion 'Things' Shared via Open Graph Daily: It won't be long now before Facebook cofounder and CEO Mark Zuckerberg says 10 billion "things" are shared on Facebook every day," July 26, 2012, http://news.cnet.com/8301-1023_3-57481153-93/facebook-1-billion-things-shared-via-open-graph-daily/, retrieved December 11, 2012.

33. McGee, Matt, "By The Numbers: Twitter Vs. Facebook Vs. Google Buzz," February 23, 2010, http://searchengineland.com/by-the-numbers-twitter-vs-facebook-vs-google-buzz-36709, retrieved December 11, 2012.

34. "Explore Flu Trends Around the World," copyright 2012 Google, www.google.org/flutrends/, retrieved December 11, 2012.

35. www.foxbusiness.com/technology/2012/07/26/facebook-growth-slows-shares-tumble/, retrieved December 11, 2012.

36. "#numbers," March 14, 2011, http://blog.twitter.com/2011/03/numbers.html, retrieved December 11, 2012.

37. Brown, Anna, "Leading the Analytics Charge: A Call for Talent," www.allanalytics.com/author.asp?section_id=2208&doc_id=253770, retrieved December 11, 2012.

38. Matlis, Jan, "QuickStudy: Predictive Analytics," October 9, 2006, www.computerworld.com/s/article/267042/Predictive_Analytics, retrieved December 11, 2012.

39. "Law of Large Numbers," 2012, www.investopedia.com/terms/l/lawoflargenumbers.asp#ixzz2Ap4Fcor3, retrieved December 11, 2012.

40. Everitt, B.S. (2002) *The Cambridge Dictionary of Statistics*, CUP. ISBN 0-521-81099-X, retrieved December 11, 2012.

41. Simon, Phil, "Metadata and Collaborative Filtering," July 5, 2001, http://mike2 .openmethodology.org/blogs/information-development/2011/07/05/metadata-and-collaborative-filtering/, retrieved December 11, 2012.

CHAPTER 4

Big Data Solutions

Data is not information, information is not knowledge, knowledge is not understanding, understanding is not wisdom.

—Clifford Stoll

From the last chapter, we know that Big Data is a bit of a catch-all term. So where do we go from here? This chapter provides an overview of the most prevalent Big Data tools and resources at reasonably high levels.* This chapter will not delve into highly technical details. Don't expect complicated schematics. This is a book about the business case for Big Data, not an implementation guide for any one application. As discussed in Chapter 1, old tools like relational database management system (RDBMSs) just can't efficiently handle Big Data. Different times call for different solutions, and it's time to get familiar with Hadoop, NoSQL, columnar databases, and other emerging Big Data tools.

---

* This will be a high-level overview, not a how-to section.

Note that this is the closest thing to a technical chapter in the entire book. Here I endeavor to keep things at a relatively high level, not to inundate the reader with needless complexity. Yes, database schemas, nodes, clusters, in-memory databases, data compression, parallel processing, and other technical concepts are essential concepts that underscore Big Data. However, here they are intentionally kept to a bare minimum. This isn't that type of book. The main point of this chapter is that Big Data encompasses a variety of new data sources and types, as well as increased data volumes and velocity. As such, to effectively utilize Big Data, organizations need to deploy new tools, such as the ones found in the following pages. For the most part, traditional row-based databases just can't handle Big Data very well, a point shared by many industry experts like Rich Murnane, Director of Enterprise Data Operations at iJET International. "Let's say that an organization hires me to build a data system that needs to receive and store hundreds of millions of sensor data records per day," Murnane told me. "If I advise the organization to try to use a relational database such as I have in the past, that client should probably run out and get a new consultant."[1]

 BIG DISCLAIMERS

I'll try here to preempt those who are probably already frothing at the mouth right about now. I am convinced that some folks have read the first two paragraphs of this chapter and are getting ready to slam me on Twitter, write me a nasty e-mail, or comment on my blog. The gripe: Big Data does not necessarily require new databases and tools because traditional data warehouses, data marts, and databases are evolving.

Without question, most large software vendors are not standing still. They are augmenting their current products and launching new ones. As far as I can tell, their general goal is to allow their clients to better handle the massive amounts of semi-structured and unstructured data available today. For instance, consider Sybase, a company founded in 1984. The company sells products in data management, analytics, and mobility, among others. In May 2010, SAP acquired it, keeping the Sybase brand. (Sybase now describes itself on its site as "an SAP company.") Despite the acquisition, the innovation at Sybase has continued. It is not simply there to support its legacy products. The company now sells Big Data solutions.[2] Also, as we'll see later in this chapter, the latest version of Microsoft's SQL Server 2012, its relational database, integrates with and simplifies Hadoop—or at least Microsoft claims as much.[3]

My point in this chapter is *not* that the more established tools are objectively inferior to the newer ones across the board. Nor do I mean to imply that the traditional software vendors will never alter or improve their current offerings. As the following pages will show, that's clearly not the case. Rather, those looking to take advantage of Big Data should understand that mature data warehouses, relational databases like dB2, SQL Server, Oracle, and other solutions are often not, by themselves and as currently constituted, ideal for these purposes. New technologies and solutions meet legitimately new business needs—and deal with data the scale of which we have heretofore never seen. Yes, organizations have available to them more data than ever (read: increased velocity, variety, and volume). To combat these Big Data "problems," there's an increasing array of powerful solutions. Today, there's never been more choice and, without any particular bias, this chapter explores these options.

Now, I am not claiming that the traditional data warehouse no longer serves a valuable purpose and that it will never evolve. I am not that presumptuous, and I am certainly not omniscient. I only wish to alert the reader to new technologies that are arguably much better suited for Big Data than many well-trodden solutions developed fifteen years ago. As a general rule, we just can't handle new data sources and types with the same legacy tools.

Next, organizations should not throw the baby out with the bath water. I don't foresee a day in which Big Data solutions can do what customer relationship management (CRM), enterprise resource planning (ERP), and other essential enterprise applications can do. More likely, applications like Hadoop will replace existing data warehouses, datamarts, and ad hoc querying and reporting tools.

Next, these tools are constantly changing—and new ones are being developed as we speak. For instance, it's entirely possible that current limitations of Hadoop (like the lack of real-time reporting) as of this writing cease to be limitations by the time you read this book. Yes, Big Data solutions are evolving that quickly.

Finally, please note that, by design, this chapter covers topics in a manner best described as wide, not deep. Many big books have been written about most of the solutions covered here. As such, this chapter should serve as a primer—a launching pad for more detailed discussions about an organization's specific Big Data needs. It is not intended to be remotely comprehensive.

With these disclaimers out of the way, let's move on to the specific Big Data solutions that many organizations are currently using.

PROJECTS, APPLICATIONS, AND PLATFORMS

It's hard to think of Big Data solutions as applications in the traditional sense. For instance, Microsoft Excel and Outlook seem to better fit the definition of an *application*. Yes, each can do some pretty amazing things, but to compare them to Big Data software is analogous to saying that the Eiffel Tower is a just another building. It just doesn't seem right.

Irrespective of moniker, though, Big Data doesn't just happen by itself. Even an individual Big Data technique like A/B testing or sentiment analysis still necessitates some type of service, project, software program, or platform. This section examines some of the more mainstream ones.

Hadoop

Any conversation today about Big Data tools has to start with Apache Hadoop, the large collection of open-source projects that distributes and processes data. Collectively, the Hadoop stack and its different components allow organizations to store and make sense of vast amounts of semi-structured and unstructured data. GigaOM calls Hadoop "the world's *de facto* Big Data platform."[4] Today, Yahoo!, Facebook*, LinkedIn, American Airlines, IBM, Twitter, and scores of other companies use Hadoop. Its popularity can be attributed to a number of factors, including these:

- It can handle many different types and source of data, including structured, unstructured, log files, pictures, audio files, communications records, and e-mail.
- It scales easily and across multiple servers (i.e., it is schema-less).
- It has high fault tolerance.
- It's extremely flexible.

---

* Facebook used Hadoop to create strategic analytic applications involving massive volumes of user data.

■ It's an open-source project that has spawned its own ecosystem, a community that seeks to improve the product.

At present, there is no one "official" Hadoop *stack* or standard configuration. As of this writing, Hadoop includes more than a dozen dynamic components or subprojects, many of which are complex to deploy and manage. Installation, configuration, and production deployment at scale is often challenging.[5] For a much more comprehensive technical look at Hadoop and some of its components, check out a book like *Hadoop: The Definitive Guide* by Cloudera engineer Tom White.

Importantly, Hadoop's origins stem from Google's MapReduce and the Google file system,* topics certainly worth exploring here. MapReduce takes a unique approach to processing vast amounts of relatively new data types. (In its first incarnations, Hadoop only performed MapReduce jobs, but those days are officially over.) Without getting too technical here, MapReduce works as follows:

■ It breaks Big Data problems into much more manageable subproblems.

■ It distributes those subproblems to myriad "processing nodes."

■ It reaggregates them into more digestible datasets.

In this sense, Hadoop is not a database per se, at least in the traditional sense of the term.[6] Rather, it is a *file system*. More formally, the Hadoop Distributed File System (HDFS) stores vast amounts of data used by other parts of the Hadoop stack. HDFS works closely with another component: MapReduce, the distributed programming framework designed to run on commodity hardware. "MapReduce doesn't provide access to real-time data, but that's changing thanks to newer Hadoop components like HBase," Scott Kahler tells me. Kahler is the Big Data Architect of Adknowledge, the fourth largest advertiser marketplace.[7]

HBase, the open-source implementation of Google's NoSQL architecture, is becoming an increasingly key part of the Hadoop stack.

---

*At its highest level, a file system organizes data on a storage device for future retrieval.

Think of it as a distributed and scalable Big Data store. HBase and Impala allow for traditional data indexing and in-memory storage, allowing users more instantaneous access to data. (The scale of HBase is enormous: it can support *billions* of rows and millions of columns, while concurrently ensuring that both write and read performance remain constant.) Many IT executives are asking pointed questions about HBase and its offshoots. For instance, the HBase NoSQL database is built on top of HDFS. It shows what's possible when Hadoop is freed from the constraints of MapReduce.

While not entirely mature, Hadoop has certainly evolved from its early days. "It's an exciting time today for Hadoop and its users. The ability to do near-real-time queries on a massive data storage and processing framework is finally becoming a reality," continues Kahler. "It has been a godsend and represents a major shift in the Big Data world. We now can worry less about how we handle the data and more about the actual insights that we can drive from it."

The Hadoop Ecosystem

Near the end of my last book, *The Age of the Platform*, I examined smaller companies that are embracing platform thinking. Amazon, Apple, Facebook, and Google might run the world's largest platforms, but by no means are they the only ones. Today, WordPress, Salesforce.com, HubSpot, and scores of other companies are allowing—and even encouraging—others to take their products and services in new and exciting directions. Not surprisingly, the same thing is happening with Hadoop.

Because of its open-source origins and rising popularity, Hadoop continues to evolve, as does its ecosystem. Since its inception, complementary projects have leveraged Hadoop's core functionality—and extended it in different directions. Hive and Pig are two of the most prominent Hadoop extensions, supported by companies like Cloudera and Talend.[8] While Hadoop is enormously useful as presently constituted, its popularity also stems from the fact that many people believe that it will continue to evolve and improve over time. The history of technology teaches us that software programs have limited shelf lives, but Hadoop seems like a solid bet, at least for the foreseeable future.

Of course, true open-source projects do not need the permission of senior management at a private company or the imprimatur of a government agency. Anyone with the technical chops and desire can start or contribute to an open-source application and see where it goes. Projects like WordPress, Linux, and Firefox all benefit from active and knowledgeable communities of users and experts who often volunteer their skills after they come home from their day jobs.

The Hadoop community is a vibrant one full of smart cookies. Many communicate online or see each other at events like Hadoop World,[9] a conference with attendance that has quintupled in size over the past three years. Regardless of where and how they meet, members of the Hadoop community are taking the product in new and exciting directions. Entire companies are building products on top of Hadoop (extending the product's core or native functionality) and supporting it in the enterprise.

Cloudera

We'll see later in this chapter how Google makes some of its powerful Big Data tools available for public usage. Still, most of Google's Big Data software is proprietary and lies behind closed doors. Five years ago, that reality started to irk Google employee Marcel Kornacker, so he decided to do something about it. As Kornacker told *Wired* magazine, "I wanted to work on something similar to what I had been doing but in a more publicly accessible context."[10]

Kornacker left Google and baked bread for two weeks before joining a little company named Cloudera in 2008. Based out of Palo Alto, California, the enterprise software company provides Hadoop-based software, support, services, and training. In short, it helps enterprises become more data driven. Thanks to products like Impala, as of this writing, Cloudera has become the biggest vendor of commercial Hadoop technology.

Kornacker believes that Google "sees its custom data center creations as a competitive advantage that should be guarded from rivals. It builds this software only for itself—although plenty of others use it. By contrast, Cloudera builds software for everyone."[11] Kornacker's smart, but I don't fully share his viewpoint. As this chapter will show, Google makes many of its products and services available for others to use, including some of its Big Data solutions.

Hortonworks, MapR, and Splunk

Cloudera may be one of the elephants in the Hadoop room, but it's by no means the only provider or partner. Other companies recognize the tremendous business opportunity available to them and have moved quickly to position themselves as major Hadoop players. These include Hortonworks, a company "focused on accelerating the development and adoption of Apache Hadoop software."[12] For its part, MapR makes "managing and analyzing Big Data a reality for more business users."[13] It has created a commercial distribution of Hadoop and implements its own proprietary file system. (We'll see in Chapter 5 that Quantcast did something very similar.)

You may be wondering how any organization can create its own file system based upon Hadoop. After all, no one can legally fork a version of Oracle's enterprise applications or Microsoft SQL Server. Because Hadoop is open source, this behavior isn't only legal: it's encouraged. Plus, unlike traditional ERP and CRM vendors, there is no official sanctioning body for Hadoop certification. Anyone can start a Hadoop service firm or development shop without a type of imprimatur. Such is life in the software world. (Note, however, that Hadoop has a governing body of sorts. Its committers review product patches, new code, and enhancements. Many large-scale open-source projects work like this. Committers are usually small and closely coordinated communities of senior contributors to a project.)

Increasingly, machines are generating more and more data, something that will only intensify as the Internet of Things accelerates. (This is discussed in more detail in Chapter 8.) Founded in 2003 (five years before Hadoop existed), Splunk has carved out an interesting niche for itself. According to its website, the company "indexes and makes searchable data from any app, server, or network device in real time including logs, config files, messages, alerts, scripts, and metrics."[14] These files can often grow to sizes simply unmanageable by many mainframes, often forcing organizations to store a limited amount of data and archive the rest.

Splunk's clients include Groupon, Zynga, Bank of America, Akamai, and Salesforce. As of this writing, it employs nearly 500 people and has even been issued a U.S patent. To its credit, Splunk management quickly realized the power of Hadoop and soon pivoted, offering a number of powerful Hadoop-related offerings. Perhaps Splunk's most interesting offering is Hadoop Connect, a user-friendly product that "helps integrate and move data easily between Splunk Enterprise and Hadoop. Conversely, data already in Hadoop can be sent to Splunk for analysis without users having to write code."[15] In other words, Splunk recognizes the power of getting data into and out of Hadoop. Given the size and variety of potential uses of Big Data, flexibility is king.

Emerging Hadoop-Based Start-Ups

Later in this chapter, we'll explore the differences between traditional RDBMSs and columnar alternatives. For now, suffice it to say that different databases are probably best at handling very different types of data. But what if you could handle all types of data in a single, hybrid "system" or database? That's the thinking behind Hadapt, another promising Hadoop offshoot. And the idea has legs, as evinced by the fact that it has already received nearly $10 million in venture capitalist (VC) funding.[16] From the company's website, its patent-pending technology features a hybrid architecture that brings

> the latest advances in relational database research to the Apache Hadoop platform. RDBMS technology has advanced significantly over the past several decades, but current analytic solutions were designed prior to the advent of Hadoop and the paradigm shift from appliance-based computing to distributed computing on clusters of inexpensive commodity hardware.[17]

Hadoop serves as Hadapt's foundation. It offers one-stop shopping—an all-in-one system for structured, unstructured, and multistructured data.

But don't think for a minute that Hadapt is the only Hadoop-based start-up or project. Far from it. Start-ups as we speak are working on hybrid tools that handle structured and unstructured data in a single system. RainStor seeks to turn an organization's historical (and "frozen") Small Data into Big Data. Its product "uses sophisticated data compression and de-duplication techniques to reduce the storage footprint by 95%+ less. Data retained in RainStor can be queried and analyzed directly using SQL, your favorite BI tool, or MapReduce on Hadoop without restoring or re-inflating the data."[18] RainStor stores data in partitions (i.e., large blocks that organizations can easily manage using standard file systems, HDFS, and low-cost storage platforms). The result is a low overall total cost of ownership.

Like Hadapt, VCs believe that Rainstor is on to something. The company has raised $12 million.[19] And it continues. Backed with $20 million from Battery Ventures, Andreessen Horowitz, and Sutter Hill Ventures, Platfora "aims to do that with an intuitive user interface that has advanced data science functions built in, rather than making users perform queries."[20] Many folks as we speak are building analytic apps that sit on top of Hadoop.

Existing Enterprise Vendors

No one would ever call Oracle Corporation a new company or a start-up with its storied history and a market capitalization around $150 billion.[21] Led by bombastic CEO Larry Ellison, Oracle is famous for acquiring companies at a frenetic pace. Given the popularity of Big Data, it should be no surprise that Oracle sells a number of proprietary, closed-source products that help organizations store and interpret vast amounts of unstructured data.[22] More shocking to some, though, is the fact that Oracle has developed products that work with Hadoop.[23] And Oracle isn't the only large enterprise software vendor to integrate open-source solutions into its product lines. IBM years ago recognized the power of Linux and bet big on it.[24] After years of pooh-poohing open source solutions, Microsoft got a little bit pregnant with shared source.[25] Many traditional software vendors are recognizing the power of open-source Big Data tools—and Hadoop in particular.

And Oracle is not alone here in jumping on the Hadoop train. IBM sells Infosphere BigInsights, an analytics platform that lives on top of Hadoop. SAP launched its HANA platform that tightly integrates with Hadoop.[26] In late-October 2012, as expected, Microsoft announced that it had launched a fully Windows-compatible Apache Hadoop distribution.[27] The HDInsight Server is designed to work with (but does not include) Windows Server and Microsoft SQL Server. For its part, EMC claims offering a Hadoop-friendly, "unified, and high-profit-margin, Big Data system."[28]

Bottom line: Large software vendors aren't standing still; they are reacting to the Big Data trend. Many of their clients are expressing strong interest in Big Data. Making Big Data happen requires the ability to store, retrieve, and analyze vast amounts of information. To the extent that organizations prefer integration over data silos, more familiar business intelligence (BI) and data warehousing tools have to play nice with new Big Data solutions like Hadoop.

Limitations of Hadoop

While enormously powerful, Hadoop is anything but perfect. First, as of this writing, it does not provide real-time information—although it can get pretty close thanks to supplemental components HBase and Impala. Second, programming in Hadoop is not for the faint of heart. What's more, data consolidation may pose its own set of problems. "Aggregating data into one environment . . . increases the risk of data theft and accidental disclosure," says Richard Clayton, a software engineer with Berico Technologies, an IT services contractor for federal agencies.[29] In other words, data silos may in fact be more secure than data marts, although I'd vehemently argue that the cons of these data islands far exceed their pros. Why "fix" one problem by failing to address another more serious one? Finally, as of this writing, as mentioned at the beginning of this section, Hadoop lacks formal industry standards. James Kobielus of IBM writes, "The Hadoop market won't fully mature and may face increasing obstacles to growth and adoption if the industry does not begin soon to converge on a truly standardized core stack."[30]

Because of this and some technical considerations, plenty of people believe that Hadoop's days are numbered.[31] Based upon my research for this book, however, I strongly disagree. More likely, Hadoop will evolve and improve over time—and process an increasing share of the world's data. Many skilled people and organizations are working on reducing the technical and knowledge gaps that exist today.

OTHER DATA STORAGE SOLUTIONS

Chapters 1 and 2 showed that, as a general rule, Big Data just doesn't play nice with native relational databases and SQL. All of this data has to be stored somewhere and, if stalwarts like Oracle and SQL Server aren't suitable, what's an enterprise curious about Big Data to do?

NoSQL Databases

The past few years have seen the rise of the NoSQL "database."* Before continuing, it's essential to make three points. First, I put the word "database" in quotes for a specific reason. A NoSQL database is only a *database* in a very general sense. When most people think of proper databases, they conjure up images of the relational kinds rife with tables described in Chapter 1. (See Tables 1.1 and 1.2 and Figure 1.2.) Perhaps more accurately, one should think of these NoSQL databases as "data stores." Second, the term *NoSQL* connotes a binary, as in SQL databases rely upon SQL, while NoSQL databases do not. In reality, though, NoSQL databases use "not only SQL." That is, they don't rely exclusively upon SQL. Finally, many organizations concurrently use both SQL and NoSQL databases for different purposes. Using one in no way obviates or precludes using the other.

The NoSQL movement began in 2009 and took off quickly. Reasons include its general utility, the limitations of RDBMSs, and the price of many NoSQL solutions (read: free). As of this writing, there are already more than 120 projects listed on the site nosql-database .org. At a high level, NoSQL databases generally break down into four main types, as presented in Table 4.1.

As the examples in Table 4.1 illustrate, there are many types of NoSQL databases. Rather than just thinking about a single NoSQL database, it's better to think of NoSQL as an entirely new *category* of databases. In point of fact, this isn't uncommon. In the open-source world, there may be several current or sanctioned or mainstream versions of a particular application, but typically different alternatives abound. NoSQL is no exception to this rule.

Like Hadoop, NoSQL databases suffer from a fair number of drawbacks. For one, *by themselves*, they offer few facilities for ad hoc queries and analysis. Even a simple query requires significant programming expertise, and commonly used BI tools do not provide connectivity to NoSQL.

Some relief is provided by the emergence of new Hadoop extensions, such as Hive and Pig. These projects can provide easier access to data

---

* Some people consider Hadoop a NoSQL solution, while others don't. For the sake of organization, this section focuses on Hadoop alternatives.

Table 4.1 The Four General Types of NoSQL Databases

Type	Description	Examples
Key-Values Stores	The main idea here is using a hash table where there is a unique key and a pointer to a particular item of data. The key/value model is the simplest and easiest to implement. But it is inefficient when you are only interested in querying or updating part of a value, among other disadvantages.	Tokyo Cabinet/ Tyrant, Redis, Voldemort, Oracle BDB
Column Family Stores	These were created to store and process large amounts of data distributed over many machines. There are still keys, but they point to multiple columns. The columns are arranged by column family.	Cassandra, HBase, Riak
Document Databases	These were inspired by Lotus Notes and are similar to key-value stores. The model is basically versioned documents that are collections of other key-value collections. The semi-structured documents are stored in formats like JSON. Document databases are essentially the next level of Key/Value, allowing nested values associated with each key. Document databases support querying more efficiently.	CouchDB, MongoDb
Graph Databases	Instead of tables of rows and columns and the rigid structure of SQL, a flexible graph model is used which, again, can scale across multiple machines. NoSQL databases do not provide a high-level declarative query language like SQL to avoid overtime in processing. Rather, querying these databases is data-model specific. Many of the NoSQL platforms allow for RESTful interfaces to the data, while others offer query application programming interfaces (APIs).	Neo4J, InfoGrid, Infinite Graph

Adapted from "Picking the Right NoSQL Database Tool" by Mikayel Vardanyan[32]

held in Hadoop clusters and, perhaps eventually, other NoSQL databases. Quest Software has developed Toad for Cloud Databases, a product that provides ad hoc query capabilities to a variety of NoSQL databases.[33]

Table 4.1 lists the different types of NoSQL databases and, to be sure, some are more popular than others. However, one warrants a longer mention here. Launched in 2008, Apache Cassandra[34] is a relatively mature, fault-tolerant, high-performance, and extremely scalable database used by companies such as Netflix, Twitter, Constant Contact, Reddit, Cisco, and scores of others. These companies share one common characteristic: they rely upon enormous amounts of data to power their business. Cassandra integrates with Hadoop and supports MapReduce.

I have not used Cassandra and can't say with certainty that it's fundamentally "better" on some term than other NoSQL databases—not to mention those not included on Table 4.1. When looking at NoSQL solutions, cost and quality are but two considerations. For any open- or closed-source solution, it's important for organizations to ensure that an adequate support network exists, even if external hires are planned. Remember that, like all Big Data tools, NoSQL is relatively new. Existing expertise is lacking. In the case of Cassandra, because of the project's high level of demand, a vibrant third-party network has sprouted.[35] Make sure that you're not going down a largely unsupported road.

NewSQL

Think of RDBMSs and SQL as old and reliable cars. Untold numbers of people and organizations have used both extensively for decades, including yours truly. (Five years ago, I made nearly all my income off consulting gigs involving RDBMSs, SQL, and general reporting.) Those automobiles worked fine then, and they still run today. However, they were manufactured in an entirely different era. Their vintage feels aside, those cars cannot possibly take advantage of huge improvements in fuel efficiency, advances in engineering and manufacturing, and so on. And let's not forget to mention bells and whistles like iPod connectivity (a must-have for me), GPS, Bluetooth, OnStar, and many others. It should be no surprise, then, that cars today can do things not possible three decades ago. Today, from a technology perspective, even $25,000 gets you quite a bit of car. Should it be any surprise that RDBMSs and SQL are evolving as well?

Companies like VoltDB are working on an entirely new generation of RDBMSs based upon a totally different architecture—SQL 2.0, or NewSQL, if you like.* From the VoltDB company website, "Traditional RDBMSs . . . are based on a one-size-fits-all model we refer to as *OldSQL*. This model is challenged by the exponential transaction growth that led to the evolution of non-relational data stores,** collectively referred to as *NoSQL*. A new generation of RDBMSs, known as *NewSQL*, take[s] a radically different approach that combines the speed and scale of NoSQL with the proven capabilities of OldSQL."[36]

What if a traditional RDBMS could combine all that's good about OldSQL, but without the baggage? At least that's the promise of NewSQL. Before jumping in with both feet, though, understand that NewSQL is still playing out, and it's not nearly as mature as software like NoSQL and columnar databases—at least yet. Still, NewSQL is worth keeping an eye on. Too many brilliant people like "database high priest" Mike Stonebraker are working on NewSQL*** to ignore it altogether.

Columnar Databases

Way back in 1996, enterprise storage company Sybase IQ recognized the long-term limitations of the relational data model. In that year, Sybase launched the first columnar database. Today, it has plenty of company. Vertica (acquired by HP in 2012), newcomers like Infobright and ParAccel, and vendors like Teradata and Oracle have all either developed or acquired column-oriented databases.

Some people have a difficult time understanding the need for columnar databases, primarily because they are so accustomed to thinking about data in terms of rows and relational tables. Consider the following example. Let's say that a customer table contains 25 fields and 100,000 records. (See Table 1.1 for a simplified version of such a table.) A business needs to determine which products sold on what date and in what store. In a row-based table, one can certainly query and count all zip codes, product stock-keeping units (SKUs), and sale dates. That's easy enough to do, and I've written many thousands of queries like that in my consulting career. However, behind the scenes,

---

* Note that VoltDB does not "own" NewSQL. NewSQL is a very broad term.
** A data store is a repository of integrated objects that contain data.
*** For more on NewSQL, check out http://newsql.sourceforge.net.

that SQL statement needs to look at each field in each database record. Even though only three fields of that record concern us, the other 22 have to come along for the ride. In order words, the query needs to look at customer name, address, account number, and the like 100,000 times despite the fact that we really don't care about that data.*

Now, truth be told, on a relatively tiny table like this, such a technical limitation has a negligible impact on performance, especially with this type of structured, transactional data. I would never recommend to an organization with data of this size that it buy and implement a columnar database (and transform its data in the process) just to shave one second off of a five-second query run weekly. There's just no point. Traditional RDBMSs and SQL work just fine with Small Data, especially the structured type.

But forget tables with 100,000 records with 5 or 10 or 20 fields. I'll see you and raise you. An SQL statement may work reasonably well on large tables with 50 or even 200 million records of this type of transactional data, but not with tables of 1 billion or more. What happens when you have to analyze terabytes or even petabytes of unstructured data? Bottom line: here traditional tools just don't cut it.

Perhaps the single greatest limitation of row-oriented databases is speed. No one is going to wait 24 hours as a traditional SQL statement examines every field in every row, especially when time is of the essence. As an alternative, organizations are increasingly using faster-performing columnar databases. For a more technical explanation of why columnar databases offer superior performance relative to RDBMSs, consider the words of William McKnight, a longtime datawarehousing expert:

> Columnar storage reduces input/output (I/O), which has gradually become the unquestioned bottleneck in analytic systems today. As you will see, columnar databases not only greatly limit the volume of storage going through the I/O channels, but also help ensure that whatever does go through I/O is very useful to building the query results. The I/O has become the bottleneck over the years due to increasing data sizes and the overwhelming need to consume that

---

* Of course, as any good DBA will tell you, it's not hard to create separate temp tables and perform other back-end tricks, but let's keep the example simple here.

data. All data that is part of the I/O consumes resources that other I/Os cannot consume. If that data is page metadata or columns clearly uninteresting to the query, it is still consuming I/O resource. Hence, the I/Os bottleneck.[37]

Let's extend McKnight's comments a bit further. When considering whether to purchase and deploy a columnar database, the overriding question is *not* whether standard SQL statements and RDBMSs can theoretically handle some types of Big Data. At a high level, the answer is a highly qualified yes. I'll grant that some Small Data tools can technically handle relatively small amounts of Big Data. Even if an organization can live with suboptimal performance of smaller datasets, there's another factor to consider: cost. Columnar databases offer far superior data compression compared to their row-based counterparts—often seven to eight times better. Greater compression means lower data storage costs. While these costs have certainly plummeted, they remain a significant expense for many IT departments.

Before concluding this section, it's important to note that organizations may not have to decide between row- and column-orientation. (Yes, databases can use either one, although most today are "long," not "wide.") Sure, organizations may find it necessary to store and manage very different types of data in very different types of databases. That doesn't change the fact that it's messy. What if organizations could manage both Big Data and Small Data in the same place?

I'm far from the only one asking that question. As of late, the distinction between columns and rows has begun to blur. For instance, version 14 of Teradata's database "supports both row-store and column-oriented approaches. EMC Greenplum, Microsoft (via the most recent incarnation of SQL Server), and Aster Data (now owned by Teradata) have also recently blended row-store and column-store capabilities."[38] Today, organizations and IT departments have greater choice than ever as more and more Big Data solutions and services emerge.

Google: Following the Amazon Model?

Some people don't realize the size of Amazon's other (read: non-book) lines of business. Excluding books, Amazon sells 160 million products on its website as of mid-2012. To power so much traffic, commerce, and, above all, data, the company has built immense data centers and bet heavily on cloud computing. For nearly two decades now, Jeff Bezos has run a future-oriented company, often to the chagrin of profit-hungry investors. He has always invested in the long term and understands all too well the power of scale. (It's interesting to note that Amazon offers its own Big Data play. Redshift is a fast and powerful, fully managed, petabyte-scale data warehouse service in the cloud.)

Amazon doesn't need to use all the compute power generated by its servers and data centers. Rather than letting it fly into the ether and go to waste, Amazon decided to sell that excess to businesses of all types. In early 2006, the company launched Amazon Web Services (AWS) and, after a few years of experimentation and pricing refinements, it's been nothing less than a blockbuster. While Amazon won't split revenue and profits from its different lines of business, Wall Street analysts believe that, in 2011, the company made nearly $750 million in essentially pure profit from AWS. In 2014, that number could be as high as $2.5 *billion*.[39]

At Google, we may well be seeing a parallel, Amazon-like pattern playing itself out with respect to Big Data. Google has developed a number of powerful Big Data tools that helps it store, access, interpret, and retrieve ungodly amounts of data. Like Amazon seven years ago, Google has realized that some of its own internal information needs may match those of many companies today. (Hmmm, maybe there's a business here?) To that end, Google has made some of its internal tools available for third parties to use for free or license. This section describes some of these tools. (In point of fact, we already saw early in this chapter how Hadoop can trace much of its origins to Google tools: MapReduce and the Google file system come to mind.)

At present, some of the bullets in the Google Big Data chamber are presented in Table 4.2.

WEBSITES, START-UPS, AND WEB SERVICES

More mature and established tools do the lion's share of the Big Data work in many organizations. However, we are living in an era of open-source software, cloud computing, open APIs, and historically low

Table 4.2 Google Big Data Tools

Tool	Description
BigQuery	Enables users to "run SQL-like queries against very large datasets, with potentially billions of rows. This can be your own data, or data that someone else has shared for you. BigQuery works best for interactive analysis of very large datasets, typically using a small number of very large, append-only tables."[40]
BigTable	Google's seminal NoSQL database, BigTable is designed to scale into the petabyte range across "hundreds or thousands of machines, and to make it easy to add more machines [to] the system and automatically start taking advantage of those resources without any reconfiguration."[41]
Dremel	A "scalable, interactive ad-hoc query system for analysis of read-only nested data. By combining multi-level execution trees and columnar data layout, it is capable of running aggregation queries over trillion-row tables in seconds. The system scales to thousands of CPUs and petabytes of data, and has thousands of users at Google."[42] In English, this means that Google seems to have figured out a way to make Big Data look more like Small Data, especially with respect to querying times.[43]
MapReduce	As discussed in the "Hadoop" section earlier in this chapter, MapReduce served as the initial foundation for Hadoop.

start-up costs. As such, a great deal of exciting innovation is occurring in the Big Data world. As we'll see in the following section, some interesting start-ups are taking Big Data to the masses, trying to solve important business and societal problems in the process.

This section presents a few of the many companies pushing the Big Data envelope. Note that this is in no way a comprehensive list; it merely represents some of the highlights of my research in writing this book.

Kaggle

What if you created a company that was equal parts funding platform (like Kickstarter and IndieGoGo), crowdsourcing company (like Innocentive), social network, wiki, and job board (like Monster or Dice)?

And what if you added a dash of gamification* to this little stew of a company? You'd wind up with Kaggle:

> an innovative solution for statistical/analytics outsourcing. [It is] the leading platform for predictive modeling competitions. Companies, governments and researchers present datasets and problems—the world's best data scientists then compete to produce the best solutions. At the end of a competition, the competition host pays prize money in exchange for the intellectual property behind the winning model.
>
> The motivation behind Kaggle is simple: most organizations don't have access to the advanced machine learning and statistical techniques that would allow them to extract maximum value from their data. Meanwhile, data scientists crave real-world data to develop and refine their techniques. Kaggle corrects this mismatch by offering companies a cost-effective way to harness the "cognitive surplus" of the world's best data scientists.[44]

Founded in April 2010 by Anthony Goldbloom and Jeremy Howard, Kaggle seeks to make data science a sport. It is a mesmerizing hybrid of a company, and I could write an entire book about it. Anyone can post a project by selecting an industry, type (public or private), participatory level (team or individual), reward amount, and timetable. A look at some existing Kaggle competitions[45] shows an amazing variety of current contests, including the following:

- **Medicine: Merck Molecular Activity Challenge:** To help develop safe and effective medicines by predicting molecular activity.

- **Politics: Follow the Money: Investigative Reporting Prospect:** To find hidden patterns, connections, and ultimately compelling stories in a treasure trove of data about U.S. federal campaign contributions.

- **Financial: Benchmark Bond Trade Price Challenge:** To develop models to accurately predict the trade price of a bond.

---

*The site lets users rate other users.

■ **Science: Mapping Dark Matter (Supported by NASA and the Royal Astronomical Society):** A cosmological image analysis competition to measure the small distortion in galaxy images caused by dark matter.

The San Francisco–based company attempts to match those with rare skills and interests (data scientists) with people and organizations with real problems to solve—and the data that, in the right hands, could yield a solution. Sound niche? Well, it's a pretty big niche. Kaggle sports a community of more than 40,000 predictive modeling and machine-learning experts from 100 countries and 200 universities.

Before starting a project, you need to have a goal in mind (see previous list). But what if you just own a bunch of data and aren't sure about what to do with it? You suspect that there's some value in it, but what do you know? You're not a data scientist. Kaggle's got you covered with Prospect, a way of asking its community what to do with your trove of information. Users can suggest uses for owners of large datasets.

Other Start-Ups

Organizations looking to date before they get married to Big Data (see Table 4.3) might want to consider 1010 data. The company specializes in cloud-based analytics and claims that it can quickly analyze trillions of records. For their part, the folks at Precog believe that Big Data need not mean Big Complexity. Company CEO John De Goes is on record saying that "Hadoop is stupid." Not surprisingly, the company has bucked the trend to follow others that are building on top of Hadoop. Instead, Precog chose to create its proprietary-only Big Data solution.[46] The goal: to make Big Data less complex than current alternatives.

I could list a dozen more start-ups here, each of which promises a slightly different take on Big Data, analytics, and other topics covered in this chapter. While I'm not completely oblivious to the VC world, I'll let a true expert have the final say on the matter in this section.

A great deal of activity, investment, and innovation is taking place in the Big Data space. As with any emerging trend, it is sometimes difficult to separate fact from fiction. To that end, I reached out to Brad Feld, an early stage investor and entrepreneur for more than twenty years.

BIG DATA: A VENTURE CAPITALIST'S PERSPECTIVE

Like many technology terms, "Big Data" has progressed on the typical curve from a clever description of a set of technologies to a buzzword that is overused and now refers to anything and everything. It also has suddenly and magically appeared as something new and mystical, replacing historic (and perfectly descriptive, but worn-out) terms like analytics, which replaced terms from the 1970s like executive information systems and data warehouses.

Twenty years from now, the thing we call Big Data will be tiny data. It'll be microscopic data. The volume that we're talking about today, in 20 years, is a speck.

When everything is suddenly Big Data, it gives us an opportunity to redefine what it means and what matters about the term. And that's where we find ourselves today, as Big Data has merely become a label describing a phenomenon. Since everything is Big Data, we can focus on what *Big Data* actually means, and what the implications of it are.

I encourage entrepreneurs to go one level deeper than the surface definition and talk about what they are doing in the context of an exponentially increasing amount of data. There are a lot of entrepreneurs who assert that they're doing magical new things with data, that we can't tell you about because it's so incredible, and just trust this black box and give us some money—and we'll give you amazing things out the other end. This is garbage, and the more hand waving there is, the more nonsensical the entrepreneur.

Instead, assume that there is a broad phenomenon of exponentially increasing data and that it will continue for a long time. Assume that the connections between machines, applications, and networks are progressing faster than many of us are really aware of or can comprehend. Assume that the machines have already taken over and are just waiting patiently for us. They have no incentive to exterminate us—humans killing humans is a human construct, not a machine construct, so assume the machines are going to treat us as pets.

Sounds silly, right? Yet today's smartphones would have been called supercomputers 30 years ago. And what today's smartphone can do pales in comparison to what it'll be able to do in a couple of years, if it's even called a smartphone anymore. Why do we even need a smartphone? Shouldn't we be able to assume that we'll have implants that are processing all the data we want in real time?

As the amount of data generated and consumed continues to expand geometrically, across many different vectors, the software that processes this data will continue to have to evolve. Whether this is at the data level, the system level, or the application level, there will regularly be new technological approaches to handling hundreds or thousands of times more data in the same time frame.

This phenomenon simply won't stop in the foreseeable future. Imagine every cell in the body being instrumented and generating data about itself. What if every physical thing on the planet is able to act as a transmitter about a variety of data about it? And every other physical thing has the ability to process the inputs from these transmitters in real time. Now we are talking about Big Data.

As an investor, I'm interested in what people are doing at all three levels. I care a great deal about instrumenting things at the data level, such as the human being. My investment in Fitbit[47] is an example of this—I believe that Fitbit is version 0.1 of our ability to fully instrument ourselves as humans. I care about this at system level—investments in companies like Mobiplug[48] connect existing sensors together into one integrated whole. And I care about this at the application level, with investments in companies like Gnip[49] connecting together all of the generators of real time data with the consumers of real time data.

We are at the very beginning of a Cambrian explosion of data. While it's big right now, it'll be ginormous before we know it. And then humongous after that. Don't get tangled up in the buzzword. Focus on being involved in the phenomenon.

Brad Feld is currently the Managing Director at Foundry Group. He has penned several books, including the award-winning *Startup Communities: Building an Entrepreneurial Ecosystem in Your City*.

HARDWARE CONSIDERATIONS

At this point, it should be obvious that traditional, row-store databases just can't handle Big Data—at least not in any meaningful way. As any IT professional knows, however, software is just part of the equation.

For a while now, organizations have been able to effectively obviate the need for purchasing and configuring expensive hardware by going to "the cloud." In reality, though, many organizations will continue to host many of their own applications. Put differently, the cloud represents just another option for CIOs; it is hardly the only one. Each organization has to look at cost, security, and control issues when deciding whether or not to abandon the on-premise software model. This is as true with ERP and CRM applications as it is with Big Data.

Are hardware considerations being neglected in all the current Big Data hubbub? It's a fair question to ask. To this end, ZDNet blogger

Larry Dignan recently interviewed Univa CEO Gary Tyreman about the impact of Big Data on existing hardware and infrastructure. Univa bills itself as a high-performance computing (HPC) company that "provides the evolution of Grid Engine, the most widely deployed, distributed resource management software platform used by enterprises and research organizations across the globe."[50] The company counts NASA and Motorola Mobility among its clients. The following are excerpts from that interview:

Are hardware issues overlooked in all the Big Data talk?

I don't know if they are forgetting or just not appreciating the challenges. Hadoop nodes today are 10 or less so it's not hard to get it working. Companies are underestimating how much it takes to roll into production and get it running. In a nutshell, there's a jump from a Hadoop pilot to actually scaling it.

What's the solution?

Clusters today are one way to get Big Data environments set. The time has to be put in to configure the software behind the infrastructure, set storage, and fix network settings. If those configurations take two days it's not a big deal, but then it is rolled into production and there are more complications.

Why isn't hardware a consideration?

At this juncture, companies are primarily focused on the outcome of Big Data and what can be done. Enterprises need to focus on the outcome as well as what they want to know. Existing business intelligence tools also have to be considered.[51]

Let's say that an organization's existing hardware can support new applications like Hadoop. But a new installation is missing something big: the truly enormous amounts of data that Hadoop will be asked to store and interpret. Tyreman's answer to the first question is indicative of a much larger IT problem: organizations tend to underestimate requirements across the board, and Big Data is no exception to this rule. At the same time, though, no chief information officer (CIO) wants to spend millions of dollars on hardware purchases and upgrades only to discover that the money could have been much better spent elsewhere. What to do?

Recognize that current Big Data tools continue to evolve and new applications pop up seemingly every day. The question isn't whether the cost of "doing" Big Data will decline over time. The answer is clearly yes. With respect to Big Data, the intelligent organization will ask a much different and banal question: Are the expected benefits of getting on the Big Data train worth their perceived costs? To this query, there are three possible answers, represented in Table 4.3.

Brass tacks: Although Big Data does not require big hardware, organizations need to recognize that Big Data cannot just be "rolled up" or "folded into" existing Oracle, SQL Server, or DB2 databases. As a stopgap, they may want to consider Big Data appliances from vendors

Table 4.3 Is Big Data Worth It? Hardware Considerations

Is Big Data Worth It?	Hardware Considerations
Yes	It's full steam ahead. You've run the numbers, and the business case for Big Data is a no-brainer. You certainly can make the requisite investments in necessary hardware and software, but don't rule out the cloud. Just because you can do everything in-house doesn't mean that you should.
No	One of two things has happened. Either: 1) this book hasn't sold you on Big Data; or 2) you buy into the benefits of Big Data but your organization is just not ready to go down this road—and you know it. Fear not. It's much better to realize this now, not after massive IT expenditures, expensive consultants, and project failures. Reevaluate in six months. Wait until your organization matures, the expected benefits increase, or the costs decline.[*]
Maybe/Not Sure	Date before you get married. Forget about massive hardware upgrades and purchases for the time being, *unless you need to make them for other essential business purposes*. Try using lower-cost, secure, cloud-based services to see if the squeeze is worth the juice. Understand that, in the long term, it may well be cheaper to move to an on-premise solution.

[*] Note that Big Data need not be deployed only at an organizational level. Departments, teams, groups, and divisions may still benefit a great deal from Big Data solutions even if the organization isn't ready to jump in.

like Oracle[52] and Teradata (Extreme Data Appliance).[53] These appliances purport to load unstructured data into larger database tables and traditional data warehouses.

Bottom line: Organizations intent on using their own hardware to harness the power of Big Data will in all likelihood have to make some pretty big purchases. As Eric Savitz writes on *forbes.com*, "Traditional database approaches don't scale or write data fast enough to keep up with the speed of creation. Additionally, purpose-designed data warehouses are great at handling structured data, but there's a high cost for the hardware to scale out as volumes grow."[54] Know this going in.

THE ART AND SCIENCE OF PREDICTIVE ANALYTICS

As discussed before, we have never before seen data with the volume, variety, and velocity of today. Compared to ten years ago, many of today's data sources and types may be different, but in a way nothing fundamental has changed. We're still just trying to look at data to understand what's going on—and why. With that information, we can derive knowledge to more confidently predict the future. Yes, the term *Big Data* is certainly new, but its objectives are not.

As we'll see in the case studies in Chapter 5, new and improved data mining and predictive technologies are here—and organizations of all types are using them to do some pretty remarkable things.

Before concluding this chapter, permit me a few words on the limitations of predictive analytics. Yes, organizations can purchase and deploy best-of-breed applications such as those from vendors like SAS.[55] You'll get no argument from me on the merits of these solutions: you can only do so much with Small Data tools. However, those with unrealistic expectations are bound to be disappointed. One should not confuse reducing future uncertainty with eliminating it. Not too many predictive models saw the Arab Spring coming in 2011. Yes, an organization may well be able to get a better handle around future sales, but those estimates will still be just estimates; they will not be perfect. Too many other variables are at play. On occasion, software salespeople have been known to stretch the truth. Take the loftiest of claims with more than a grain of salt.

Think of it this way: Coupled with Big Data, predictive tools can reduce the degree of uncertainty your organization faces (both generally speaking and with respect to individual business decisions). But make no mistake: analytics aren't crystal balls. Organizations will *always* face some level of uncertainty, even those that use Big Data well. As discussed in Chapter 2, some things can and always will be understood only in hindsight.

SUMMARY

This chapter provided a summary of some of the main Big Data technologies, applications, platforms, and web services. Yes, volume, velocity, and variety of Big Data require new tools. Given that, we examined some of those specific solutions.

Because even very large amounts of structured and transactional Small Data pale in comparison to Big Data, companies require new solutions. To that end, technologies such as Hadoop, NoSQL, and columnar databases fill important needs. Also, keep an eye on emerging start-ups and new web- and cloud-based services like Kaggle. Collectively, these new tools are allowing organizations to take Big Data from theory to practice. Finally, even though highly sophisticated predictive applications can do amazing things, they are far from perfect.

Now that we know how these new technologies can be used, let's turn to how they are actually being used. Chapter 5 presents three case studies of organizations using Big Data to achieve fascinating results.

NOTES

1. Personal conversation with Murnane, November 17, 2012.
2. "SAP Sybase IQ," 2012, www.sybase.com/products/datawarehousing/sybaseiq, retrieved December 11, 2012.
3. "Big Data Solution Brief," 2012, http://download.microsoft.com/download/F/A/1/FA126D6D-841B-4565-BB26-D2ADD4A28F24/Microsoft_Big_Data_Solution_Brief.pdf, retrieved December 11, 2012.
4. Harris, Derrick, "Startup Precog Says Big Data Doesn't Need to Be So Complex," September 27, 2012, http://gigaom.com/data/startup-precog-says-big-data-doesnt-need-to-be-so-complex/, retrieved December 11, 2012.
5. Walker, Michael, "Hadoop Technology Stack," August 22, 2012, www.analyticbridge.com/profiles/blogs/hadoop-technology-stack, retrieved December 11, 2012.

6. Shapira, Gwen, "Hadoop and NoSQL Mythbusting," October 4, 2011, www.pythian .com/news/27367/hadoop-and-nosql-mythbusting/, retrieved December 11, 2012.

7. Personal conversation with Kahler, November 26, 2012.

8. "Big Data," 2012, www.talend.com/products/big-data, retrieved December 11, 2012.

9. "What Can Hadoop Do for You?," 2012, www.hadoopworld.com/, retrieved December 11, 2012.

10. Metz, Cade, "Bread Baker Frees Software Secrets from Google Empire," October 29, 2012, www.wired.com/wiredenterprise/2012/10/kornacker-cloudera-google, retrieved December 11, 2012.

11. Ibid.

12. "Architecting the Future of Big Data," 2012, http://hortonworks.com/, retrieved December 11, 2012.

13. "MapR," 2012, www.mapr.com/, retrieved December 11, 2012.

14. www.splunk.com/view/SP-CAAACVK, retrieved December 11, 2012.

15. Yasin, Rutrell, "How to Make Big Data More Useful, Reliable—and Fast," November 5, 2012, http://gcn.com/articles/2012/11/05/splunk-big-data-useful-reliable-fast .aspx, retrieved December 11, 2012.

16. Harris, Derrick, "Hadapt Raises $9.5M for Hadoop Data Warehouse," October 21, 2011, http://gigaom.com/cloud/hadapt-raises-9-5m-for-hadoop-data-warehouse/, retrieved December 11, 2012.

17. "Product | Hadapt," 2012, http://hadapt.com/product/, retrieved December 11, 2012.

18. "RainStor: "Cost-Effective Big Data Management," 2012, http://rainstor.com/prod- ucts/overview, retrieved December 11, 2012.

19. Harris, Derrick, "RainsStor Raises $12M to Make Your Big Data Small," October 4, 2012, http://gigaom.com/data/rainstor-raises-12m-to-turn-your-big-data-small/, retrieved December 11, 2012.

20. Harris, Derrick, "Platfora Gets $5.7M to Make Hadoop Mainstream," September 8, 2011, http://gigaom.com/cloud/platfora-gets-5-7m-to-make-hadoop-mainstream/, retrieved December 11, 2012.

21. "Yahoo! Finance: Oracle Corporation (ORCL)," 2012, http://finance.yahoo.com/ q?s=ORCL, retrieved December 11, 2012.

22. "Oracle and Big Data," 2012, www.oracle.com/us/technologies/big-data/index .html, retrieved December 11, 2012.

23. "Oracle Loader for Hadoop," 2012, www.oracle.com/technetwork/bdc/hadoop- loader/overview/index-1454316.html, retrieved December 11, 2012.

24. "IBM and Linux," 2012, www.-03.ibm.com/linux/, retrieved December 11, 2012.

25. "Shared Source Initiative," 2012, www.microsoft.com/en-us/sharedsource/default .aspx, retrieved December 11, 2012.

26. "SAP Further Extends Real-Time Data Platform with 'Big Data' Capabilities," May 16, 2012, www.sap.com/corporate-en/press.epx?pressid=18920, retrieved December 11, 2012.

27. Microsoft Corporation, "Big Data: Microsoft SQL Server," November 2, 2012, www .microsoft.com/sqlserver/en/us/solutions-technologies/business-intelligence/ big-data.aspx, retrieved December 11, 2012.

28. Harris, Derrick, "EMC Throws Lots of Hardware at Hadoop," September 20, 2011, http://gigaom.com/cloud/emc-throws-lots-of-hardware-at-hadoop/, retrieved December 11, 2012.

29. Vijayan, Jaikumar, "IT Must Prepare for Hadoop Security Issues," November 9, 2011, www.computerworld.com/s/article/9221652/IT_must_prepare_for_Hadoop_security_issues, retrieved December 11, 2012.

30. Kobielus, James, "True Hadoop Standards Are Essential for Sustaining Industry Momentum: Part 1," October 9, 2012, http://ibmdatamag.com/2012/10/true-hadoop-standards-are-essential-for-sustaining-industry-momentum-part-1/, retrieved December 11, 2012.

31. Miller, Mike, "Why the Days Are Numbered for Hadoop as We Know It," July 7, 2012, http://gigaom.com/cloud/why-the-days-are-numbered-for-hadoop-as-we-know-it/, retrieved December 11, 2012.

32. Vardanyan, Mikayel, "Picking the Right NoSQL Database Tool at Uptime and Performance Tips," May 22, 2011, http://blog.monitis.com/index.php/2011/05/22/picking-the-right-nosql-database-tool/, retrieved December 11, 2012.

33. Harrison, Guy, "10 Things You Should Know About NoSQL Databases," August 26, 2010, www.techrepublic.com/blog/10things/10-things-you-should-know-about-nosql-databases/1772, retrieved December 11, 2012.

34. "Welcome to Apache Cassandra," November 30, 2012, http://cassandra.apache.org/, retrieved December 11, 2012.

35. Hobbs, Tyler, "Third Party Support: Cassandra Wiki," September 6, 2012, http://wiki.apache.org/cassandra/ThirdPartySupport, retrieved December 11, 2012.

36. "VoltDB: NewSQL Benefits," August 18, 2012, http://voltdb.com/blog, retrieved December 11, 2012.

37. *Columnar Databases* by William McKnight, published on BeyeNETWORK.com. Read the full article at http://www.b-eye-network.com/view/15506.

38. Henschen, Doug. "Big Data: Fast, Complex, Varied, Costly." *Information Week*. October, 2011. 28.

39. Hickey, Andrew R., "Amazon Cloud Revenue Could Exceed $500 Million in 2010: Report," August 3, 2010, www.crn.com/news/applications-os/226500204/amazon-cloud-revenue-could-exceed-500-million-in-2010-report.htm;jsessionid=6qcAPhELp1er9Vy-CZZSqQ**.ecappj02, retrieved December 11, 2012.

40. "Google BigQuery," November 14, 2012, https://developers.google.com/bigquery/docs/overview, retrieved December 11, 2012.

41. O'Reilly, Tim, "Database War Stories #7: Google File System and BigTable," May 3, 2006, http://radar.oreilly.com/archives/2006/05/database_war_stories_7_google.html, retrieved November 11, 2012.

42. Melnik, Sergey; Gubarev, Andrey; Long, Jing Jing; Romer, Geoffrey; Shivakumar, Shiva; Tolton, Matt; Vassilakis, Theo, "Dremel: Interactive Analysis of Web-Scale Datasets," 2010, http://research.google.com/pubs/pub36632.html, retrieved December 11, 2012.

43. Metz, Cade, "Google's Dremel Makes Big Data Look Small," August 16, 2012, www.wired.com/wiredenterprise/2012/08/googles-dremel-makes-big-data-look-small/, retrieved December 11, 2012.

44. "Kaggle: We're Making Data Science a Sport," 2012, www.kaggle.com, retrieved December 11, 2012.

45. "Kaggle: Competitions," 2012, www.kaggle.com/competitions, retrieved December 11, 2012.

46. Harris, Derrick, "Startup Precog Says Big Data Doesn't Need to Be So Complex," September 27, 2012, http://gigaom.com/data/startup-precog-says-big-data-doesnt-need-to-be-so-complex, retrieved December 11, 2012.

47. www.fitbit.com, retrieved December 11, 2012.

48. www.mobiplug.co, retrieved December 11, 2012.

49. www.gnip.com, retrieved December 11, 2012.

50. "Our Story," 2012, www.univa.com/about, retrieved December 11, 2012.

51. Dignan, Larry, "Big Data Projects: Is the Hardware Infrastructure Overlooked?," October 18, 2012, www.zdnet.com/big-data-projects-is-the-hardware-infrastructure-overlooked-7000005940/, retrieved December 11, 2012.

52. "Oracle Big Data Appliance," 2012, www.oracle.com/us/products/database/big-data-appliance/overview/index.html, retrieved December 11, 2012.

53. "Teradata Extreme Data Appliance: Deep-Dive Analytics at an Entry-Level Price," 2012, www.teradata.com/extreme-data-appliance/#tabbable=0&tab1=0&tab2=0&tab3=0, retrieved December 11, 2012.

54. Bantleman, John, "The Big Cost of Data," April 16, 2012, www.forbes.com/sites/ciocentral/2012/04/16/the-big-cost-of-big-data/, retrieved December 11, 2012.

55. "Predictive Analytics and Data Mining," 2012, www.sas.com/technologies/analytics/datamining/index.html, retrieved December 11, 2012.

CHAPTER 5

Case Studies: The Big Rewards of Big Data

A problem well defined is a problem half-solved.

—John Dewey

U p to this point, we've defined Big Data and its elements. We then described many of the technologies that organizations are using to harness its value. Now it's time to see some of these technologies in action. This chapter examines three organizations in depth, exploring how they have successfully deployed Big Data tools and seen amazing results. Let's start with a company that makes handling Big Data its *raison-d'etre*.

QUANTCAST: A SMALL BIG DATA COMPANY

How do advertisers reach their target audiences online? It's a simple question with anything but a simple answer. Traditionally, advertisers reached audiences via television based on demographic targeting.

As discussed in Chapter 2, thanks to the web, consumers today spend less time watching TV broadcasts and more time in their own personalized media environments (i.e., their own individual blogs, news stories, songs, and videos picked). While good for consumers, this media fragmentation has scattered advertisers' audiences. Relative to even twenty years ago, it is harder for them to reach large numbers of relevant consumers.

But just as the web lets consumers choose media more selectively, it lets advertisers choose their audiences more selectively. That is, advertisers need not try to re-create the effectiveness of TV advertising; they can surpass it. For example, an hour-long prime-time show on network TV contains nearly 22 minutes of marketing content.[1] If advertisers could precisely target consumers, they could achieve the same economics with just a few minutes of commercials. As a result, TV shows could be nearly commercial free. Ads on the web are individually delivered, so decisions on which ad to show to whom can be made one consumer at a time.

Enter Quantcast.

Founded in 2006 by entrepreneurs Konrad Feldman and Paul Sutter, Quantcast is a web measurement and targeting company headquartered in San Francisco, California. Now with 250 employees, Quantcast models marketers' best prospects and finds similar or lookalike audiences across the world. Connecting advertisers with their best customers certainly isn't easy, never mind maximizing yield for publishers and delivering relevant experiences for consumers. To do this, Quantcast software must sift through a veritable mountain of data. Each month, it analyzes more than 300 billion observations of media consumption (as of this writing). Today the company's web visibility is second only to Google. Ultimately, Quantcast attempts to answer some very difficult advertising-related questions—and none of this would be possible without Big Data.

I wanted to know more about how Quantcast specifically uses Big Data, so I asked Jim Kelly, the company's VP of R&D, and Jag Duggal, its VP of Product Management. Over the course of a few weeks, I spoke with them.

Steps: A Big Evolution

> It is not the strongest of the species that survives, nor the most intelligent that survives. It is the one that is the most adaptable to change.

> **Charles Darwin**

Quantcast understood the importance of Big Data from its inception. The company adopted Hadoop from the get-go but found that its data volumes exceeded Hadoop's capabilities at the time. Rather than wait for the Hadoop world to catch up (and miss a potentially large business opportunity in the process), Quantcast took Hadoop to the next level. The company created a massive data processing infrastructure that could process more than 20 petabytes of data per day—a volume that is constantly increasing. Quantcast built its own distributed file system (a centerpiece of its current software stack) and made it freely available to the open source community. The Quantcast File System[2] (QFS) is a cost-effective alternative to the Hadoop Distributed File System (HDFS) mentioned in Chapter 4. QFS delivers significantly improved performance while consuming 50 percent less disk space.[3]

In a Big Data world, complacency is a killer. New data sources mean that the days of "set it and forget it" are long gone, and Charles Darwin's quote is as relevant now as it was 100 years ago. In 2006, like just about every company in the world, Quantcast practically ignored data generated from mobile devices. Most Internet-related data originated from desktops and laptops before iPhone and Droids arrived. Of course, that has certainly changed over the past five years, and Quantcast now incorporates these new and essential data sources into its solutions.[4] This willingness and ability to innovate has resulted in some nice press for the company. In February 2010, *Fast Company* ranked Quantcast forty-sixth on its list of the World's Most Innovative Companies.[5] To this day, the company continues to expand and diversify its analytics products.

From its inception in 2006, Quantcast focused on providing online audience measurement services, a critical part of the advertising industry for both advertisers and publishers. TV and radio stations need to use a mutually agreeable source for determining how many people they are reaching. Companies like Arbitron and Nielsen had provided similar services for radio and TV for decades. These companies used panels of users to extrapolate media consumption across the entire population.

For the most part, these companies' Small Data approaches consist of simply porting their panel-based approaches to the Internet. As discussed in earlier chapters, Small Data tools and methods typically don't work well with Big Data, something that Quantcast understood early on. It built a Big Data–friendly system tailored to the web's unique characteristics. Millions of popular sites, social networks, channels, blogs, and forums permeate the web. Consumption is fragmented, making extrapolating from a panel extremely difficult. Luckily, since each web page is delivered individually to a user panel, such extrapolation is unnecessary. On the web, Quantcast measures the "consumption" of each page directly.

Buy Your Audience

In 2009, Quantcast began development of an "audience-buying" engine. With it, the company could leverage its vast troves of consumer data on online user media consumption. As real-time ad exchanges such as the DoubleClick AdExchange arose, Quantcast quickly got on board. Today, Quantcast is a major player in a market that auctions off *billions* of ad impressions each day.

In November 2012, Quantcast released Quantcast Advertise. The self-service platform enables advertisers, agencies, and publishers to connect Big Data with discrete brand targets.[6] With the right solutions, Big Data allows organizations to drill down and reach very specific audiences. "A flexible compute infrastructure was critical to our ability to produce more accurate audience measurement services. That same infrastructure produced more accurate ad targeting once ad inventory started to be auctioned in real-time," Duggal told me.

We saw earlier in this book how Amazon, Apple, Facebook, Google, and other progressive companies eat their own dog food. Count Quantcast among the companies that use its own Big Data tools. What's more, like Google, Quantcast makes some of its own internal

Big Data solutions available for free to its customers.[7] Quantcast audience segments allow users to understand and showcase any specific audience group for free. Once implemented, these segments appear in users' full publisher profile on Quantcast.com. As a result, they can better represent their audiences. Figure 5.1 shows some sample data from its Quantified dashboard.

To be sure, "regular" web traffic, click-through, and purchase metrics might be sufficient for some business. However, Quantcast knows that it can't serve myriad clients across the globe with a mind-set of *one size fits all*. No one company can possibly predict every Big Data need. Different businesses face vastly different data requirements, challenges, and goals. To that end, Quantcast provides integration between its products and third-party data and applications. What if customers could easily integrate their own data and applications with Quantcast-generated data? What if its clients wanted to conduct A/B testing, support out-of-browser and offline scenarios, and use multiple, concurrent analytic services—without impacting performance?

"Integration is central to everything we're doing here," says Kelly. "It's the source of all the data we work with and the means

Combined Topix Sites Netw...			Monthly **14.6M** US **19.3M** Global	
2Sites | 100% US People from Sites | 1% US People from Syndicators				
combined			Monthly **14.2M** US **18.9M** Global	
+Favorites			Share	United States
Segment Name		**US People**	**US People %**	**Global People**	**Global People %**
local		8,767,849	61.9%	9,434,692	50.0%
homepage		4,503,987	31.8%	4,598,495	24.4%
news		2,009,817	14.2%	3,802,894	20.2%
adult		915,637	6.5%	1,836,651	9.7%
politics		1,418,532	10.0%	1,486,190	7.9%
health		838,890	5.9%	1,265,051	6.7%
life		458,261	3.2%	1,232,330	6.5%
ent		675,301	4.8%	1,053,554	5.6%
member		363,022	2.6%	465,907	2.5%
sports		346,923	2.4%	400,757	2.1%
business		253,928	1.8%	381,344	2.0%
autos		210,463	1.5%	273,457	1.4%

Figure 5.1 Quantcast Quantified Dashboard
Source: Quantcast.com

by which it becomes relevant to the world." And that advanced integration isn't stopping anytime soon. Case in point: Quantcast created and offers an API built off the Microsoft Silverlight Analytics Framework.[8]

Results

Consider the following results from some of Quantcast's recent customer campaigns:

- A national after-market auto parts retailer relied upon digital advertising to attract new customers and drive online sales. Quantcast built predictive models to convert customers who had actually completed an online purchase, distinguishing between passersby and converting customers. The campaign all but eliminated the majority of superfluous clicks, achieving a return on investment (ROI) greater than 200 percent.

- A major wireless phone company achieved a 76 percent increase in conversion rates above its optimized content-targeted campaign. Quantcast lookalike data allowed lead generation to garner significantly higher conversion rates over content-targeted inventory purchased from the same inventory sources.

- A leading hotelier gained deep insights into the demographic, interests, behaviors, and affinities of its customers. In the process, it ultimately doubled its bookings.

Lessons

Compared to many organizations, Quantcast is a relatively small company. This proves the point that an organization doesn't need to be big to benefit from—and innovate with—Big Data. There's no secret sauce, but embracing Big Data from its inception starts a company on the right path. Also, it's critical to realize that Small Data tools just don't play nice with Big Data. Understand this, and then spend the time, money, and resources to equip your employees and customers with powerful self-service tools.

EXPLORYS: THE HUMAN CASE FOR BIG DATA

In January 2011, U.S. health care spending reportedly topped $3 trillion.[9] That is, more than one in every seven dollars in the U.S. economy is spent on health care. While figures vary, much of that astronomical number stems from behavioral, operational, and clinical waste. Factors here include dated technologies, risk-averse doctors, perverse incentives, administrative inefficiencies, and plain old bad data. A slightly dated PricewaterhouseCoopers report from 2008 titled "The Price of Excess" puts annual health care waste at $1.2 trillion.[10] And it gets worse. By some estimates, health care expenditures will grow more than 7.5 percent in 2013,[11] two to three times the rate of inflation. In a nutshell, health care in the United States is a complete and unsustainable mess with dire long-term economic implications. As the Chinese say, there is opportunity in chaos—and Big Data is a big part of that opportunity.

As discussed in Chapter 2, Big Data is not an elixir to any problem, much less one as complex and large as health care in the United States. There's no doubt, though, that it represents a big part of the solution. At a bare minimum, Big Data has the opportunity to profoundly improve the delivery of health care and reduce superfluous expenses.

Having already led a Big Data transformation in other market sectors, in 2009, Stephen McHale, Charlie Lougheed, and Doug Meil recognized the tremendous opportunity in front of them. When they met up with Dr. Anil Jain, MD, cofounder and current Senior VP and Chief Medical Information Officer who had developed breakthrough approaches to traditional database search strategies in clinical informatics at Cleveland Clinic, the four realized that Big Data could have a big impact on health care. That year, in a spinoff deal with Cleveland Clinic, they founded Explorys. Based out of Cleveland, Ohio, today the company employs nearly 100 people.

Explorys's DataGrid unlocks the power of Big Data by integrating clinical, financial, and operational data to provide superior delivery of care. According to Jain, health care is the perfect sector to leverage a Big Data platform given the volume, variety, and velocity of data that health care systems generate. Moreover, improving health care quality while reducing cost is a noble goal worth pursuing, and their customers are not seeing decreasing cost in traditional data technologies. Over the past three years, they developed a health care Big Data platform that combines real-time collection, secure transport, storage, processing, web services, and apps that are now used by some of the nation's largest integrated health care delivery networks. Sounds promising, so I tracked down Lougheed (the company's cofounder and president) and talked to him at length about how Explorys uses Big Data to provide better health outcomes at drastically lower costs.

Better Healthcare through Hadoop

It's not much of an exaggeration to say that Hadoop accelerated the growth of Explorys. The company built DataGrid, a high-performance computing platform based on Cloudera Enterprise. DataGrid processes an enormous amount of data to provide real-time exploration, performance, and predictive analytics of clinical data. DataGrid users include several of the largest integrated delivery networks in the United States: Cleveland Clinic, MedStar, University Hospitals, St. Joseph Health System, Iowa Health System, Centura Health, Catholic Health Partners, and Summa Health System.

DataGrid provides subsecond ad hoc search across populations, providers, and care venues. Users can also build and view key performance metrics across providers, groups, care venues, and locations that identify ways to improve outcomes and reduce unnecessary costs. Explorys also offers EPM: Engage, an integrated application and framework for coordinating rules-driven registries, prioritized patient and provider outreach, and messaging.

Explorys uses MapReduce to process, organize, and curate large batches of incoming data very quickly into HDFS and HBase. Data sources include HL7,[*] claims data, and third-party feeds from electronic health record (EHR) providers such as Epic, Eclipsys, Microsoft Amalga, McKesson, Meditech, and Cerner. Explorys developed proprietary engines that take that data and materialize it into structures that can be rapidly accessed and analyzed via off-the-shelf tools or custom-built applications. Those applications then send the data back into the

---

[*] Health Level Seven International (HL7) is the global authority on standards for interoperability of health information technology, with members in over 55 countries.

Explorys platform for other processing needs. Analytics powered by Hadoop (among other technologies) facilitate clinical quality measure generation, measure calculations for registries, manage proactive care, and perform other critical tasks.

Explorys uses Hadoop-powered analytics for a variety of purposes. For example, to better serve its community, a county hospital might want to explore why people go to the emergency room (ER) rather than a primary physician for nonemergency care. This practice is hardly ideal. It is expensive for the hospital and the patient. What's more, patients here are starting from scratch. They don't receive the continuity of care that a primary physician would provide.

Twenty years ago, one would be limited to analyzing the hospital's ER record system and manually attempting to cull data from disparate sources. Even then, the true answer would prove elusive. With the support of a Hadoop infrastructure, Explorys's customers can easily analyze the demographics of a given population, their past medical history, their patient locations, and whether or not care is available in their neighborhoods. Rather than having to run reports, Explorys provides these analytics daily and automatically. In the end, decision-makers can take immediate action. Providers and care coordinators can reach out to patients over secure methods to guide them through their treatment processes. What happens when patients receive the right care at the right venues at the right time? The quality of patients' overall care increases, while superfluous costs disappear.

This type of proactive health care just isn't feasible when clinical information is stored among a bevy of relational databases or traditional data warehouses. Organizations that try to retrofit Big Data into old tools will quickly find themselves frustrated. For instance, let's say that a hospital crams petabytes of unstructured clinical data into relational database management systems (RDBMSs). Health care practitioners who understand something specific about a population or segment of data will have to go to their IT departments and then wait days or weeks for that information. "We wanted to provide a platform that would give them an answer as fast as if they were searching on Google, but at the same time in a way that respects HIPAA and privacy concerns," says McHale.

This is wise. Remember, we live in a self-service age. People are used to finding their own answers. We routinely use Google to answer questions for ourselves. We prefer to fish for ourselves, not wait for IT to return two weeks later with the fish they think we wanted.

Many organizations maintain data silos, and health care providers are some of the worst culprits. (I've worked in many a hospital in my consulting career.) Explorys took a vastly different, more integrated approach to data management. Rather than storing and managing clinical, financial, and operational data in three data silos, Explorys consolidated all that data. As Lougheed explained to me, "It's about merging the three elements and telling a story about how an organization is doing, because ultimately what we want to do is improve health care and do it at a lower cost. With over 17 percent of the nation's GDP being spent on health care services, we've got to find a better way to deliver health care for less."

The variety of data would also present a challenge. As discussed in Chapter 3, EHRs are finally becoming more prevalent in the United States. "There are more and more devices that generate massive amounts of data. Patients are providing data and feedback on how they're doing. They have devices in the home that provide data," says Lougheed. "There's a ton of data variety coming in, and it's more than the health care space can really handle with traditional data warehousing."

Explorys needed to find a cost-efficient technology that would help the company address these Big Data challenges. Hadoop met both of these criteria, and Cloudera stood out to Explorys as the most credible company delivering an enterprise-ready Hadoop solution. McHale, Lougheed, and Meil attended the first Hadoop World conference hosted by Cloudera in 2009. During the conference, the three were sold both on the value of Hadoop and on Cloudera's ability to deliver. They also appreciated Cloudera's contingent of on-staff Hadoop Committers. As an early Hadoop adopter, Explorys knew that it would need help in supporting production deployments that would ultimately drive the direction of the technology. "Our platform needed to support the ever-complex world of health care data, not to mention the evolving transformation of the health care delivery system," says Jain. "It's clear that we do not know what questions we may be asking of our health care data five years from now. We knew that we needed a solution that [would] grow with us."

Steps

After deploying the DataGrid platform on CDH (Cloudera's official distribution of Apache Hadoop), Explorys moved to the Cloudera Enterprise (CE) subscription. CE bundles CDH with Cloudera Support and Cloudera Manager, a software application that delivers visibility into and across Hadoop clusters for streamlined management, monitoring, and provisioning. CE allowed Explorys to continue operating its mission-critical Hadoop environment with a lean staff that could focus on the core competencies of its business. In other words, Explorys shows that Big Data need not require a big staff.

Explorys relies upon CDH to provide the flexibility, scalability, and speed necessary to answer complex questions on the fly. Lougheed believes that the window for analysis would have been 30 days using traditional technologies. With Explorys's CDH-powered system, that number shrank to seconds or minutes.

Now also an HBase Committer at the Apache Software Foundation, Meil has his own take on things. "We didn't invent clinical quality measures, but the ability to generate those measures on a rapid basis, support hundreds of them, implement complex attribution logic, and manifest that with a slick user interface on top—that's revolutionary," he explains. "Cloudera provides the technology that allows us to address traditional challenges in medicine and in operational reporting with a radical new approach."

Results

Because Hadoop uses industry standard hardware, the cost-per-terabyte of storage is, on average, ten times cheaper than a traditional relational data warehouse system. "We'd be spending literally millions more dollars than we are today on relational database technologies and licensing," says Lougheed. "Those technologies are important, but they're important *in their place*. For Big Data, analytics, storage, and processing, Hadoop is a perfect solution for us. It has brought opportunities for us to rechannel those funds, that capital, in directions of being more innovative, bringing more products to bear, and ultimately hiring more people for the company as opposed to buying licenses."

Lougheed summarized, "We were forced to think about a less expensive, more efficient technology from the beginning, and in hindsight, I'm glad that we were. For us—needing storage, high capacity index, and analytics—Hadoop really made a lot of sense. And from a partner perspective, Cloudera is one of the most influential that we've had throughout the years."

Lessons

As discussed in Chapter 4, NoSQL means *not only SQL*. Explorys uses several open source technologies and has developed many proprietary engines to process data efficiently. Sometimes an organization can get a technology to do something it was not originally designed to do, but results are typically mixed. Sometimes that works well and produces breakthroughs. Other times, you hit the wall, especially given the scale of Big Data. As Explorys has shown, for an organization to successfully leverage Big Data, its engineering teams need to recognize this key tenet. It's imperative to learn, adapt, and be creative.

NASA: HOW CONTESTS, GAMIFICATION, AND OPEN INNOVATION ENABLE BIG DATA

There's no doubt that individual private companies like Quantcast and Explorys can devote significant internal resources to Big Data—and reap big rewards in the process. And if relatively small for-profit companies like these can harness the power of Big Data, then surely very large organizations can as well. But what about nonprofits and government agencies? And should an organization develop its own internal Big Data solutions just because it can? In other words, what's the relationship among Big Data, collaboration, and open innovation? Before answering that question, let's take a step back.

In 2006 Don Tapscott and Anthony D. Williams wrote *Wikinomics: How Mass Collaboration Changes Everything*. In the book, the authors discuss the dramatic effects of crowdsourcing on the economy and even the world. The effects of the Internet are impossible to overstate with respect to collaboration and innovation. For instance, Wikipedia isn't the property of any one individual. It's effectively run by and for the collective, and its results have been astounding. For instance, in 2005, a study found that Wikipedia is as accurate as Britannica[12] despite the fact that, with some notable exceptions, anyone can edit anything at any time.

Fast-forward six years, and many new and mature organizations are realizing the benefits of open innovation, crowdsourcing, and gamification. (Case in point: private funding platforms like Kickstarter and IndieGoGo are redefining business, but that's a book for another day.) Open innovation is allowing individuals, groups, and even large organizations to accomplish that which they otherwise could not. What's more, individuals with unorthodox methods are finding unexpected solutions to vexing real-world problems at a fraction of the expected cost. If Wikipedia stems from the unpaid efforts of tens of thousands of unpaid volunteers, imagine what can be accomplished when organizations offer significant monetary prizes for solving big problems.

Open innovation, crowdsourcing, and gamification lend themselves to many areas of business—and Big Data is no exception. Remember from Chapter 2 that Big Data is less about following items on a checklist and more about embracing the unknown. When done right, Big Data is fundamentally exploratory in nature. Crackpot ideas from all corners of the globe may be crazy enough to work (i.e., to find a solution to a vexing problem or discover hidden value in massive datasets).

In Chapter 4, I briefly discussed how Kaggle is using these trends to democratize Big Data. It turns out that Kaggle is hardly alone in understanding how Big Data can benefit from the wisdom of crowds.* Many people and organizations get it. Count among them the folks at NASA.

Background

NASA, Harvard Business School (HBS), and TopCoder collectively established the NASA Tournament Lab (NTL). Not unlike Kaggle

---

* In his 2004 book *The Wisdom of Crowds: Why the Many Are Smarter Than the Few and How Collective Wisdom Shapes Business, Economies, Societies and Nations*, James Surowiecki discusses how groups can use information to make decisions that are often better than could have been made by any one member of the group.

(discussed in Chapter 3), TopCoder brings together a diverse community of software developers, data scientists, and statisticians. It runs contests that seek to produce innovative and efficient solutions for specific real-world challenges.[13] For its part, NASA wants to do "space stuff" (i.e., deploy free-flying satellites, conduct planetary missions and laboratory experiments, and observe astronomical phenomena). Like any research institution, HBS is interested in the research potential and field experiment output of these data competitions.

Yes, institutions such as NASA and Harvard have at their disposal myriad human, physical, and financial resources. With a 2012 budget of more than $17 billion,[14] organizations don't get that much larger than NASA. However, with big budgets come big demands. To that end, even large, resource-laden organizations like these are starting to realize the vast benefits of looking *outside* of the organization to innovate. And this is certainly true with respect to Big Data. NTL is one of many organizations currently running data competitions through TopCoder. The site operationalizes NASA's challenges, in effect satisfying the needs of both NASA and HBS. TopCoder helps marry problems with problem solvers, and not just for the public sector. "We have many times more nongovernment clients than government ones," says McKeown. A look at existing TopCoder projects dazzles the mind. For instance, as I write this, the City of Boston is running a risk-prevention contest. Whoever writes the algorithm that best predicts the riskiest locations for major emergencies and crime will receive a share of the $10,000 prize purse.[15]

Examples

As the Director of Advanced Exploration Systems Division at NASA, Jason Crusan works closely with the TopCoder community to develop contests. In each data contest, smart cookies from across the globe compete with each other to develop innovative and efficient solutions to NASA's specific real-world challenges—challenges as diverse as image processing solutions to help categorize data from missions to the moon on the types and numbers of craters to specific software required to handle the complex operations of a satellite. Submissions take place right on the TopCoder website. Real-time data tells potential contestants the number of submissions for each contest. Contestants can even comment on the contest via online forums.

Crusan serves as the Director of the Center of Excellence for Collaborative Innovation (CoECI). Established in 2011, CoECI advances the use of open innovation methods across the federal government. A major focus is the use of prizes and challenges. CoECI provides guidance to other federal agencies, and NASA centers on implementing open innovation initiatives, defining problems, designing appropriate incentives, and evaluating post-submission solutions.[16] It's interesting to note that the same TopCoder community conceived of and built both the CoECI and NTL platforms throughout the competition process. As we saw earlier in this chapter with Quantcast, Big Data companies practice what they preach—and TopCoder is no exception to this rule.* "We eat our own dog food whenever we do anything, internally and for clients," says Jim McKeown, TopCoder's Director of Communications.

A Sample Challenge

Over the past thirty years, NASA has recorded more than 100 terabytes of space images, telemetry, models, and more from its planetary missions. NASA stores this data within its planetary data system (PDS) and makes it available to anyone with an Internet connection and sufficient interest.** That's all well and good, but what other research, commercial, and educational uses can come from that data? With that amount and variety of data, opinions run the gamut. Rather than put a bunch of employees on the project, NASA decided to run a data contest, presented next.

PLANETARY DATA SYSTEM IDEA CHALLENGE: CONTEST OVERVIEW[17]

The purpose of this challenge is to generate ideas for potential applications to allow exploration and analysis of the PDS databases. PDS is located at http://pds.nasa.gov.

(Continued)

---

* We'll see in Chapter 6 how Sears does the same.
** Anyone can access this data. Just go to http://pds.nasa.gov and knock yourself out.

While rich in depth and breadth of data, the PDS databases have developed in a disparate fashion over the years with different architectures and formats, thereby making the acquisition of data problematic. Consequently, the major challenge is how the data provided by PDS can be used and possibly combined to generate interesting applications (e.g., visualizations, analysis tools, educational applications, mash-ups).

The goal of this challenge is to generate ideas for these applications, not finished applications. However, keep in mind, a future challenge could consist of programming an application programming interface (API). Submissions should include

- A description of the overall idea.
- A description of the target audience (who might be interested in this application?)
- The benefits of the application for the target audience.
- The nature of the application (how should the application be implemented? As a web-based system, on a mobile device, a Facebook application, integrated into Eyes on the Solar System, etc.).
- Which existing PDS data sources are used, and which data sources will need to be created or modified in order for the application idea to function.
- Limitations.
- Any examples of the process flow or the interface behavior of the application. Mock-ups would be a bonus.

Overall, submissions are expected to be around two to three pages of text, including figures, tables, and images. No code or software is necessary. Please make sure that submissions are as comprehensive as possible.

Duration: The contest registration and submission processes will both last for two weeks from Monday, April 4, 2011 at 9:00 a.m. EDT until Monday, April 18, 2011 at 9:00 a.m. EDT.

Background: The PDS is an archive of data products from NASA planetary missions, which is sponsored by NASA's Science Mission Directorate as a basic resource for scientists around the world. All PDS-produced products (imagery, geolocation data, etc.) are peer-reviewed and well documented via a system of online catalogs organized by planetary disciplines. Datasets from the following missions are included:

- A grand prize of $1,000 will be awarded to the highest-scoring submission as evaluated by the expert panel.
- Up to three $500 prizes will be awarded to additional submissions based on the discretion of the expert panel.

- A $750 community choice award will be awarded to the submission with the highest number of TopCoder community votes based on the voting procedure held at the conclusion of the submission phase.
- T-shirts and stickers to be given to the first 50 distinct submitters who submit ideas that pass basic screening criteria. To be considered for this prize, submissions must contain a valid idea and meet all other criteria outlined within the competition specifications.

All cash prize winners will be recognized by NASA.

In the two weeks that this first contest ran, 212 people registered, and 36 submitted proposals for the contest. The winning entry came from Elena Shutova, a twenty-something woman in Kiev, Ukraine.[18] Shutova's "White Spots Detection" proposal involved creating a database that would determine which areas, parameters, and objects of planetary systems are well researched and what objects are "white spots" (i.e., PDS has little knowledge on them). Shutova also developed a PDS document parser, processor, and validation tool that minimized the manual work required. In the end, NASA employees were able to easily see the data collected, fix it if necessary, and add supplemental record or metadata. Users could then query the database and immediately see the results in the system's user interface (UI).

Shutova shows the type of innovation and problem solving that can emanate from anywhere on the planet. From NTL's perspective, $1,000 is a minimal sum of money. At the same time, though, it provides sufficient incentive for creative and intelligent people just about anywhere, especially in developing countries. In the end, everybody wins. Other noteworthy NTL challenges have included vehicle recognition[19] and crater detection.[20]

Lessons

To effectively harness Big Data, Crusan is quick to point out that an organization need not offer big rewards. What's more, money is not always the biggest driver. In fact, offering too much money may signal the wrong thing (read: it's too complicated). Crusan has learned that there is no one recipe to follow in pricing data contests. Pricing is more art than science, and many elements should be considered. It turns out that the hardest part of each challenge is not determining which parts of projects NTL should post on TopCoder. "Rather, the real trick is stating the problem in a way that allows a diverse set of potential solvers to apply their knowledge to the problem," Crusan tells me. "The problem decomposition process by far takes the longest amount of time. However, it's the critical piece. Without it, it's impossible to create a compelling Big Data and open innovation challenge."

SUMMARY

This chapter has demonstrated how three dynamic organizations are embracing Big Data. It has dispelled the myth that only big organizations can use—and benefit from—Big Data. On the contrary, size doesn't matter. Progressive organizations of all sizes, types, and industries are reaping big rewards. They have realized that Big Data is just too big to ignore.

Chapter 6 will offer some advice for individuals, groups, and organizations thinking about getting on the Big Data train.

NOTES

1. "Average Hour-Long TV Show Is 36% Commercials," May 7, 2009, www.marketingcharts.com/television/average-hour-long-show-is-36-commercials-9002, retrieved December 11, 2012.
2. "QFS: Quantcast File System," September 27, 2012, http://quantcast.github.com/qfs/, retrieved December 11, 2012.
3. "Quantcast File System: Bigger Data, Smaller Bills," 2012, www.quantcast.com/about/quantcast-file-system, retrieved December 11, 2012.
4. "Quantcast Measure: Mobile Web Traffic," 2012, www.quantcast.com/measurement/mobile-web, retrieved December 11, 2012.
5. Ibid.
6. Mandese, Joe, "Quantcast Unveils Self-Serve Platform: Enables Brands, Publishers to Define Real-Time Audience Segments," November 15, 2012, www.mediapost.com/publications/article/187358/quantcast-unveils-self-serve-platform-enables-bra.html#ixzz2CqhijD3L, retrieved December 11, 2012.
7. "Quantcast Measure," 2012, www.quantcast.com/measurement, retrieved December 11, 2012.
8. "Learning Center: Quantcast Silverlight API Guide," 2012, www.quantcast.com/learning-center/guides/quantcast-silverlight-api-guide/, retrieved December 11, 2012.

9. Munro, Dan, "U.S. Healthcare Hits $3 Trillion," January 19, 2012, www.forbes.com/sites/danmunro/2012/01/19/u-s-healthcare-hits-3-trillion/, retrieved December 11, 2012.

10. "The Price of Excess: Identifying Waste in Healthcare Spending," March 14, 2008, http://hc4.us/pwcchart, retrieved December 11, 2012.

11. Morgan, David, "Healthcare Costs to Rise 7.5 Percent in 2013: Report," May 31, 2012, www.reuters.com/article/2012/05/31/us-usa-healthcare-costs-idUSBRE84U05620120531, retrieved December 11, 2012.

12. Terdiman, Daniel, "Study: Wikipedia as Accurate as Britannica," December 15, 2005, http://news.cnet.com/2100-1038_3-5997332.html, retrieved December 11, 2012.

13. Keeler, Bill, "Human Exploration and Operations," November 30, 2011, www.nasa.gov/directorates/heo/ntl/, retrieved December 11, 2012.

14. Berger, Brian, "NASA 2012 Budget Funds JWST, Halves Commercial Spaceflight," November 18, 2011, www.spacenews.com/article/nasa-2012-budget-funds-jwst-halves-commercial-spaceflight#.ULkjX5IoeMI, retrieved December 11, 2012.

15. "Marathon Match, Contest: HMS Challenge #4," 2010, http://community.topcoder.com/longcontest/?module=ViewProblemStatement&compid=29272&rd=15458, retrieved December 11, 2012.

16. Lewis, Robert E., "Center of Excellence for Collaborative Innovation," December 7, 2012, www.nasa.gov/offices/COECI/index.html, retrieved December 11, 2012.

17. "Conceptualization: Planetary Data System Idea Challenge," April 4, 2011, http://community.topcoder.com/tc?module=ProjectDetail&pj=30016974, retrieved December 11, 2012.

18. "Conceptualization: Planetary Data System Idea Challenge," April 4, 2011, http://community.topcoder.com/tc?module=ProjectDetail&pj=30016974, retrieved December 11, 2012.

19. "Marathon Match, Contest: Marathon Match 4," 2010, http://community.topcoder.com/longcontest/?module=ViewProblemStatement&compid=29272&rd=15458, retrieved December 11, 2012.

20. "Marathon Match, Contest: Marathon Match 2," 2010, http://community.topcoder.com/longcontest/?module=ViewProblemStatement&compid=29272&rd=15459, retrieved November 11, 2012.

CHAPTER **6**

Taking the Big Plunge

I don't see the logic of rejecting data just because they seem incredible.

—Fred Hoyle

In the previous chapter, we moved from theory to practice. We saw how three organizations have used Big Data and related solutions to move their needles. Much can be extrapolated from those case studies and the other examples discussed in the book—and that's the point of this chapter. The following pages offer sage advice for getting started with Big Data.

BEFORE STARTING

Perhaps the three case studies in Chapter 5 inspired you to take action. Maybe your brain is overwhelmed with possibilities right now about what Big Data can mean for your organization, and you just can't wait to get started. If so, I'm glad. Now, I don't want to rain on your parade, but before continuing, don't start just yet. Airplanes don't take off without undergoing a swath of diagnostics. By the same token, on an enterprise level, jumping into Big Data without first asking a few questions is ill advised. Consider these four things before starting the ignition.

Infonomics Revisited

How can an organization possibly benefit from Big Data if its culture and employees only rely upon empiricism? What if they don't recognize the inherent value of information? (See the discussion in the Introduction titled "Google and Infonomics.") Short answer: they can't. Unfortunately, employees in many organizations regularly ignore or reject information and data. Instead, they rely exclusively on hunches, intuition, policy, and routine.

All else being equal, organizations that view *and utilize* information in this manner will realize greater benefits from Big Data than those that don't. (And, I'd argue, they will be more successful.) Organizations that fail to recognize the value and power of information should probably hold off on Big Data for the time being, although individual employees, groups, and departments may be able to succeed despite considerable obstacles. In an era of open-source software and bring your own device (BYOD), it's never been easier to fly under the radar.

Big Data Tools Don't Cleanse Bad Data

At one point in my career, I consulted for a prestigious *Fortune* 500 company in a hybrid capacity. (Let's call that company ABC here, although it's obviously a pseudonym.) I spent about 60 percent of my time implementing new technologies and the other 40 percent working on the company's bevy of legacy systems. To say the least, it was an eye-opening experience; one day I would work on the future, and the next I'd be pulled back into the past. I couldn't believe that the internal systems and data of such a storied organization could be, quite frankly, such a mess. Rather than retiring many applications that were more than a little long in the tooth, the company just bolted on more. What's worse, ABC bought and highly customized PeopleSoft (then a best-of-breed enterprise resource planning [ERP] system) to integrate— and I use that term very loosely—with its morass of internal systems.

Simple questions like, "How many people work in Asia?" and, "What's the size of our U.S. sales force?" took a minimum of two weeks to answer—and even then the number was off.

On several occasions, I was able to interact with ABC's senior folks. I remember a specific meeting that I attended with the senior vice president (SVP) of HR (we'll call her Diane, although it's also a pseudonym) along with some of her colleagues at other organizations. Diane proudly told others about ABC's wonderful new technologies. Most recently, she remarked, the company had implemented People-Soft along with a new BI application. What magnificent reports it produced! Now, HR could *finally* be a true strategic partner, not just "the personnel department."

Diane either didn't know or didn't care that, in reality, those pretty reports didn't emanate from PeopleSoft or ABC's business intelligence (BI) application. Rather, a bunch of her underlings spent a great deal of time cobbling together information from ABC's eye chart of systems. What's more, even after all that scrambling, those new reports were rife with inaccurate information, causing employees to ignore them or become frustrated. Many senior folks erroneously believed that the fault lay with the new software: they must be faulty applications. In point of fact, ABC's problems had nothing to do with its new tools. They were just the messengers; both were loaded with bad data.

The main lesson from this little yarn: any application or enterprise system is only as good as the data it contains. I've always preferred a simple Excel spreadsheet with accurate data to the most sophisticated application on the planet with inaccurate, duplicate, and incomplete information. By bastardizing its new applications and loading them with bad data to boot, ABC ignored a longstanding law of data management: garbage in, garbage out (GIGO). That law is as true with columnar and NoSQL databases as it is with PeopleSoft and other enterprise systems.

The Big Question: Is the Organization Ready?

Let's leave aside the fact that ABC's new applications only served as a repository for its truly awful data. For many reasons, the organization just wasn't ready for any ERP system or BI application, a lesson that it spent more than $5 million learning.

As we saw earlier, ABC learned the hard way that deploying new technologies for the sake of doing so is more than pointless; it's actually detrimental. Let me explain. Let's say that I could have waved my magic wand and populated ABC's new applications with comprehensive and completely accurate information. It wouldn't have mattered in the slightest. People at ABC—at least, those with whom I regularly interacted—usually did not use data to make decisions. In fact, during the few times that I carried the data flag into combat, I was quickly overruled and reminded of my place on the totem pole.

So what does this mean for Big Data? On many levels, mid-1990s, best-of-breed ERP systems and BI applications have little in common with today's best Big Data tools. However, the same general principle applies in each case. Before moving forward with Big Data, consider the following broad questions:

- What are you going to do with Big Data in the short and long terms? (This topic is addressed in the next section.)
- What types of questions do you plan to ask?
- Are you ready to ask new, entirely unexpected questions?
- Are you really prepared for the unexpected answers that Big Data will probably provide?
- What's the larger business objective?

The honest answers to questions like these will give employees, departments, teams, and organizations key insights into their actual Big Data readiness. If not ready, then do not pass go and collect $200. Organizations should hold off on Big Data if they are loath to embrace data, don't take Small Data seriously, or can't overcome other obstacles. Doing it wrong is always much, much worse than not doing it at all. Green fields are always easier to cultivate than brown fields—or black fields.

Don't be dissuaded if the entire organization isn't ready to embrace Big Data. As I know all too well, waiting for everyone to be on the same page often wastes valuable time. If you believe that the benefits of Big Data far exceed their costs, you're in luck: an individual group, team, department, or division can take advantage of Hadoop, NoSQL, and the other Big Data solutions discussed in Chapter 4 even if the organization as a whole isn't ready.

Think Free Speech, Not Free Beer

A point from Chapter 2 bears repeating here. Open-source tools like Hadoop and NoSQL databases are freely available online. However, one shouldn't confuse free speech with free beer. The chief information officer (CIO) who believes that her organization can leverage Big Data without a proper budget, headcount, external consulting, or training is sorely mistaken. We saw in Chapter 5 how Explorys worked closely with Cloudera on its Hadoop deployment, how Quantcast invested significant resources on its own version of Hadoop, and how NASA offered prizes via TopCoder. Think of Big Data as any business output: for it to be successful, it requires some inputs.

STARTING THE JOURNEY

The first part of this chapter was meant to provide a necessary Big Data stop sign. Rather than just bolting ahead, it behooves readers to ask themselves if their organizations are *really* ready to embrace a data-oriented mind-set. If that is indeed the case, the following tips should prove beneficial.

Start Relatively Small and Organically

The beauty of solutions like Hadoop is that they allow Big Data to take root organically within an organization. To get going with Big Data, a chief executive officer (CEO) or CIO does not need to submit formal requests for information (RFIs) and requests for proposals (RFPs). Multi-million dollar budgets aren't prerequisites. Unlike 1998, an organization need not perform a laborious customer relationship management (CRM)- or ERP-like procurement and deployment process. In fact, depending on your organization's budget, current human resources, and general level of technical sophistication, it can take steps today to use—and benefit from—Big Data in relatively short periods of time.

You'll get no argument from me about the business case for Big Data. After all, that's why I wrote this book. Still, it's hard for me to see the logic in an organization earmarking a small fortune for Big

Data activities from the get-go. (Of course, this is no hard and fast rule of thumb. The National Security Administration is building a state-of-the-art $2 billion data center in Utah.[1]) For the most part, I am skeptical of such large initial expenditures. Boiling the ocean rarely works, and a modicum of caution is probably in order, at least at the beginning. Why not start a bit conservatively with reasonable investments in hardware, software, and additional headcount? And don't forget that cloud solutions may essentially obviate the need for hardware purchases and upgrades.

First Aim for Little Victories

Now, let's take a step back. Big Data is just like any new technology: to succeed with it, an organization has to be ready. But, let's not confuse readiness with clairvoyance. In no way am I implying that CIOs and steering committees must figure *everything* out years in advance. Part of the power (dare I say, the *beauty*?) of Big Data is its serendipity, its dynamism. Embrace it.

It's essential to know this going in because Big Data can be more than a bit daunting. Employees who have traditionally made "data-less" decisions will probably feel overwhelmed if given access to datasets in the petabytes, unfamiliar tools, and a mandate to "make it happen" in a few weeks. Also, since Big Data is so new, all but a handful of organizations are starting from scratch, and goals should be tempered appropriately. For instance, how can an organization that has struggled managing its Small Data expect to accurately predict customer behavior in six months? It can't. Table 6.1 represents some simple short- and long-term goals with respect to Big Data.

In other words, don't try to do everything at once, especially from day one. While Big Data is certainly powerful, it is also unwieldy, often unpredictable, highly dynamic, and probably a bit intimidating at first. Realize that it's a journey, not a destination—and your organization isn't going to find the Holy Grail in two weeks.

For Big Data to have a big impact, it may be wise to start with a relatively inefficient or expensive business function. (This is not to say that already well-functioning and efficient operations can't be improved, but quick hits may build momentum throughout the

Table 6.1 Big Data Short- and Long-Term Goals

Group	Short-Term Goals	Long-Term Goals
Customers	Gather unstructured data on current and former customers Increase understanding of user and customer behavior on website Improve company website design and product offerings based upon customer behavior and specific metrics	Predict which products will gain traction Reduce customer churn, particularly of less valuable or bad customers Retain most valuable customers Proactively contact customers who are about to defect, perhaps by providing real-time offers (without annoying them)
Employees	Gather more structured data on current and former employees If possible, attempt to collect unstructured data like performance reviews, exit interview notes, and the like Increase understanding of current workforce	Predict which employees will be successful Minimize or eliminate bad hires Reduce regrettable employee turnover Proactively approach valuable employees who are likely to leave

company.) For instance, consider what retailer Sears has done. As Doug Henschen writes in *Information Week*,[2] the company's bloated IT architecture prevented it from obtaining anything close to meaningful analytics on its customers. Reports would take months to produce and, as a result, Sears lost additional sales and market share to big-box retailers like Walmart and Target, as well as online behemoths like Amazon. By embracing Hadoop, Pig, and some of the other Big Data solutions discussed in Chapter 4, Sears was able to increase earnings 163 percent for the quarter ending July 28, 2012 (relative to the previous quarter). Based upon Sears's initial successes, executive vice president (VP) and chief technology officer (CTO) Phil Shelley is poised to ramp up the company's use of Big Data.

Knocking 1 percent off of already-low data storage costs five years down the road may not represent the best initial objective for a Big Data project.

New Employees and New Skills

Beyond hybrids who can help bridge the traditional gap between lines of business (LOBs) and IT, however, organizations looking to leverage Big Data should consider sending high-potential employees to hands-on physical or virtual training classes. (Yes, there's even a Big Data University,[3] and some vendors will come to you.[4]) Schools across the world are starting to recognize the importance of matriculating students with big knowledge of Big Data. Consider a course on "Very Large Information Systems" now offered by my alma mater, Carnegie Mellon University (CMU),* that covers "the theory, design, and implementation of text-based information systems. The Information Retrieval (IR) core components of the course include important retrieval models (Boolean, vector space, probabilistic, inference net, language modeling), clustering algorithms, automatic text categorization, and experimental evaluation. The course covers a variety of current research topics, including cross-lingual retrieval, document summarization, machine learning, and topic detection and tracking."[5]

Trust me: even though tech-savvy Carnegie Mellon is at the forefront of the most current technology trends, the school didn't offer a Big Data program when I was there nearly twenty years ago. Like all good schools, CMU adapts. Today, it is one of a growing cadre of universities that has recognized the need to incorporate data science and Big Data into its curriculum. Rather than merely providing standalone courses, the school now offers a master's degree in technology strategy, with a concentration in "Big Data and Analytics" to boot. In the fall of 2012, New York City awarded Columbia University $15 million to start a new data-science institute.[6] Expect more colleges and universities to follow suit in the coming years. If they don't adapt to current and future marketplace trends (and Big Data specifically), they will perish.

Organizations embarking on the Big Data road would do well to remember the multifaceted skills of true data scientists. Simply putting a bright but untrained financial or marketing analyst into a data scientist position is unlikely to yield the same benefits as a proper external hire with related training, education, and experience. Even traditional

---

* It's not relevant here, but I couldn't resist commenting on two things. The school's nickname (The Tartans) and its colors (plaid) are just plain awful.

statisticians may not be immediately suitable for these positions, depending on their backgrounds.

Training for Big Data is on the rise—and not just for technical areas like installing Hadoop and configuring columnar databases. Eager to meet the burgeoning demand for data scientist, organizations are starting to offer formal programs. Consider what EMC did in July 2010 after acquiring Big Data firm Greenplum.[7] EMC decided that "the availability of data scientists would be a gating factor in its own—and customers'—exploitation of Big Data. So its Education Services division launched a data science and Big Data analytics training and certification program. EMC makes the program available to both employees and customers, and some of its graduates are already working on internal Big Data initiatives."[8]

Of course, training new data scientists takes time. Many organizations will want to buy—not grow—their data scientists. Those in the latter camp should aggressively target graduating and newly minted data scientists and act quickly in gobbling them up. People with Big Data skills won't last on the labor market for too long because there just aren't too many of them. (See the McKinsey quote in the Introduction, "Why Now? Explaining the Big Data Revolution.") Next, understand that making a few key "specialists" isn't going to cut it. Everyday (read: nontechnical) employees will need to become more comfortable working with data. Much like communication skills, proficiency with data and analytics will become requisite skills across the organization—and outside of it. Finally, if you can't find or afford to bring data scientists aboard, consider using the services of consulting firms or posting projects on crowdsourcing sites like Kaggle (discussed in Chapter 4).

Experiment with Big Data Solutions

> If things seem under control, you are just not going fast
> enough.
>
> **Mario Andretti**

In many ways, Big Data is a bit of a luxury. (This might seem like an odd statement given much of the content in this book, but keep reading.) For better or worse, at least in the short term, many organizations can keep their lights on without Big Data (i.e., while they essentially ignore the vast amounts of structured and unstructured data available to them). Big Data in this way is the antithesis of mission-critical applications such as e-mail, CRM, and ERP. Organizations cannot expect to survive for very long if they cannot accurately produce financial statements, book sales, track their inventory, pay their vendors' invoices, and cut employee checks.

Think of the "nonessential" nature of Big Data as a potential point of differentiation among organizations.

Let's say that a company experiments with Hadoop, populating it with a feed of call detail records (CDRs), a Twitter firehose, and other sources of unstructured data. Then, without warning, these feeds suddenly shut off. (If configured properly, this should be uncommon, as Hadoop was built with a high degree of fault tolerance. However, on occasion Twitter goes down, hence the term *fail whale*.) What to do? While not good news, it should not affect truly essential operations like those described in the previous paragraph. Ideally, Big Data will become less of a luxury. I believe strongly that Big Data will soon become indispensable. I see a future in which employees increasingly rely upon analytics for daily planning, decision-making, and strategy purposes.

But no two organizations are alike, and Big Data certainly doesn't change that. Employees should be encouraged to play around with new and different data sources. Fight the urge to become complacent. Think of the Mario Andretti quote at the beginning of this section. Why not push the envelope? Why not run a business by relying upon valuable key performance indicators (KPIs), analytics, insights, and outputs?

Big Data is ultimately *not* about aping the setup, data sources, and processes of comparable organizations. As starting points, they may be fine. It's downright natural to ask what others have done and how they've done it. However, the creative, exploratory element of Big Data should not cease when an organization "goes live." The fun is just beginning, and employee curiosity is a good thing. Data scientists swim in data and, as such, they are likely to make unexpected discoveries.

New trends, events, and data sources may result in new, valuable, and unexpected insights, analytics, and patterns. Just like "real" scientists, they don't create checklists, follow scripts, and adhere to rigid routines.

Gradually Gain Acceptance throughout the Organization

Like any new technology or trend, it's unlikely that an organization and all its employees will embrace Big Data overnight. This is especially true with large, mature companies and public sector agencies. Based on myriad factors, certain enterprises and employees will realize the benefits of Big Data sooner than others.

Chapter 8 discusses some problems related to employee resistance of Big Data at some length. For now, suffice it to say that it's unlikely that *everyone* will gravitate toward Big Data and data-oriented decision-making. Pay the naysayers no heed. As your organization gets its arms around Big Data and starts to see its benefits, it's likely that others will follow. Part and parcel to this is publicizing the use of new tools, data, and mind-sets. Look for internal publicity on company wikis, intranets, and social networks, but don't stop there. Many sites, magazines, conferences, and journals are looking for Big Data success stories. For instance, if your organization deployed RFID technologies with great success, why not contact the *RFID Journal*? Perhaps a case study will win an award, further cementing your organization's reputation as an innovative, future-looking place to work. Perhaps sought-after data scientists will actively seek out *your* organization.

Open Your Mind

After minimizing the noise inherent in Big Data, it's entirely likely that new, entirely unexpected, and potentially counterintuitive insights will emerge. For instance, what if you ran a gigantic retail store in the Midwestern United States and you knew that a hurricane was coming? What would you do? You would stock more staples like batteries, canned goods, and bottled water than normal, right?

It seems like a solid and logical plan, but you'd be leaving money on the table. Consider what the mother of all retailers discovered through Big Data. Say what you will about Walmart as a corporation, but its use of operational and analytical systems is almost without parallel. In truth, one feeds the other. That is, Walmart's analytical systems would be almost useless without its exceptionally large and accurate trove of customer transactional customer data.

In 2004, Walmart employees mined the company's historical data before expected hurricanes and storms. Its data scientists (or rough equivalents) found that stores affected by severe weather did indeed sell more of certain products, but not just the usual flashlights. "We didn't know in the past that strawberry Pop-Tarts increase in sales, like seven times their normal sales rate, ahead of a hurricane," said CIO Linda M. Dillman, "And the pre-hurricane top-selling item was beer."[9]

The larger point here is that, to get the most out of Big Data, you have to open your mind. Findings are often surprising and even counterintuitive. For a fancier psychological term, we must avoid things like the *availability heuristic* or bias. This is a mental shortcut that all of us use to make judgments about the likelihood of events by the ease with which examples come to mind. Amos Tversky and Daniel Kahneman first studied the concept in 1973.[10] Big Data challenges the notion that, "if you can think of it, it must be important."

Let the Data Model Evolve

The pure relational data model so efficient with structured data and discussed in Chapter 1 just doesn't apply to Big Data. Relational database management systems (RDBMSs) ship with a highly structured data schema and, to fulfill their promise, all legacy enterprise data needs to be crammed into existing tables. (Of course, database administrators [DBAs] can create their own tables, but that can pose risks beyond the scope of this book.) For its part, Hadoop holds data in its raw form. As a result, nothing needs to be converted or transformed before being loaded, at least in the traditional sense. To continue with the Sears example from earlier in the chapter, CTO Phil Shelley believes that "ETL* must die," although not everyone agrees with his viewpoint. Established technologies and methods have a way of sticking around.

---

* As discussed in Chapter 1, ETL stands for *extract, transform, and load*. It is a common way to move data in and out of different systems.

Hadoop and other Big Data solutions represent a fundamentally more flexible, ad hoc, and organic approach to data modeling. Meeting a business need trumps following regimented, predefined data schema and models. Ignore Steven Covey's advice here: you don't need to begin with the end in mind.

Tap into Existing Communities

I began this book by discussing a conference that I attended in Las Vegas on analytics and Big Data in 2011. Earlier in this chapter, I mentioned that I went to a data science summit in early 2012. At each, I learned more about Big Data, Hadoop, and the revolution currently taking place in predictive analytics. I'll be the first to admit that watching a few talks and having a few conversations does not a Big Data expert make. Big Data is far too big for that. Without question, however, I learned a great deal and met some interesting folks, some of whom I interviewed for this book.

Conferences are only one real-world means of expanding one's knowledge of Big Data. Meetup groups are also beneficial.[11] If Big Data is too broad a category for you and you'd like to know more about specific applications like Hadoop, you're probably in luck. Depending on where you live, you may not have to travel very far. Given the Data Deluge, the number and variety of these groups will only get increase.

And that's just the physical world. The resources online are nothing less than astounding. Information on specific applications is abundant, something that could certainly not be said of early ERP and CRM projects that predated the web. Groups, websites, and wikis may not be able to answer every conceivable question, but there's big data on Big Data (Big Metadata?). And if you don't find a resource that covers your topic in sufficient detail, just start one.

Realize That Big Data Is Iterative

As discussed in the Introduction, the city of Boston launched an early version of Street Bump as more of a proof of concept than anything else. Subsequent versions improved upon the initial release. When (not if) new data sources can further increase the app's performance, accuracy, and utility, expect them to be integrated.

Big Data doesn't stand still (i.e., an organization is never "done" with Big Data). On the contrary, we're in the second or third inning of the game. Many things need to play out. The tools described in Chapter 4 will invariably evolve and improve—and new applications and web services will come and go. So will data sources. And let's not forget that user, consumer, employee, and citizen behavior change as well. Their populations are not static. The same tools and data may tell us very different things from one year to the next.

AVOIDING THE BIG PITFALLS

Aside from following the advice in the previous section, organizations should avoid the five Big Data pitfalls discussed in this section.

Big Data Is a Binary

If you think of Big Data as an all-or-nothing proposition, you are mistaken. There are *levels* to using Big Data. Don't for a second believe that your organization needs to import, load, or link to "all" data out there—or even all data in a particular area. Such an undertaking is probably not feasible, much less cost effective, even for very large, resource-laden organization. Getting all the data isn't even remotely possible, as Figure 2.2 showed on the Deep Web.

Like cell phones, the Internet, and fax machines, Big Data is subject to network effects. All else being equal, more data (when used right) yields better analytics, deeper insights, and more accurate predictions. Even though different data sources may come with a high noise-signal ratio,[*] the techniques and solutions mentioned in Chapters 3 and 4 can help companies dial down that noise, exposing additional business value in the process. Big Data solutions, mentioned in Chapter 4, coupled with the low cost of data storage mean that organizations can store more data than ever, even if they don't have the current means to analyze it. When cost and performance cease to be factors, it's always better to keep more data than less.

---

[*] In electrical engineering, a signal conveys information. Noise represents a superfluous or random addition to the signal. Problems arise when the noise drowns out the signal.

Big Data Is an Initiative

Organizations that mismanage their Small Data generally don't function properly. They often struggle to keep the lights on and, after much hemming and hawing, may call in consultants or data quality experts. Perhaps they will embark on a master data management (MDM) project. They wind up spending a great deal of time, money, and resources cleansing their data, implementing new procedures, and the like.

Unfortunately, many of these projects ultimately fail because employees correctly see them as "one-off" initiatives, the endeavors du jour of their peripatetic chief officers who will soon move on to newer and shinier things. Once the consultants leave or a new project begins, old employee and organizational habits revert. Bad data begins to creep back into the picture, undermining much of the work that had been done. New processes are ignored because people hate change and aren't held accountable for their actions—or lack thereof.

Getting the most out of Big Data requires doing much more than reading books like this one, although I like to think that texts like these will help generate internal momentum. Big Data is not just about downloading Hadoop and buying and deploying a columnar database. These types of things are *necessary conditions*. They sound cutting edge when CIOs tell their colleagues about them but, by themselves, they represent wholly *insufficient conditions* to unleash the true power of Big Data. To really move the needle here, data-oriented decision-making needs to be ingrained in an organization's culture, its DNA, and its individual employees.

Now, let's not overdo it here. Data cannot and should not be used to make every conceivable type of decision. Where should we go to lunch, and what should I order? What time should we hold this meeting? What does the data say? Still, at a bare minimum, major decisions vis-à-vis research and development (R&D), finance, marketing, sales, and human resources should involve established and emerging types and sources of information available to the organization. Ignoring or minimizing Big Data at senior levels sends a powerful message that echoes throughout the organization: it's just not that important, especially for "real" matters.

Saying that Big Data should factor into most organizational decisions is not tantamount to saying that Big Data should be *the only* factor.

As discussed in Chapter 2, Big Data is a complement to both Small Data and human judgment. Foolish is the person who thinks of Big Data as an elixir or a substitute for those other critical inputs. Employees still need to interpret information presented to them, and Big Data should not hijack the decision-making process. But Big Data should not be ignored.

Big Data Is a Side Project

Let's say that you work in a large company. Perhaps your day job involves supporting legacy systems or marketing, a job that keeps you pretty busy. You'd like to know more about Big Data, and you surf the Internet on your lunch break.

Hopefully, your research leads you to at least one conclusion: you don't add Big Data to the already-full workload of an individual employee, team, or department and expect meaningful results. In this sense, Big Data is like search engine optimization (SEO). It's not too hard to understand the basics of SEO pretty quickly and even take a few simple steps to increase the visibility of your website. Still, there's a reason that large companies employ highly paid folks with titles like SEO Engineer, Director of SEO, and Director of Search Engine Marketing. For their part, many small businesses that cannot afford to make full-time hires contract firms that specialize in SEO.

All of my years working with enterprise systems, emerging technologies, programming languages, and different applications have taught me one thing: no one learns a new technology in weekly 15-minute chunks—and I'm certainly no exception. On a personal level, over the years, I taught myself Crystal Reports, Microsoft Access, some SQL Server, and WordPress by spending hundreds of hours working with each. Lamentably, all too often people take a two- or three-day class on a new application and then return to their day jobs. For whatever reason, they don't play around with the application, losing the opportunity to reinforce what they have learned. Then, six months or a year later, they dust off that training manual and unsuccessfully try to solve a problem, build an application, or write a complex report. It just doesn't work that way.

Big Data is no different in this regard. As we have seen in this book, organizations of all types and sizes are starting to recognize its power. To this end, the intelligent ones are hiring specialists and data scientists who can help them take advantage of it. Search for "Big Data jobs," and you'll be overwhelmed at the results. For instance, JIVE software brands itself as "the pioneer and world's leading provider of social business solutions," so why would the company ignore Big Data? It doesn't and, as of this writing, it's actively recruiting Hadoop experts, among others.[12]

There Is a Big Data Checklist

In this book, I've compared Big Data to golf and chess. Now it's time for an anti-analogy: Big Data is nothing like a baking a cake. It's an ongoing process, not a set of instructions to follow.

Yes, best practices are helpful to follow—one of the reasons that I wrote this book. At the same time, though, transformative technologies like Big Data don't lend themselves to recipes and often-trite checklists. This is doubly true when the trends and their accompanying solutions are still in their relative infancies. This is clearly the case with Hadoop, NoSQL, and the other solutions described in Chapter 4.

Big Data may have one overarching business goal that transcends industry, geography, and organizational type and size: to better understand what's going on and try to do something about it. However, that's where the ubiquity ends. As the case studies and examples in this book have shown, Big Data is being used in different ways (and for different reasons) by different organizations. One size certainly doesn't fit all, and your mileage may vary.

IT Owns Big Data

For years, many organizations have struggled with a fundamental disconnect between two general groups of employees: technical (IT) and functional folks representing different lines of business (LOBs). This concept is widely known as *the IT/business divide*. Many IT projects have failed because of this chasm, and I have seen this dysfunction in action more than a few times. At a fundamental level, each group speaks a different language and believes that it has to meet different objectives. In the end, much often gets lost in translation, and new systems and applications fail to live up to their promise.

In my first book, *Why New Systems Fail*, I wrote about the need for organizations to hire and train *hybrids*: employees who can effectively speak both languages and understand the goals of each group. Hybrids are techno-functional folks who are often worth their weight in gold. While you won't find the term *Big Data* in that book, the same need for hybrids exists here. (Even the most talented hybrids cannot do what good data scientists can do). For any organizational Big Data effort to be successful, IT and the LOBs need to work together. This even holds true in a world full of clouds and open-source software. It's not advisable for IT to be kept in the dark on something as big as Big Data. By the same token, expecting IT to "own" data in general—and Big Data in particular—is misplaced.

On the *Harvard Business Review* site, Tom Redman makes this very point. Redman, the author of *Data Driven: Profiting from Your Most Important Business Asset*, writes that

> management responsibility should lie with the parties that have the most to gain or lose. Business departments gain mightily when they create new value from data. In contrast, IT reaps little reward when data is used to improve a product, service, or decision. This point is increasingly relevant in light of the increasing penetration of data into every nook and cranny of every business department.[13]

Redman is absolutely right. At its core, Big Data serves the same purpose as any other technology: it advances the business. Big Data should not be viewed as an IT responsibility like provisioning laptops or configuring servers. If Big Data is going to be successful in any organization, IT and the line will have to collaborate—and LOBs should own their data.

Remember the Goal

This chapter concludes with an important reminder about the point of Big Data. It's not a contest, and he who stores the most data doesn't win. In a sense, Big Data is just another means toward solving business problems.

HOW DO YOU SOLVE A PROBLEM LIKE THE DATA SCIENTIST?

The newest aphorism du-jour in the Big Data world is this: "It's not Big Data—it's just data." As debates on both the definition and value of Big Data continue, this argument has some validity. The struggle to find, assess, cleanse, annotate, integrate, standardize, and provision data predates not only the Big Data trend, but computing itself.

Information Week warned readers of the consequences of "infoglut" back in 1995 under the heading "New Tools That Can Help Tame an Ocean of Data." Mixed metaphor aside, the article confirmed what had been keeping business and IT managers up at night: how to harness proliferating and ever-more complex amounts of data. The rise of Big Data means that these challenges will only get harder.

"Most of the complex problems we tackle should involve some sort of initial data exploration," explains Bill Rand, Assistant Professor of Marketing at the University of Maryland and Director at the university's Center for Complexity in Business. Rand personifies the expanding role of the data scientist, professionals who not only explore diverse datasets but determine how the use of the data can help their companies compete.

Rand and his team have been applying analytical skills to examine diverse social media data to understand behavior patterns and propensities that could aid marketers. "Social media players aren't a bunch of people working on a common problem," he explains. "They're individuals working on separate problems. Data scientists need to explore large volumes of detailed data to understand the realm of possible social media actions. Only after the initial analysis can they determine how to apply subsequent analytic models."

The keyword here isn't "analyze," but "apply." The people with the job title dubbed "The Sexiest Job of the 21st Century" by authors Tom Davenport, Ph.D, and D.J. Patil, are no longer expected to simply run mathematical models against diverse datasets. They're now just as likely to suggest how to leverage the data to drive cross-selling techniques, suggest supply chain efficiencies, predict fraud, and determine a customer's next likely purchase.

"Data scientists, by definition, combine business acumen with data acumen," explains P.K. Kannan, Professor of Marketing Science and Marketing Department Chair at University of Maryland's Smith Business School (and Rand's boss). "From a knowledge perspective, a data scientist has keen insights into the business models driving the firm, its products, and services, while simultaneously possessing

(Continued)

mastery of data creation and data analysis. In that sense, they're different from traditional statisticians not only in their business domain knowledge but also in terms of their broader scope."

This is one lofty job description and one that, without the right set of guidelines, standards, and skills, is primed for failure. On the one hand, IT personnel are likely to have begun implementing data governance, establishing clear policies for the access, usage, and deployment of information from a variety of sources. They may have also adopted enabling technologies such as data quality, master data management, and metadata repository tools to help automate repeatable tasks. Depending on how it's defined, the data scientist's role could erode data governance policies, or worse, contradict them.

On the business side, the phenomenon of data hoarding is alive and well and making no apologies. Even in the age of Big Data, knowledge is (still) power, and line of business staff are loathe to share data that might bestow the sheen of indispensability. So the customer address data is shared, but the online behaviors are shielded from customer support reps. Or the electronic health record is shared with clinicians, but the patient's survey data is shared only with administrators. A data scientist (or business analyst or visualization tool user) can hardly deliver value if she can only access a portion of the data—however big—she needs to do her job.

Managers have to do the hard but sometimes unpleasant work of inventorying incumbent skills and even consolidating data management roles or functions. Circumscribing role boundaries is key, not only to prevent duplication of effort, but to stem confusion among incumbent data experts. Failing to do so can result in staff disaffection. "I guess I always assumed I was one of the firm's data authorities," an actuary at an insurance company confided recently. "Now I'm being 'coached' on how to do the job I've done for twelve years. Maybe if I called myself a data scientist I'd have more clout."

With the increase of systems generating the data—both within and outside of the firewall—operationalizing the flow and usage of information is the biggest barrier to becoming a data-driven organization. At Baseline Consulting we called it "the data supply chain," and it's an apt term for Big Data's interdisciplinary skill sets and cross-functional reach. Because no matter how big or complex the data is, the "it's not the size, but how you use it" aphorism is as true as it ever was.

Jill Dyché is an internationally recognized author, speaker, and business consultant. Dyché was a partner and cofounder of Baseline Consulting, the premier provider of specialty consulting for business analytics, data management, and data integration. SAS acquired Baseline in 2011.

SUMMARY

This chapter has provided tips for jumping on the Big Data train. An organization that downloads Hadoop isn't finished; in fact, it's just getting started. It has shown that ambitious long-term goals should give way to more reasonable and attainable short-term objectives. With Big Data, you have to walk before you can run. Big Data is a big commitment, and people have to disavow themselves of the notion that they can leverage the power of the technology with minimal commitment.

Chapter 7 looks at the flip side of Big Data. We'll see that it's not all lollipops and roses. With Big Data, there is big danger.

NOTES

1. Bamford, James, "The NSA Is Building the Country's Biggest Spy Center (Watch What You Say)," March 15, 2012, www.wired.com/threatlevel/2012/03/ff_nsadata-center/, retrieved December 11, 2012.
2. Henschen, Doug. "Big Data, Big Questions." *Information Week*. November, 5, 2012. 22.
3. "Big Data University," 2012, http://bigdatauniversity.com/, retrieved December 11, 2012.
4. "LearnComputer—Hadoop Overview for Managers Training Course," 2012, www.learncomputer.com/training/hadoop/hadoop-overview/, retrieved December 11, 2012.
5. "Master of Information Technology Strategy (MITS)—Big Data Analytics Elective Courses," 2012, www.cmu.edu/mits/curriculum/concentration/bigdata.html, retrieved December 11, 2012.
6. "NYC Awards Columbia $15 Million for New Data-Science Institute," 2012, http://magazine.columbia.edu/news/fall-2012/nyc-awards-columbia-15-million-new-data-science-institute, retrieved December 11, 2012.
7. "Press Release: EMC to Acquire Greenplum," July 6, 2010, www.emc.com/about/news/press/2010/20100706-01.htm, retrieved December 11, 2012.
8. Davenport, Thomas H.; Patil, D.J., "Data Scientist: The Sexiest Job of the 21st Century," October 2012, http://hbr.org/2012/10/data-scientist-the-sexiest-job-of-the-21st-century/ar/3, retrieved December 11, 2012.
9. Hays, Constance L., "What Wal-Mart Knows About Customers' Habits," November 14, 2004, www.nytimes.com/2004/11/14/business/yourmoney/14wal.html?_r=0, retrieved December 11, 2012.
10. Tversky, Amos; Kahneman, Daniel, "Availability: A Heuristic for Judging Frequency and Probability," September 1973, www.sciencedirect.com/science/article/pii/0010028573900339, retrieved December 11, 2012.
11. "Big Data Meetup Groups," 2012, http://big-data.meetup.com/, retrieved December 11, 2012.
12. "Big Data: From Big Problems to Big Solutions," 2012, www.jivesoftware.com/about/careers/big-data, retrieved December 11, 2012.
13. Redman, Thomas C., "Get Responsibility for Data Out of IT," October 22, 2012, http://blogs.hbr.org/cs/2012/10/get_responsiblity_for_data_out.html, retrieved December 11, 2012.

CHAPTER **7**

Big Data: Big Issues and Big Problems

What hath God wrought.

> —First message in American Morse code sent by
> Samuel F. B. Morse to officially open the Baltimore-Washington
> telegraph line, May 24, 1844, quoting *Numbers*, 23:23

In May 2012 Google once again found itself in a heap of trouble. After a few years of successfully getting away with it, the U.S. government discovered that the company's Street View software had been furtively collecting data on open Wi-Fi networks. (Yes, many people never bother to lock down their wireless routers.) In a *Wired* piece on the matter, David Kravets reported that a "Federal Communications Commission (FCC) document "showed for the first time that the software in Google's Street View mapping cars was 'intended' to collect Wi-Fi payload data, and that engineers had even transferred the data to an Oregon Storage facility. Google tried to keep that and other damning aspects of the Street View debacle from public review, the FCC said."* True ignorance is one thing. Outright deception and mendacity is another. As Kravets reports, this was a far cry from saying, "Hells bells, Margaret. We didn't know we were gathering this information." That Google denied it was surreptitiously collecting this data seems to be yet another violation of its own "Don't be evil" credo.

As the case studies and examples in this book have manifested, the potential of Big Data is both vast and unprecedented. Up until now, we have barely touched upon fundamental ethical questions like, Is Big Data good for us? Is Big Data a net positive? What are some of the downsides of a Big Data world?

The term *Big Data* may be new, but the issues it broaches are not. We have seen this movie before,[1] although perhaps not on a screen quite so large. Case Western Reserve University history professor Melvin Kranzberg once famously said, "Technology is neither good nor bad; nor is it neutral." His quote illustrates that any transformative technology (and its components) forces us to rethink many established legal, societal, and ethical precepts. And Big Data is no exception. While I happen to believe that the pros of Big Data outweigh its cons, it is high time to discuss its legitimate issues in some depth. To be clear, I am very much a Big Data advocate, but foolish is the person or organization that refuses to acknowledge the very real concerns brought about by telemetry, massive data centers, ubiquitous technology, smartphones, radio-frequency identification (RFID) tags, and the like.

PRIVACY: BIG DATA = BIG BROTHER?

With respect to Big Data, privacy represents the elephant in the room. Companies that effectively leverage Big Data often face a great deal of media scrutiny, PR issues, and vocal individual detractors. (Perhaps some companies do Big Data *too well*?) Amazon, Apple, Facebook, Google, and others have all to varying extents come under criticism for privacy and security concerns.

Let's go back to Google for a moment. A disturbing pattern is emerging at the company; Cargate was not an isolated incident. Only a few months later, the company again found itself in hot water.

---

[1] During the height of the dot-com boom, I consulted for Internet advertiser DoubleClick, a company that caused plenty of controversy. Ironically, Google acquired DoubleClick.

In August 2012, the Federal Trade Commission (FTC) "fined Google $22.5 million on Thursday to settle charges that it had bypassed privacy settings in Apple's Safari browser to be able to track users of the browser and show them advertisements, and violated an earlier privacy settlement with the agency."[2] The fine represents "the largest civil penalty ever levied by the commission." This should be no surprise; it has been cracking down on tech companies for privacy violations. What's more, the FTC is investigating Google for antitrust violations. Google again claimed that its actions were "unintentional," but others justifiably have their doubts, as do I.

No company is made of Teflon, Google included. At some point, the sum total of Google's "privacy-challenged" actions may stick to it. The results may be government action, lawsuits, the decline of its brand, and a mass consumer exodus. Think about it. No one *needs* to use Google for search—or anything else for that matter. While the company owns more than two-thirds of the U.S. search market as of this writing, there are plenty of other shows in town. Forget the other big names like Yahoo! and Bing. New companies are building privacy right into their business models (i.e., defining themselves based on how they treat user data). For example, consider DuckDuckGo, a search engine that "provides a clean interface together with a no-tracking privacy policy."[3] Social network Diaspora bills itself as "the privacy-first Facebook competitor."[4] And Google isn't alone in giving Big Data a bad name. Facebook operates under a well-deserved cloud of suspicion about how it treats user data.

As I discuss in *The Age of the Platform*, because of the consumerization of IT, today people use the products or services of Amazon, Apple, Facebook, Google, and others because they want to, not because they have to. This is a critical distinction. (Apple's iPad may be the chic tablet to own today and Amazon may be the world's largest bookstore, but there are alternatives to each company's products and services.) Continued gaffes and negative PR will hurt those individual companies and, in the process, make people and regulatory agencies more suspicious of Big Data.

Organizations that rely upon Big Data—and effectively make it even bigger—face another issue in this regard. The Introduction to this book covered the impact of platforms and ecosystems on Big Data. To summarize that section of the book here: the bigger the platform, the more users it can support, and by extension, the more data generated by these platforms. Unlike the Google Wi-Fi sniffing issue described earlier, sometimes privacy controversies stem not from the direct actions of "platform companies," but from the actions of their partners, external developers, and third-party apps. For instance, consider what happened with iOS app Path in early 2012:

> Path bills itself as a social network that cares about privacy. For a while it was also an App Store outlaw. When iPhone users downloaded it through Apple's popular storefront, the software surreptitiously sent a user's entire contacts list—including e-mail addresses, names, and phone numbers—to the company's servers. That wasn't just creepy, it was a violation of Apple's rules.[5]

An engineer in Singapore revealed the transgression on his blog in February of 2012. Soon after, Apple CEO Tim Cook summoned Path cofounder Dave Morin into Apple's headquarters, according to people familiar with the meeting but not authorized by Apple to discuss it. And Path was not alone here. As the controversy unfolded, it became evident that several other popular apps uploaded contacts as well, violating Apple's terms of service.

While Apple acted quickly and decisively in trying to stop the bleeding, the Path incident demonstrates that even relatively closed platforms cannot completely police everything. Apple iPhone customers can download more than 600,000 apps in the AppStore as of this writing (and growing). There's no easy way for the company to prevent violations of its terms of service. One can only imagine the privacy breaches taking place on much more open platforms such as Android. No one can completely answer the question, "What are our partners doing with the data they collect?"

Plenty of people don't trust Amazon, Apple, Facebook, and Google. But protecting privacy means much more than avoiding these four ubiquitous companies. Let's return for a moment to our example of car insurance and Big Data from the Introduction. Some people don't want their driving habits to be tracked, either by insurance companies or the police. What to do? For starters, they can buy noPhoto, "a smart license frame that prevents traffic enforcement cameras from taking photos of [their] license plate."[6] This IndieGoGo project may be the first of its kind, but it sure won't be the last. Others will no doubt attempt to cash in on the desire of many people to "stay off of the grid." The larger point is that just because we have the ability to generate more data doesn't mean that everybody will want to do just that. Privacy still matters, and Big Data is bringing many of these related issues to the forefront.

Many fear Big Brother, the fictional character in George Orwell's 1949 classic *Nineteen Eighty-Four*. Note, though, that Big Brother didn't just punish innocent civilians for independent thinking as thought-crimes. Big Brother caught legitimate criminals as well, and Big Data can, too. For instance, insurance companies believe that Big Data and predictive analytics can take a huge bite out of the $60 billion to $250 billion that it loses to fraud each year. With so much claim-related data, the possibilities are limitless. Consider the words of Scott Horwitz, a senior director in the insurance practice at credit-scoring company FICO.

> "Link analysis works by ferreting out related claims that may not appear to be related. For instance, a suspicious auto body shop may be handling an unusually high number of accident repairs. Link analysis might show that the body shop is not the culprit—or at least, not the only culprit. There may be a pool of crooked attorneys, 'victims', and vehicle owners who take vehicles to the same shop. *When viewed individually, each claim may look legitimate. But when viewed in a broader context, the fraudulent pattern becomes clear.*"[7] [Emphasis added]

Horwitz makes two key points here. First, patterns emerge when we look at data *en masse*. The patterns would elude us if we insisted upon looking at cases individually and without context. This is a key precept of Big Data. Second, Big Data is not just about increasing revenue or finding customer insights. Big Data can also catch fraudsters—and lower insurance premiums for law-abiding citizens.

Google and other companies can do some amazing things with Big Data. Progressive management thinkers clearly understand the power and importance of Big Data. I believe firmly in the business case for it.

But we should not be so blind that we don't pay heed to the potential abuses described in this section. My only hope is that senior executives at these organizations understand that just because they *can* do something doesn't mean that they *should*.

BIG SECURITY CONCERNS

Privacy is hardly the only problem associated with Big Data. Some people become disheveled when they find out that Google tracks their searches and YouTube videos viewed. In October 2010, then-CEO Eric Schmidt spoke to *The Atlantic* about a wide range of issues, including privacy. He offered up a bunch of juicy sound bites, including, "We know where you are. We know where you've been. We can more or less know what you're thinking about."[8]

Was Schmidt overstating things here? Hardly. Google's trove of user information is perhaps only rivaled by that of Facebook. Even if you believe in the benevolence of Google (not exactly a given these days), the company's use and sheer amount of data collectively represent another major problem: security. In other words, you may be comfortable with what Google knows about you—and what it does with that information. Perhaps you understand as I do that Google is a business, and businesses need to make money. Since the majority of Google's products and services are free, you accept the fact that *you* are the product. Maybe the relevant ads that appear in your Gmail messages don't bother you. (If you're like me, you just block them with an extension in your web browser.)

So you understand the trade-off implicit in using Google products and services. But what happens if nefarious sorts gain access to Google's data? Big Data attracts big interest from hackers, especially when that data is so complete, so personal. (Google Wallet and NFC-enabled Droids only up the ante.) Don't think for one minute that unsavory folks aren't targeting these companies and others—and not because they care about the apps you download or the books you read. Apple has a reported 400 million customer credit cards on file,[9] and Amazon is rumored to be in the same ballpark.

To hackers, the Holy Grail is represented by banks, credit card companies, and behemoths like Amazon, Apple, Facebook, and

Google. But today *every* organization has to worry about data pirates. Consider online shoe and clothing retailer Zappos, owned by Amazon .com. In January 2012, the company "began e-mailing its 24 million customers . . . advising them that its site had been hacked, and some customers' personal details and account information [were] likely stolen. But Zappos said that no credit or debit card information had been accessed by attackers."[10] Then, five months later, a hacker stole and posted 8 million usernames and passwords from LinkedIn,[11] prompting a $5 million lawsuit. With nearly 200 million registered users as of this writing, count LinkedIn among the many companies that use and generate a boatload of valuable data.

The bad guys know that Big Data is a big target. The bigger the data, the bigger the target. Maintaining network security has never been a simple endeavor, and I for one cannot imagine a hacker-free world. The fleas come with the dog. Organizations shouldn't make the mistake of protecting only *their* internal Small Data; external Big Data can be just as important, especially when breaches become public and lead to negative press.

BIG, PRAGMATIC ISSUES

Even though the term may change, I for one don't see an end in sight to Big Data. In this way, it's like the Internet. While I would argue that, in each case, the pros outweigh the cons, several Big Data issues beyond security and privacy warrant discussion here.

Big Consumer Fatigue

In 2002, early social networks like Friendster and MySpace showed us a glimpse of a much different future. These social media first-movers laid the groundwork for the giants of today. It's hard to pinpoint an exact date at which social media crossed the chasm, but it certainly occurred at some point in the mid-2000s. Perhaps it was September 26, 2006, the date at which Facebook finally did the inevitable and opened up its gates to everyone—at least, everyone over age 13 with a valid e-mail address. (Facebook used to be reserved to only those with an *.edu* e-mail domain.) After that point, Facebook mushroomed in popularity, soon followed by other social networks like Twitter, Google+, and others. While founded in 2002, LinkedIn no doubt benefited from Facebook's rising tide. It lifted all boats.

By 2011, however, many people were suffering from social media fatigue, to paraphrase the title of a blog post by author and social media guru Chris Brogan.[12] There were only so many hours in a day to tweet, like, follow, share, friend, blog, comment, and +1. The novelty was starting to wear off. Unlike the early days of Twitter, by 2010 no one could even pretend to keep track of everything going on. When venture capitalists say, "Social media is dead," they don't literally mean that it's lacking a pulse and it will go the way of the Polaroid in a year. Rather, they mean that the growth—and opportunity for significant returns on their investments—has largely disappeared. They have to look for the next big thing, the next game-changer. History tells us that social media may very well become far less important than it is today, but it's unlikely that a new social network will usurp Facebook, Twitter, and LinkedIn. (This is why each of these companies has a multi-billion-dollar valuation.)

Of course, this hasn't stopped some companies from crashing the party, even if the bartender is about to announce last call. In May 2012, Microsoft launched So.cl, a student-centric social network.[13] For the most part, though, the social media ship has all but sailed. As we saw in Chapter 4 (see "Big Data: The Venture Capitalist's Perspective"), venture capitalists (VCs) are betting on what's next.

I can see a similar pattern playing out with Big Data over the next few years. While machines will not get tired of Big Data, it's entirely possible that many consumers will stop actively generating as much data as they are today, especially on social networks. This does not mean that Big Data is ephemeral. It isn't going anywhere and, in fact, it will only get bigger.

Without question, Big Data early converts and zealots will make their fair share of mistakes. At the same time, though, they will also be better poised to take advantage of it than its naysayers and detractors. Despite the hype, Big Data presents an enormous opportunity for organizations, not to mention software vendors, consulting firms, VCs, and others. This opportunity may well not exist in five years *to the same extent*, especially as early Big Data adopters move into new markets, develop important new customer insights, and capitalize on the inertia of their competition. There's no end in sight to Big Data, and fatigue hasn't crept in just yet.

Rise of the Machines: Big Employee Resistance

What happens when a machine can do your job—or at least management at your company thinks so? While I see them on *Mad Men*, I have not met anyone in the past twenty-five years with the formal job title of *typist*. Word processing programs and computers did away with them years ago. The trade-off between humans and machines has been with us for centuries, although many of us have only had to face it relatively recently. For a long time, bank tellers and travel agents held relatively "safe" jobs. Of course, that's changed thanks to the rise of ATMs and do-it-yourself (DIY) travel sites like Travelocity and Expedia, respectively.

Now, I mean no disrespect here to bank tellers, travel agents, and other people who have suddenly had to find new jobs. This is just the nature of capitalism. The creative destruction of Austrian American economist and political scientist Joseph's contribution is alive and well more than sixty years after his death. Generally speaking, however, the typical day of a bank teller, typist, and travel agent involved a great deal of repetitive tasks. Yes, individual judgment was required from time to time, and those positions have not been *completely* eliminated. (I'm sure that some company out there still employs a formal typist, perhaps for the near-retirement CEO who still refuses to use a computer.) One can persuasively argue, though, that those types of jobs were ripe for extinction. It was only a matter of time.

As technology has advanced over the past fifty years, it has given rise to a new type of employee—one that has had to analyze and synthesize information, think critically, perform nonroutine tasks, and use judgment on a regular basis. Enter the *knowledge worker*, a term coined by management guru Peter Drucker in 1959. By way of contrast, the knowledge worker for the most part did not exist in the world of Frederick Taylor's scientific management. In short, knowledge workers think for a living. The term has a certain ring to it and, as such, entered the business zeitgeist. Politicians began talking about the need to create not just jobs, but "good" jobs that paid more and were less likely to be replaced by machines or outsourced to developing (read: low-wage) countries.

For decades, knowledge workers have had a pretty good run. In the United States, they have largely withstood the movement of jobs overseas, although there have been notable exceptions. The same can be said for other industrialized countries.

 ## THE MYTH OF THE KNOWLEDGE WORKER

Many knowledge workers historically were not true knowledge workers at all. I'd put these people into three general groups:

- Poseurs
- Those with bad intentions
- Those with good intentions

First, let's discuss the poseurs, the folks who have had data at their fingertips but actively refused to use it to make better business decisions. I have heard directors defiantly say in meetings things like, "I don't need the data to tell *me* why employees are leaving!" (If you think that this sounds quite a bit like Art Howe in the Introduction of the book, you're absolutely right—and we know now what happened to him.) I also have seen employees in organizations manipulate data to advance some personal or political agenda, and something tells me that I'm not exceptional here.

Second, on much larger and more public scales, there are data-related implosions like Enron, Tyco, and Bernie Madoff. While I've never talked to Drucker about it, I sincerely doubt that the man had these types of behaviors in mind when he originally conceived of the prototypical knowledge worker. Color me an optimist, but I like to believe that in business, foul play like the earlier examples represents the exception, not the rule.

And finally, let's not forget the well-intentioned knowledge workers who tried to live up to Drucker's ideal but, for a slew of reasons, could not. It's simply naïve to think that knowledge workers always considered data when making decisions, much less the right data at the right time. Perhaps they felt time constraints or could not access key information.

What does the arrival of Big Data mean for most knowledge workers? Are they going the way of typists and bank tellers? I wouldn't go quite that far (at least yet), but Big Data will challenge many of them—and disintermediate more than a few. No, we're not at the point envisioned by movies like *The Matrix* and *Terminator*, but we're getting closer. Machines and data can inform human decision-making more than ever if we let it.

The Big Data revolution is being televised. It is doing much more than forcing many employees to deal with new sources of data in the workplace, in faster and in larger amounts than ever before. Many people will have to get out of their comfort zones. Big Data is going way beyond that. New technologies, data, and applications like those mentioned in Chapter 4 are creating entirely new categories of jobs (e.g., the data scientist) while concurrently destroying others. To this end, organizations should expect a fair amount of employee resistance, especially from those who believe that they possess unique skills and judgment. In other words, they are "above" using data. Yes, plenty of folks think that, "It ain't broke, so why fix it?" Because they have made decisions sans data during their careers, they will in turn view Big Data as a big nuisance.

Is this ultimately a problem? Well, yes and no. Big Data will ultimately force many employees and organizations to adapt or perish. I am careful to qualify that statement. We saw in Chapter 3 how the health care industry has grown to dizzying heights despite being glacially slow to adopt much-needed technologies like electronic health records (EHRs) and Natural Language Processing (NLP). Notable exceptions, however, like Dr. Pho make me optimistic that some of those stubborn dominoes will eventually fall. Maybe Pho will be the Billy Beane of medicine and exhort the establishment to finally enter the twenty-first century.

Health care doesn't get a pass, though. Even here, employers would do well to know as soon as possible which employees are comfortable with a more data-oriented approach to work and management—and which are not. Think of the arrival of Big Data as tantamount to going to the doctor's office for a checkup. You may not like what the doctor has found, but the consequences of *not* discovering the tumor or malady are probably much worse.

Let's stay on the subject of doctors for a moment. Many knowledge workers will reject Big Data and data-oriented thinking for the same reason that many doctors hate the Internet. Most doctors spent many years, countless hours, and hundreds of thousands of dollars becoming experts in their specific fields. Then, circa 1997, many of their patients starting researching different diseases, conditions, and symptoms online. In their commercials, pharmaceutical companies not so gently advised people to "talk to their doctor" about [insert name of drug]. Many people would simply shop for doctors until they found ones that would give them the pills they thought they needed (whether they actually did or not). To this extent, the web partially usurped doctors' monopoly on information and expertise—and most doctors were none too pleased. People who watched a 30-second commercial or read an article online came to believe they knew as much as or more than people who devoted most of their professional careers to the study of medicine.

Big Data is no different. Many will resist or reject, minimize, or ignore Big Data because it may challenge their authority and judgment culled from years of experience in their fields. Big Data will sometimes contradict their intuition, their recommendations, and their own personal experience. And, above all, Big Data will force many to learn new skills and rely upon parts of their brain that have remained mostly dormant since they took college statistics. Bottom line: expect resistance—and perhaps a great deal of it. We saw in Chapter 3 how the health care industry has been slow to embrace much-needed technologies like EHRs and NLP.

Employee Revolt and the Big Paradox

Fatigue and resistance aren't the only problems related to Big Data. I'd be shocked if we didn't see a certain amount of outright workplace rebellion with respect to Big Data in the coming decades. After all, while on the clock, do most of us really want to constantly question what we know? Do we *always and only* want to look at data when making business decisions? These are all fair questions, and Michael J. Mauboussin partially addresses the last one in his 2012 book *The Success Equation: Untangling Skill and Luck in Business, Sports, and Investing.* As Mauboussin writes, a "survey of 250 seasoned investors found that almost two-thirds of them agree with the statement

'As a forecasting / recommendation task becomes more complex and difficult, I tend to rely more on judgment and less on formal, quantitative analysis.'[14] In the face of complexity, investors default to a simpler and more intuitive mode." That is, as problems get bigger and more complex (along with the data behind them), some of us actually want to use less data, not more. Call this *the big paradox*.

Think about it. Let's say that I wave my magic wand. Presto! Tomorrow all of us will be able to easily go to the data and find the correct answers to every problem at work. Big Data always knows best, right? Would this appeal to many of us? Will "data slaves" feel any pride or sense of accomplishment? Who among us wants individual judgment completely eliminated from our jobs? I certainly don't, and I suspect that I'm not alone. While Big Data may not inform the majority of decisions *yet*, continued technological advances are only increasing the amount of time that many professionals are expected to interact with gadgets and data. Today, our thinking has evolved from centuries ago. Few intelligent management folks believe that employees are motivated exclusively by money. It remains to be seen if the economic imperative will win out over the desire of many employees to feel that they are contributing in a personal way at their desks.

SUMMARY

Supreme Court Justice Potter Stewart once said, "Ethics is knowing the difference between what you have a right to do and what is right to do." While Stewart wasn't talking specifically about Big Data, his line is entirely apropos here. Yes, Big Data is cool, but it is also scary; it is concurrently beneficial and potentially malevolent. We have established that Big Data is no panacea to business problems. Fair enough, but it clearly has the potential to vastly improve business decision-making and provide profound insights. At the same time, though, Big Data actually amplifies some existing workplace and ethical issues. It also introduces some new ones that we should not ignore. Responsible organizations should take the requisite privacy- and security-related steps to minimize the chance that Big Data results in big headaches.

NOTES

1. Kravets, David, "An Intentional Mistake: The Anatomy of Google's Wi-Fi Sniffing Debacle," May 2, 2012, www.wired.com/threatlevel/2012/05/google-wifi-fcc-investigation/, retrieved December 11, 2012.

2. Miller, Claire Cain, "F.T.C. Fines Google $22.5 Million for Safari Privacy Violations," August 9, 2012, http://bits.blogs.nytimes.com/2012/08/09/f-t-c-fines-google-22-5-million-for-safari-privacy-violations/, retrieved December 11, 2012.

3. "DuckDuckGo Privacy," December 8, 2012, http://duckduckgo.com/privacy.html, retrieved December 11, 2012.

4. "Diaspora*—The Community-Run, Distributed Social-Network," 2012, http://joindiaspora.com/, retrieved December 11, 2012.

5. Satariano, Adam, and MacMillan, Douglas, "Anarchy in the App Store," March 15, 2012, www.businessweek.com/articles/2012-03-15/anarchy-in-the-app-store, retrieved December 11, 2012.

6. Li, Anita, "NoPhoto Prevents Speeding, Red Light Cameras From Catching You [VIDEO]," October 21, 2012, http://mashable.com/2012/10/21/nophoto/, retrieved December 11, 2012.

7. Horwitz, Scott, "Big Data: The Future of Insurance Fraud Prevention," October 1, 2012, www.insurancetech.com/security/big-data-the-future-of-insurance-fraud-p/240008192?printer_friendly=this-page, retrieved December 11, 2012.

8. Saint, Nick, "Google CEO: 'We Know Where You Are. We Know Where You've Been. We Can More or Less Know What You're Thinking About.'", October 4, 2010, www.businessinsider.com/eric-schmidt-we-know-where-you-are-we-know-where-youve-been-we-can-more-or-less-know-what-youre-thinking-about-2010-10, retrieved December 11, 2012.

9. Thomas, Owen, "Apple Is Blowing PayPal and Amazon Away in Payments with 400 Million Accounts," June 11, 2012, www.businessinsider.com/apple-payments-paypal-amazon-400-million-accounts-2012-6, retrieved December 11, 2012.

10. Schwartz, Mathew J., "Zappos Hack Exposes Passwords," January 17, 2012, www.informationweek.com/security/attacks/zappos-hack-exposes-passwords/232400441, retrieved December 11, 2012.

11. Schwartz, Mathew J., "LinkedIn Users: Change Password Now," June 6, 2012, www.informationweek.com/security/attacks/linkedin-users-change-password-now/240001623, retrieved December 11, 2012.

12. Brogan, Chris, "Social Media Fatigue," August 1, 2011, www.chrisbrogan.com/fatigue/, retrieved December 11, 2012.

13. Clay, Kelly, "Microsoft Launches New Social Network to Compete with Google," May 21, 2012, www.forbes.com/sites/kellyclay/2012/05/21/microsoft-launches-new-social-network-to-compete-with-google/, retrieved December 11, 2012.

14. Robert A. Olsen, "Professional Investors as Naturalistic Decision Makers: Evidence and Market Implications," *The Journal of Psychology and Financial Markets* 3, no. 3 (2002): 161–167.

CHAPTER 8

Looking Forward: The Future of Big Data

Without Big Data, you are blind and deaf and in the middle of a freeway.

—Geoffrey Moore

For some time now, retail giant Target has taken data mining and Big Data very seriously. Forget the fact that most retailers have had to operate at relatively low margins. For instance, supermarkets historically have been volume businesses. They make profits of approximately three cents on the dollar.[1] Adding salt to the wound, retailers like Best Buy, Walmart, and Target these days face an entirely new problem. Connected consumers are visiting traditional retail stores, looking at products, whipping out their smartphones, finding the same products online for lower prices at sites like Amazon.com, *and ordering them right in the stores*. This process has been termed *showrooming*[2] and it represents a herculean challenge for big-box retailers, especially if the purchase takes place in a state in which Amazon need not pay sales tax. Best Buy management sees the writing on the wall. The company may soon go the way of Tower Records and Blockbuster Video.

Faced with few options, Best Buy announced on October 15, 2012 that it would match Amazon's prices in its physical stores.[3] Whether this will work is anyone's guess, but competing against Amazon on the basis of price has historically been an exercise in futility. Amazon CEO Jeff Bezos understands the concept of a loss leader and has said repeatedly that he is comfortable operating at "very low margins."* (Forget *low* margins and think for a minute about negative margins. Amazon is rumored to have taken a $50/unit loss on the Kindle Fire. The company hopes to make the money back on movie, book, magazine, and music purchases. Some speculate that in the near future Amazon will give away the basic Kindle.)

But let's stay on target with Target. In September 2012, the company fired back at the Seattle-based behemoth. Target announced that it was following the lead of Walmart and ceasing sales of Amazon Kindles in its physical stores.[4] It turns out that independent bookstore owners and aficionados aren't the only ones with axes to grind against Amazon. Target might be the proverbial Paul Bunyan.

In an ultra-competitive business landscape, what's a retailer like Target to do? Funny you should ask. In the course of my daily activities and while researching this book, I came across some downright fascinating uses of Big Data. Without question, my favorite anecdote comes from Target.

PREDICTING PREGNANCY

In a February 2012 article for The *New York Times* titled "How Companies Learn Your Secrets,"[5] Charles Duhigg writes about a statistician named Andrew Pole hired by Target in 2002. Soon after he started his new job, two employees in the marketing department asked Pole a strange question: "If we wanted to figure out if a customer is pregnant, even if she didn't want us to know, can you do that?" Intrigued and up to the challenge, Pole said yes and began work on a "pregnancy-prediction

---

* Amazon's net profit margin typically hovers at around 2 percent and has trended downward over the past few years. (See: ycharts.com/companies/AMZN/profit_margin.) By way of contrast, Apple's has been north of 30 percent over the past few years.

model." He looked at products that potentially pregnant women bought, like lotions and vitamins, as well as products that they *didn't* buy. A woman four-months' pregnant is probably not going to purchase baby food and diapers and store them for five months. (Duhigg's lengthy expose is nothing short of riveting, and I highly recommend reading it.)

The marketing folks weren't just hazing Pole or giving him busy work. They had a very real business reason for approaching him. Ultimately, they used Pole's model to send custom coupons to women that Target believed to be pregnant—or, more accurately, women who were likely to be pregnant based upon Target's data.

Don't yawn yet. About a year later, the story gets really interesting. A man angrily walked into a Target outside Minneapolis, Minnesota. He demanded to see the manager. He was clutching a mailer that had been sent to his daughter. From Duhigg's article:

> "My daughter got this in the mail!" he said. "She's still in high school, and you're sending her coupons for baby clothes and cribs? Are you trying to encourage her to get pregnant?"[6]

It turns out that the manager didn't know what the customer was talking about. (Retail employees are often unaware of corporate marketing efforts.) He took a look at the mailer. The father wasn't lying; the mailer was in fact addressed to his daughter. It contained advertisements for maternity clothing, nursery furniture, and pictures of smiling babies. The manager promptly apologized to his customer. A few days later, he called the man at home to apologize again. On the phone, though, the father was somewhat humbled.

> "I had a talk with my daughter," he said. "It turns out there's been some activities in my house I haven't been completely aware of. She's due in August. I owe you an apology."

In a nutshell, *Target knew that a teenage girl was pregnant before her own father did*. Pole's pregnancy prediction model did not require individual names, and Pole certainly did not know the identity of the woman in Duhigg's story. None of that mattered. His model didn't need that information. Target's own internal sales data was plenty.

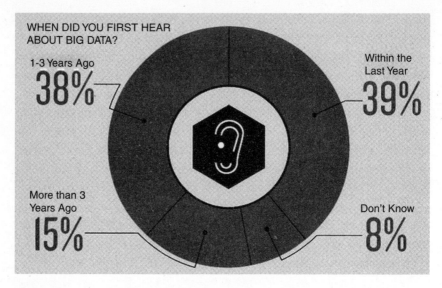

WHEN DID YOU FIRST HEAR ABOUT BIG DATA?

1-3 Years Ago
38%

Within the Last Year
39%

More than 3 Years Ago
15%

Don't Know
8%

Figure 8.1 Retail Awareness of Big Data
Source: Baynote, Inc.

Target saw the Big Data revolution before many other retailers. Consider the infographic in Figure 8.1.

In other words, Target could predict if a seventeen-year-old girl was pregnant (while her own father didn't know) way back in 2002. Imagine what the company could do today. The possibilities are limitless and, I'll admit, even a little scary. Many of today's Big Data sources, techniques, and tools weren't around or nearly as advanced ten years ago as they are today.

BIG DATA IS HERE TO STAY

Duhigg's Target article was nothing if not controversial. Just look at the 500-plus comments it generated. It's hard to read it and not have a strong opinion about the ethics of Target's data mining practices. Leaving that aside for a moment, stories like this illustrate the often-shocking power of Big Data—and more and more organizations are starting to take notice. Anecdotes like these are certainly compelling, but they represent just the beginning. More and more examples, case studies, journal articles, books, and innovative uses of Big Data are coming. And forget hyperbole from software vendors and consultancies that clearly have skin in the game. Quotes from recognized and more objective experts only add fuel to the Big Data fire. Joe Hellerstein, a computer scientist at the University of California in Berkeley, believes that we're living in "the industrial revolution of data."[7] While it's too early to say, we may look back at the 2012 presidential election as a watershed moment for Big Data—the point at which it crossed the chasm.

BIG DATA WILL EVOLVE

In his 2010 book *Where Good Ideas Come From: The Natural History of Innovation*, Stephen Johnson writes about inventors who ultimately were, quite frankly, too far ahead of their time. For instance, English mathematician, philosopher, and inventor Charles Babbage conceived of a machine that resembled the modern-day computer nearly more than a century before it could have remotely been considered commercially viable. Why such a long gap between Babbage's master plan and the modern-day computer? According to Johnson, for ideas to take hold, they must fit into something he calls *the adjacent possible*. One can certainly innovate, but innovations must rely largely upon components and materials that currently exist—or soon will. Babbage's concept of a computer could never work (in his lifetime, anyway) precisely because it was *too advanced*. That is, the majority of the parts necessary to turn his machine into a reality simply didn't exist yet—and wouldn't for decades.

And the adjacent possible is alive and well today. More recently, in February 2005, three former PayPal employees started a little site called YouTube. Think about the timing of YouTube for a moment. This happened ten years *after* Mosaic and Netscape brought the commercial web to the masses. Again, why the delay? In short, a site like YouTube just hadn't entered the adjacent possible in the mid-1990s—and even six or seven years later than that. Most people connected to the Internet via glacially slow dial-up modems, present company included. I remember the days of Prodigy and AOL. I couldn't contain my excitement when I connected at 56 kbps. Of course, those days are long gone, although evidently AOL still counts nearly three million dial-up customers to this day.[8] YouTube never would have taken hold if external factors didn't let it (e.g., online storage didn't drop in price by orders of magnitude, broadband connections hadn't mushroomed, and digital cameras and smartphones didn't democratize videos). Absent these factors, YouTube would never have been possible, much less remotely successful—and Google certainly wouldn't have gobbled it up for $1.65 billion in 2007.

Ron Adner makes a similar point about electric cars in his 2012 book *The Wide Lens: A New Strategy for Innovation.* A company may possess the technology and desire to build a gasoline-free car, but that's hardly the only relevant consideration. Nobody will actually want to buy one unless at least two critical conditions are met:

1. The car and its battery are affordable.
2. Battery charging stations are conveniently located throughout the country.

After all, we drive cars for two very simple reasons: we *need* to go places (such as to the office, the dentist, and the supermarket), and we *want* to go to other places (such as vacations, golf courses, and ballet recitals). Sure, we may hate paying $4/gallon at the pump, and most of us should know that the supply of oil is finite. But the current system works—at least for the time being. We know that we can get to where we need to go and return to our homes. The same just isn't true for electric vehicles, at least as of this writing.

Well, we may not be able to say the same for long. Based out of Israel, Better Place is not only building affordable electric cars. As discussed, that's only half the battle. The company is also working with the Israeli government on developing a network of solar-powered charging stations for its electric vehicles. One without the other just doesn't cut it. Meeting both conditions is necessary for battery-powered cars to become more than a pipe dream. Better Place is well on its way, as venture capitalists (VCs) essentially doubled down in November 2012.[9]

And Big Data is already following a similar trajectory. Organizations didn't have to worry about parsing through large videos in 1997 because no one was going to wait six hours for a video to upload (if the Internet service provider's [ISP's] dial-up connection didn't crash midway throught).

Today, that's no longer an issue and hasn't been for years. Twenty years ago, sending an e-mail was laborious, so few people bothered to do it. Now, we have the opposite problem: because it's so easy, 294 billion e-mails are sent *every day*.[10] The same can be said for the early days of blogs, radio-frequency identification (RFID) chips, social networks, and many of the other sources of unstructured data that have exploded over the past ten years. And each innovation, each progression, increases the adjacent possible. New sources of data will continue to sprout.

PROJECTS AND MOVEMENTS

Chapter 7 of this book looked at some Big Data abuses and issues like privacy and security. Without repeating them all here, suffice it to say that Big Data can yield potentially inimical consequences. As we conclude, remember the quote at the beginning of this book from Big Data pioneer Sandy Pentland. Big Data has big potential and will transform society. In fact, this is already happening. In this section, I'll briefly introduce three groups who take these issues seriously. They are currently working behind the scenes to make data not only bigger, but more democratic, portable, contextual, and relevant.

The Vibrant Data Project

Big Data can mean big abuse, but this doesn't have to be the case. So says the folks behind The Vibrant Data Project (VDP). At a high level, the group lobbies for increased transparency around all this data. It asks a critical question: how can we make our data work for us and not against? At present and as discussed in Chapter 7, large corporations like Amazon, Apple, Facebook, and Google gather, store, and utilize a tremendous amount of data on their customers and users. By and large, these organizations use this data only for their own economic purposes. VDP would like to change that. The project seeks to foster "a conversation around core challenges for empowering a much more decentralized approach—where individuals retain more control over their personal data, collaboratively discover its value, and directly benefit from it."[11]

The Vibrant Data Project is in its infancy, but it's worth keeping an eye on. Remember that the NoSQL movement did not start with

120 projects; it started with one. As Big Data becomes bigger and more powerful, expect the number of concerned citizens, groups, and government agencies to increase.

The Data Liberation Front

VDP isn't alone as an advocate of data transparency and democratization. Consider what some Google engineers are doing under the moniker *The Data Liberation Front* (DLF). DLF has a single modus operandi: to enable Google users to move their data in and out of the company's products. That is, users should be able to export their data from—and, if desired, import it into—other products.

"We help and consult other engineering teams within Google on how to 'liberate' their products," the DLF's website reads. "This is our mission statement: Users should be able to control the data they store in any of Google's products. Our team's goal is to make it easier to move data in and out."[12]

Now, some may trivialize this as a Google PR ploy. After all, the company operates under an increasing swarm of privacy concerns, and many of its wounds are self-inflicted. (Again, Chapter 7 had plenty to say about this.) For the time being, it appears as if DLF is legitimately trying to raise awareness of a key issue raised by Big Data: who owns all this data in the first place? It's a contentious issue that will only increase in importance.

Open Data Foundation

As discussed earlier, many organizations struggle with managing their own internal and structured data. These organizations lack a common understanding. For instance, Jack and Jill work for the same company, but they have different ideas about the definition of the term *customer*. (Many businesses lack a common understanding of basic but critical terms.) But what if that problem went away? What if everyone was on the same page in that company?

Now think bigger. What if people, businesses, and governments in Africa, Iceland, and the United States all used the same metadata? What if we *all* knew what we meant across different languages? Sound impossible? It's not. Metadata standards will eventually make this dream a reality, in the process improving libraries, biology, archiving, the arts, and many more areas of our lives. More formally, metadata standards are requirements intended to establish a common understanding of the meaning or *semantics* of the data. When in place, they ensure the correct and proper use and interpretation of the data by its owners and users.

To be sure, you won't overhear too many people talking about metadata standards at your local Starbucks. And they may not change your life tomorrow. Rest assured, though, they're important, they're coming, and their effects will be transformative. Metadata standards will enable and expedite the arrival of the semantic web.*

Organizations like the Open Data Foundation (ODaF) are working on these standards as we speak. According to its website, ODaF is

> a non-profit organization dedicated to the adoption of global metadata standards and the development of open-source solutions promoting the use of statistical data. We focus on improving data and metadata accessibility and overall quality in support of research, policy making, and transparency, in the fields of economics, finance, healthcare, education, labor, social science, technology, agriculture, development, and the environment.

The foundation sees this information as primarily statistical in nature. At the same time, though, it understands that these standards can be drawn from a variety of sources, some of which may be unconventional.[13]

As we saw in Chapter 2, accurate metadata makes *all* data more relevant and contextual.

BIG DATA WILL ONLY GET BIGGER . . . AND SMARTER

Without question, more of the unwired masses will connect to the Internet in the coming years. Collectively, humanity will produce even more data than it does today through an increasing array of devices. The growth of mobility is intensifying, and soon smartphones will penetrate

---

* For more here, see David Siegel's excellent book *Pull: The Power of the Semantic Web to Transform Your Business.*

the developing world. While citizens in impoverished nations may not be able to afford the latest iPhone or iPad, growth may come from one former tech bellwether that has recently fallen tough times.

Research in Motion (RIM) has all but ceded the U.S. smartphone market to the Apple, Google, HTC, and Microsoft. Desperately trying to remain relevant, RIM is aiming for the lower end of the market. In May 2012, new CEO Thorsten Heins announced that his company would be pursuing "markets in the developing world" that would account for much of the company's future revenue.[14] Whether people in Congo, Liberia, and Zimbabwe buy BlackBerrys *en masse* is anyone's guess. (I have my doubts, and I certainly won't be buying RIM shares anytime soon.) Still, smartphone prices keep falling, with no end in sight. If it's not the BlackBerry that helps close the digital divide, perhaps it will be the ultra-low-cost Aakash, an Android-based tablet computer with a 7-inch touch screen, ARM 11 processor, and 256MB of RAM.[15] Regardless of which devices bring computing to the impoverished masses, it's a safe bet that each year more and more people will connect to the Internet—making Big Data even bigger.

But let's forget human beings for a moment: there are only so of us on the planet. More and more *devices* are now independently and automatically generating data. As the following examples show, advanced technologies and smart devices are starting to supplant their "dumb" counterparts. The implication for Big Data: it will only get bigger.

THE INTERNET OF THINGS: THE MOVE FROM ACTIVE TO PASSIVE DATA GENERATION

Web 1.0 allowed hundreds of millions of people to consume content at an unprecedented scale and rate, but only very technically savvy folks could produce it. As discussed in Chapter 1, around 2005 or so, Web 1.0 gave way to Web 2.0. For the first time, laypersons (read: nontechies) were able to generate their own data. As a result, enormous amounts of text, audio, and video content flooded the web. Of course, not everyone is happy with the proliferation of "amateur" content. Perhaps the most vocal critic is Andrew Keen, author of the controversial book *The Cult of the Amateur*. Keen pines for the good old days in which the gatekeepers had a tighter grip on the means of production.

Keen can whine all he wants, but no one can put the Internet genie back in the bottle. What's more, regardless of how you feel about the ability of musicians to circumvent proper record companies and authors to self-publish their work, one thing can't be denied: the democratization of content creation tools has produced a whopping amount of data.

That data is going to grow at an even faster rate thanks to the Internet of Things, a term coined by Kevin Ashton in 1999. In short, the term represents an increasing array of machines that are connecting to the Internet just as people have—and its consequences are profound. Ten years after introducing it, Ashton reflected on where we are going:

> We need to empower computers with their own means of gathering information, so they can see, hear and smell the world for themselves, in all its random glory. RFID and sensor technology enable computers to observe, identify and understand the world—without the limitations of human-entered data.

In other words, let's say that we existed in a world in which computers knew everything there was to know—using data gathered without any help from us. In this world, we could track and count everything. In the process, we would greatly reduce waste, loss, and cost. In Ashton's view, we would know when things needed replacing, repairing, or recalling, and whether they were fresh or past their best.

Think of the Internet of Things not as more tech jargon, but as an inevitable development with profound implications. Germane to this book, it will only make Big Data, well, bigger. Machines will automatically create more and more data, perhaps even more than human beings currently do. Stated differently, the Internet of Things represents a sea change in who will be generating the most data—or, more precisely, *what* will be generating the most data.

At present, human beings are directly responsible for a high proportion of all data produced. This data begins with eyes on screens and fingers on mice, keyboards, smartphones, tablets, and PCs. Now, I don't want to overstate things here. Our own data-generating activities aren't going the way of the fax machine anytime soon. Billions of people will continue to blog, buy things, upload YouTube videos, tweet, text, make phone calls, search the web, and pin photos. All of this will still produce massive amounts of data, mostly the unstructured and semi-structured kinds. For the most part, sentient human beings have actively generated the most data. But what about more passive activities such as the myriad things that happen (or don't happen) in a supermarket? Isn't there potentially valuable data to be gleaned? The answer, of course, is yes.

Hi-Tech Oreos

For instance, Betty, a female shopper, picks up a box of Oreos, looks at it, appears to read its nutritional content, decides not to purchase it, and finally puts it back on the shelf. Historically, absent video cameras or in-store spies, not much could be gleaned from that nontransaction. Now, consider that same scenario, but in a Big Data world with ubiquitous, low-cost RFID tags, sensors, near field communication (NFC), and other powerful technologies.

What part of the packaging did Betty appear to read? Did specific images or words resonate with her more than others? What were her nonverbal expressions when she saw the number of carbs per serving? Exactly how long did she hold the box in her hands? Did Betty look at any other types of cookies, and for how long? Was she with anyone, like her children? Did her daughter say anything during that time? Was she a former Oreophile? Is this behavior markedly different in Safeway, Walmart, and other supermarkets? Why?

In the near future, consumer product companies will be able to quickly and easily capture and store immense amounts of product- and customer-specific data from physical stores. Advances in technology will allow these Oreo-related questions (and, many, many more) to be answered for the first time. Equipped with this information, the marketing folks at Nabisco can tweak the package color or fonts and analyze the effects of those changes. Perhaps they'll find "the right" combination of each. What if they find that a one-size-fits-all package doesn't make sense, even within the same country? It's entirely possible that different people buy Oreos for different reasons, and packaging can be customized just like television advertisements. Big Data and related technologies are making all this possible and, in the future, easier.

Hi-Tech Thermostats

How do you follow up the über-successful iPod? It's a question that Tony Fadell, the man who designed the hardware for Apple's breakthrough product, had to face. After working on eleven consecutive models of the iPod, Fadell left Apple and decided to take on a much different challenge. Why not try to make thermostats hip? After a good deal of tinkering, the Nest Thermostat was born.

Forget for a moment the fact that Nest just looks cool and is braindead simple to use. As a *Wired* article by Steven Levy[16] points out, the device connects to Wi-Fi networks, enabling two important things. First, Nest users can set temperature remotely via their iPhones. (One can imagine a day in the not-too-distant future in which we won't have to wonder if we've left the oven on after leaving the house. We will be able to just turn it off remotely.) The broader, more important implication of devices like Nest is that they generate data specific to each customer. This data can be easily collected and sent to websites, allowing people to track temperatures in their own homes—and even "learn" about their own personal temperature preferences. Nest will "know" that you like your home warmer at night in the winter (say, 71 degrees) but a bit cooler during the day. In the summer, your preferences change, and so will the temperature in your home—without your having to do anything.

Thermostats are only the beginning. You don't need to buy a high-tech Nest Learning Thermostat to realize some of the benefits of Big Data. Electricity as we know it is changing. Smart meters and grids are coming to a city near you—and soon. I'll be the first to admit that many people will find this odd. After all, historically, utilities haven't exactly been technological trailblazers. The reasons aren't terribly difficult to discern. Electric companies basically hold local monopolies. It's not as if their customers can easily switch from Utility A to Utility B. To boot, many are in fact nonprofits. And let's not forget what they're selling: electricity, a service that is anything but optional. (Economists describe products like these as having a *high elasticity of demand*.) There's really no substitute for electricity, although candles and a Wi-Fi connection at Starbucks helped me survive a storm and subsequent power failure in northern New Jersey for several painful days back in 2010.

Consider what one utility company is doing. Established way back in 1935, EPB is a nonprofit agency that provides electric power to the people around Chattanooga, Tennessee. It is one of the largest publicly owned electric power distributors in the country. Using a 100 percent fiber optic network as its backbone, EPB is moving ahead full-steam with smart grids. The company's digital smart meters communicate with its power system. Much like a traditional electric meter with a dial, a smart meter measures its customers' electric consumption. However, there's a key difference: a smart meter remotely reports consumer consumption every 15 minutes. By contrast, traditional meters are usually read manually, and only once per month. In what will no doubt become standard in a few years, consumption levels are displayed digitally on the meter. As of this writing, this information is available for EPB customers to view online, on a channel or application, or over a Wi-Fi network. From the company's website:

> Smart meters also help us keep an eye on things as they happen. So, by fall of 2012, if there is a power outage at your home or business, we'll know within 15 minutes and can get to work fixing the problem immediately! And if we notice an unusual or substantial increase in your power consumption, *we can notify you so you can investigate.*[17] [Emphasis added.]

An electric company that proactively notifies its customers when their usage levels increase? Perish the thought! E-mails or texts that alert people to what's happening! You can see before your bill arrives that you're on track for a $300 charge and can make adjustments accordingly. And EPB has company here. At some point in the near future, smart grids will become standard. Can water companies be far behind? What else will technology and Big Data disrupt?

Smart Food and Smart Music

We've heard for a while now about smart refrigerators (i.e., those that will read the expiration date on milk cartons and automatically remind you to buy new milk or even order it for you). But an expiration date isn't terribly personal. What about a refrigerator that will help people diet and eat better? Far-fetched? Hardly. In January 2012, I attended the Consumer Electronics Show (CES). At the event, LG announced

> an array of new products to its Smart ThinQ appliance line. At the forefront of its new line is its refrigerator, which just got a lot smarter with a health manager feature that allows you to maintain your diet, send recipes to your smart oven, and even keeps you posted when you run out of certain groceries.[18]

In the future, my refrigerator will recommend different dishes than yours, even if we own the same model. And why shouldn't it? I probably eat differently than you do. *Our data is different.*

You probably don't eat what I eat, nor do you like the same music that I do. Thanks to the Big Data revolution and attendant technologies, we can more easily "consume" only what we like. Consider Echo Nest, founded by two MIT Ph.Ds. The company utilizes Big Data tools to analyze music. It provides this data to consumer-facing music services such as iHeartRadio, eMusic, MOG, Spotify, Nokia, the BBC, and VEVO. In total, more than 15,000 developers use Echo Nest data to create and enhance apps. Echo Nest's Fanalytics service analyzes the usage patterns and history of every person using a music service, "including the person's music collection, listening habits, and other factors. Then applications can match similar profiles. In addition, the service can provide 'affinity prediction.' [I]n other words, it can predict how music preferences predict political affiliation—or perhaps eventually other consumer habits such as purchasing or brand preferences."[19]

Welcome to a world of *metapredictions*: predictions about other predictions. Think of services like Echo Nest as a kind of Netflix for music. Thanks to Big Data and related tools, your food and music are going to get smarter.

BIG DATA: NO LONGER A BIG LUXURY

Many of the factors described in this book regarding the arrival of the Big Data revolution can be summed up simply: progressive people, organizations, and institutions like Billy Beane, Quantcast, NASA, Explorys, Target, and the city of Boston are embracing Big Data because they foresaw considerable benefits. However, there's arguably a more crucial reason for leveraging Big Data: survival. In other words, we have no choice. Forget Target making a few more dollars from expecting mothers. It's an instructive example, but consider the following harrowing story.

In October 2011, the city of Harrisburg, Pennsylvania, declared bankruptcy. The *Wall Street Journal* reported that the state's capital city "filed for bankruptcy protection from creditors Wednesday, in a case closely watched by other cities and towns looking for ways out of dire financial troubles. Including Harrisburg, there have been 48 bankruptcies from cities, counties, towns and villages since 1980, according to James Spiotto,"[20] a lawyer at Chapman and Cutler LLC in Chicago, Illinois, who specializes in laws affecting distressed municipalities. It's a trend with a disturbing uptick, and many public officials are watching similar budget crises in Wisconsin, California, and other places with keen interest.

STASIS IS NOT AN OPTION

Count among the onlookers Mayor Menino of Boston, the driving force behind Street Bump. We met him in the Introduction to this book. Now, Boston doesn't appear to be on the verge of bankruptcy anytime soon, but that doesn't mean that it can't operate in a more innovative, efficient, and data-oriented manner. (What organization *can* honestly make that claim?) Rather than fight to maintain the status quo, Menino has decided to push the envelope—and he should be commended for doing so.

Menino launched Street Bump to much fanfare, but don't call it a publicity or a reelection stunt. Nor was Street Bump an attempt to brand the city as progressive or hip. Boston doesn't need much help there; increasing its "cool factor" was just an ancillary benefit. So why?

The answer lies on the New Urban Mechanics' website:

New Urban Mechanics is an approach to civic innovation focused on delivering transformative City services to Boston's residents. While the language may sound new, the principles of New Urban Mechanics—collaborating with constituents, focusing on the basics of government, and pushing for bolder ideas—are not.[21]

In fact, Mayor Menino (known as the Urban Mechanic) has been preaching this mantra for years. He uses technology and Big Data to further his constituents' specific interests. In the process, he has become Boston's longest serving mayor, and this city has received its fair share of national kudos.

More succinctly, as Menino writes on the same site, "We are all urban mechanics." Menino is smart enough to know that government *must* innovate to survive and provide the essential services demanded by its citizenry. Stasis is no longer an option.

Today, many government-funded Big Data projects are largely driven by economic imperative. The emphasis is often on avoiding sticks (very difficult fiscal and budgetary climates, looming layoffs) more than embracing carrots (increased innovation, better functionality, and generally more responsive government). I'll do my best to remain apolitical here. At least in the United States, we can blame individual politicians, Congress, Democrats, Republicans, special interests, "the system," or any or all of the above for our current budgetary predicament.

The fact remains that budgets are shrinking with no end in sight. As Thomas L. Friedman and Michael Mandelbaum write in *That Used to Be Us: How America Fell Behind in the World It Invented and How We Can Come Back*, the status quo is simply untenable. The U.S. federal, state, and municipal governments will have to do much more with less—and soon. (Outside of the United States, there's also plenty of opportunity for governments across the globe to both cut expenses and expand their current services. For instance, I've never been to Greece, but I imagine that the country has potholes to go along with its economic malaise.) In ways like this, Big Data is a means to an end—and a necessary one at that. Given the current economic and budgetary climate, expect many more Big Data projects like Street Bump in the coming years. We simply have no choice.

SUMMARY

Business leaders and government officials need to spur innovation (with Big Data playing a big part) while concurrently balancing very real privacy and security concerns. Yes, the benefits of Big Data can help the public sector combat—but not overcome—the difficult economic times we're all facing. But our elected officials need to go much deeper than react to budget crises. *Government should innovate; our politicians shouldn't need the excuse of shrinking budgets to embrace new technologies and Big Data.* Progressive public officials like Menino, San Francisco Mayor Ed Lee,* and others clearly believe in a fundamentally different way of doing things than traditional, change-resistant bureaucrats, and Street Bump is a case in point. Along these lines, Tim O'Reilly has written and spoken extensively about the need for government to become a platform. For that platform to reach its full capacity and accrue benefits to its citizens, Big Data can—nay, *must*—play an integral role. Initiatives like Data.gov** certainly represent steps in the right direction. I am one among many who would like to see much more in the way of openness, common standards, collaboration, and innovation.

NOTES

1. Heubsch, Russell, "What Is the Profit Margin for a Supermarket?," 2012, http://smallbusiness.chron.com/profit-margin-supermarket-22467.html, retrieved December 11, 2012.

2. Brownell, Matt, "Can Retailers Beat the 'Showrooming' Effect This Christmas?," October 22, 2012, www.dailyfinance.com/2012/10/22/christmas-shopping-showrooming-online-price-match/, retrieved December 11, 2012.

3. Tuttle, Brad, "Best Buy's Showrooming Counterattack: We'll Match Amazon Prices," October 15, 2012, http://business.time.com/2012/10/15/best-buys-showrooming-counterattack-well-match-amazon-prices/, retrieved December 11, 2012.

4. Owen, Laura Hazard, "Following Target, Walmart Stops Selling Kindles," September 20, 2012, http://gigaom.com/2012/09/20/walmart-following-target-stops-selling-kindles/, retrieved December 11, 2012.

5. Duhigg, Charles, "How Companies Learn Your Secrets," February 16, 2012, www.nytimes.com/2012/02/19/magazine/shopping-habits.html?pagewanted=2&_r=1&hp, retrieved December 11, 2012.

6. Ibid.

7. Cukier, K., "Data, Data Everywhere," February 25, 2010, www.economist.com/node/15557443, retrieved December 11, 2012.

---

* Lee is modernizing city government, starting with high-tech super cops. See http://tinyurl.com/a9r3ecz.

** Data.gov seeks to increase public access to high-value, machine-readable datasets generated by the Executive Branch of the Federal Government. For more, see www.data.gov/about.

8. Aguilar, Mario, "3 Million Suckers Still Pay for AOL Dial-Up," July 27, 2012, http://gizmodo.com/5929710/3-million-suckers-still-pay-for-aol-dial+up, retrieved December 11, 2012.

9. Woody, Todd, "Better Place Raises $100 Million as Investors Double Down on Electric Car Bet," November 1, 2012, www.forbes.com/sites/toddwoody/2012/11/01/better-place-raises-100-million-as-investors-double-down-on-electric-car-bet/, retrieved December 11, 2012.

10. Tschabitscher, Heinz, "How Many Emails Are Sent Every Day?," April 9, 2012, http://email.about.com/od/emailtrivia/f/emails_per_day.htm, retrieved December 11, 2012.

11. "We the Data—Why We Do This," 2012, http://wethedata.org/about/why-we-are-doing-this/, retrieved December 11, 2012.

12. "The Data Liberation Front," November 30, 2012, www.dataliberation.org/home, retrieved December 11, 2012.

13. "The Open Data Foundation," 2012, www.opendatafoundation.org/, retrieved December 11, 2012.

14. Faas, Ryan, "RIM Falls Flat Trying to Hype Third World Sales as a Major Success," May 3, 2012, www.cultofmac.com/164814/im-falls-flat-trying-to-hype-third-world-sales-as-a-major-success/, retrieved December 11, 2012.

15. http://timesofindia.indiatimes.com/home/sunday-toi/special-report/We-want-to-target-the-billion-Indians-who-are-cut-off/articleshow/10284832.cms

16. Levy, Steven, "Brave New Thermostat: How the iPod's Creator Is Making Home Heating Sexy," October 25, 2011, http://www.wired.com/gadgetlab/2011/10/nest_thermostat/, retrieved December 21, 2012.

17. Levy, Steven, "Brave New Thermostat: How the iPod's Creator Is Making Home Heating Sexy," October 25, 2011, www.wired.com/gadgetlab/2011/10/nest_thermostat/, retrieved December 11, 2012.

18. Murphy, Samantha, "A Refrigerator That Helps You Diet? LG Unveils High-Tech Smart Appliances," January 9, 2012, http://mashable.com/2012/01/09/lg-smart-refrigerator/, retrieved December 11, 2012.

19. Geron, Tomio, "Echo Nest Raises $17 Million for Big Data Analysis of Music," July 12, 2012, www.forbes.com/sites/tomiogeron/2012/07/12/echo-nest-raises-17-million-for-big-data-analysis-of-music/, retrieved December 11, 2012.

20. Corkery, Maher; Michael, Kris, "Capital Files for Bankruptcy," October 13, 2011, http://online.wsj.com/article/SB10001424052970204002304576626752997922080.html, retrieved December 11, 2012.

21. "New Urban Mechanics—About," 2012, www.newurbanmechanics.org/about/, retrieved December 11, 2012.

Final Thoughts

There are known knowns; there are things we know that we know. There are known unknowns; that is to say there are things that, we now know we don't know. But there are also unknown unknowns—there are things we do not know we don't know.[1]

—Donald Rumsfeld, while serving as U.S. Secretary of Defense, February 12, 2002

Thanks to forces like mobility, the social web, and the consumerization of information technology (IT), we are living through a permanent data deluge. Enormous data sources are emerging faster than ever. Few intelligent people believe that collectively we'll generate and consume less data tomorrow than we did yesterday. Big Data is here, and I'm far from the only one who believes that it is changing the world.[2]

Rather than ignore or fight this inevitability, individuals and organizations of all sizes, types, and industries should embrace it. At some point, just about every employee, department, and organization will face the daunting task of doing more with less. Some will face this challenge sooner than others. And this goes double for the public sector. While not elixirs for fixing the thorny fiscal and budgetary messes in which many agencies find themselves, technology and Big Data are without question part of the solution.

217

Chapter 2 described the characteristics of Big Data in some detail. Some of those characteristics are in fact limitations of what data can do, no matter how big it gets. That is, data can only tell us so much; even Big Data certainly can't tell us everything. Rumsfield's statement at the beginning of this section is as true today as it was more than a decade ago. Overly optimistic folks may believe that data in general—and Big Data specifically—will soon be able to tell us *everything*. They're wrong, and they are just as naïve as the skeptics who believe that data can't tell us anything. The truth is somewhere in between. Most reasonable folks are squarely in the "data will reveal more" camp.

Author and statistician Nate Silver (mentioned in the Introduction) made a similar point on an October 31, 2012 episode of *Charlie Rose*.[*] Silver discussed the inherent limitations of data—specifically, polling data. In other words, despite the remarkable accuracy of his own models and ultimate predictions, Silver knows all too well the limitations of his primary profession. Statisticians never bat 1.000, to use a baseball analogy. Silver sagely told Rose that there will *always* be unknown unknowns.

And that revelation should in no way preclude you from starting down the Big Data path. The revolution is here, and it's high time that organizations of all sizes recognize it. As we have seen in this book, baseball teams; retailers; municipalities; car insurance companies; universities like Carnegie Mellon, Columbia, and Princeton;[3] and scores of other organizations have already figured this out. Let the tinkering with Big Data begin across the board: public and private sectors, big and small companies, for-profits and nonprofits. Organizations and employees should be asking new and penetrating questions and letting those answers inform new ways of thinking. The uninitiated, the skeptics, and the laggards who refuse to integrate data into their decision-making—and Big Data in particular—will only be left further and further behind.

As Silver puts it, "Data-driven predictions can succeed—and they can fail. It is when we deny our role in the process that the odds of failure rise. Before we demand more of our data, we need to demand more of ourselves." I couldn't agree more. I've made the following

---

[*] Watch the episode here: http://tinyurl.com/nate-charlie-rose.

point in my other four books and I'll end with it here: it's about the people more than the data and the technology. It all starts with us.

SPREADING THE BIG DATA GOSPEL

Thank you for buying *Too Big to Ignore*: *The Business Case for Big Data*. I truly hope you have enjoyed reading it and have learned a great deal in the process. Beyond some level of enjoyment and education (always admirable goals in reading a nonfiction book), I also hope that you can apply your newfound knowledge in your job.

And perhaps you are willing to help me. I am a self-employed author, writer, speaker, and consultant. I'm not independently wealthy, and I don't have a large marketing machine getting my name out there. My professional livelihood depends in large part on my reputation, coupled with referrals and recommendations from people like you. Collectively, these enable me to make a living.

You can help this book by doing one or more of the following:

- Review the book on amazon.com, bn.com, goodreads.com, or other related sites. The more honest, the better.
- Mention the book on your blog, Facebook, Reddit, Twitter, LinkedIn, Pinterest, and other sites you frequent.
- Recommend the book to family members, colleagues, your boss, friends, subway riders, and people who might find it interesting.
- Give it as a gift.
- If you know people who still work in newspapers, magazines, television, or industry groups, I'd love a referral or reference. Although social media is big, traditional media still matters.
- Visit www.philsimon.com and read, watch, and listen to your heart's content. I frequently blog, post videos, record podcasts, and create other interesting forms of content on a variety of diverse subjects.
- Check out my other books: *Why New Systems Fail*, *The Next Wave of Technologies*, *The New Small*, and *The Age of the Platform*.

I don't expect to get rich by writing books. I'm not as big as Michael Lewis or Stephen King. Dare to dream, right? I write books for three main reasons. First, although Kindles, Nooks, and iPads are downright cool, I really enjoy holding a physical copy of one of my books in my hands. Creating something physical from scratch just feels good to me. Second, I have something meaningful to say. I like writing, editing, crafting a cover, and everything else that goes into writing books. To paraphrase the title of an album by Geddy Lee, it's my favorite headache. Finally, I believe that my books will make other good things happen for me.

At the same time, though, producing a quality text takes an enormous amount of time, effort, and money. Every additional copy sold helps make the next one possible.

Thanks again,

Phil

NOTES

1. "News Transcript: DoD News Briefing—Secretary Rumsfeld and Gen. Myers," February 12, 2002, www.defense.gov/transcripts/transcript.aspx?transcriptid=2636, retrieved December 11, 2012.

2. Hatmaker, Taylor, "5 Ways 'Big Data' Is Changing the World," October 7, 2012, www.entrepreneur.com/article/224582, retrieved December 11, 2012.

3. Smith, Mike, "Princeton University's Neuroscience Institute Deploys FileTek StorHouse for Big Data Storage of Vital Laboratory Research and User Information," September 11, 2012, http://news.yahoo.com/princeton-university-neuroscience-institute-deploys-filetek-storhouse-big-071002005.html, retrieved December 11, 2012.

Selected Bibliography

Adner, Ron. *The Wide Lens: A New Strategy for Innovation*. New York: Portfolio, 2012.

Anderson, Chris. *Free: The Future of a Radical Price*. New York: Hyperion, 2009.

Anderson, Chris. *The Long Tail: Why the Future of Business Is Selling Less of More*. New York: Hyperion, 2008.

Ariel, Dan. *Predictably Irrational*. New York: Harper Collins, 2008.

Fisher, Tony. *The Data Asset: How Smart Companies Govern Their Data for Business Success*. Hoboken, New Jersey: John Wiley & Sons, 2009.

Friedman, Thomas L., and Mandelbaum, Michael. *That Used to Be Us: How America Fell Behind in the World It Invented and How We Can Come Back*. New York: Picador, 2011.

Johnson, Steven. *Where Good Ideas Come From: The Natural History of Innovation*. New York: Penguin, 2010.

Kahneman, Daniel. *Thinking Fast and Slow*. New York: Farrar, Straus and Giroux, 2011.

Keen, Andrew. *The Cult of the Amateur: How Blogs, MySpace, YouTube, and the Rest of Today's User-Generated Media Are Destroying Our Economy, Our Culture, and Our Values*. New York: Doubleday, 2011.

Levitt, Steven, and Stephen Dubner. *Freakonomics: A Rogue Economist Explores the Hidden Side of Everything*. William Morrow, 2009.

Lewis, Michael. *The Big Short: Inside the Doomsday Machine*. New York: W.W. Norton & Company, 2010.

Lewis, Michael. *Moneyball: The Art of Winning an Unfair Game*. New York: W.W. Norton & Company, 2004.

Mauboussin, Michael J. *The Success Equation: Untangling Skill and Luck in Business, Sports, and Investing*. Cambridge: Harvard Business Review Press, 2012.

Mlodinow, Leonard. *The Drunkard's Walk: How Randomness Rules Our Lives*. New York: Random House, 2008.

Redman, Thomas. *Data Driven: Profiting from Your Most Important Business Asset*. Boston: Harvard Business School Press, 2008.

Reis, Eric. *The Lean Startup: How Today's Entrepreneurs Use Continuous Innovation to Create Radically Successful Businesses*. New York: Random House, 2011.

Siegel, David. *Pull: The Power of the Semantic Web to Transform Your Business*. New York: Portfolio, 2009.

Silver, Nate. *The Signal and the Noise: Why So Many Predictions Fail— but Some Don't*. New York: Penguin Group, 2012.

Simon, Phil. *The Age of the Platform: How Amazon, Apple, Facebook, and Google Have Redefined Business*. Henderson, Nevada: Motion, 2012.

Simon, Phil. *Why New Systems Fail: An Insider's Guide to Successful IT Projects*. Boston: Cengage, 2010.

Taleb, Nicholas. *The Black Swan: The Impact of the Highly Improbable*. New York: Random House, 2010.

Tapscott, Don, and Anthony D. Williams. *Wikinomics: How Mass Collaboration Changes Everything*. New York: Penguin, 2008.

Watts, Duncan. *Everything Is Obvious: How Common Sense Fails Us*. New York: Random House, 2011.

Weinberger, David. *Everything Is Miscellaneous: The Power of the New Digital Disorder*. New York: Holt, 2007.

About the Author

Phil Simon is a sought-after keynote speaker and the author of five books, including the award-winning *The Age of the Platform*. While not writing and speaking, he consults organizations on how to optimize their use of technology. His contributions have been featured on NBC, CNBC, The *New York Times, Inc.* Magazine, *Bloomberg BusinessWeek, The Huffington Post, The Globe and Mail, Fast Company*, and many other mainstream media outlets. He holds degrees from Carnegie Mellon and Cornell University. You can find him on Twitter at @philsimon, and his home page is www.philsimon.com. He lives in Henderson, Nevada.

index